Many Splendored Things

Many Splendored Things

Thinking Sex and Play

Susanna Paasonen

Goldsmiths
Press

© 2018 Goldsmiths Press
Published in 2018 by Goldsmiths Press
Goldsmiths, University of London, New Cross
London SE14 6NW

Printed and bound by TJ International Ltd
Distribution by the MIT Press
Cambridge, Massachusetts, and London, England

Copyright © 2018 Susanna Paasonen

A CIP record for this book is available from the British Library

ISBN 978-1-906897-82-6 (hbk)
ISBN 978-1-906897-85-7 (ebk)

www.gold.ac.uk/goldsmiths-press

Contents

Acknowledgements   vii

1   Introduction: Sharp Thrills, Sombre Hues   1

2   Magic Circles and Magical Circuits of Play   17

3   "Raising the Ordinary to the Extraordinary"   45

4   Pervy Minors and Adult Babies   73

5   Slaves, Prisoners and the Edge of Play   101

6   Ripples Across Identities   131

References   153

Index   169

Acknowledgements

This has been my pet project for the past two years and it is thrilling to see it materialise. Writing a book on such a tight schedule speaks of the intensity of the process. At the same time, it forces closure where ideas may still be dividing along previously unsuspected paths and also provides a full stop to that which one might still want to play with. Yet, here it is.

Having studied pornography and sexually explicit media since the early 2000s, I only started thinking about the interconnections of sex and play from a more conceptual angle when writing on Jan Soldat's documentary film portrait of a male slave, *Der Unfertige* (*The Incomplete*, 2013), discussed at some length in Chapter 5, late in 2015. Jan's films continue to be an inspiration for my thinking on sex and play, and many of them are addressed in this book. First and foremost, I would like to thank Jan for giving me access to his work and for enthusiastically supporting my investigations. Had I not seen his films, this book would not have come about in the shape that it has. In fact, it might have failed to come about in any shape whatsoever.

As tends to be the case with projects that come to occupy a central position in one's thoughts and activities, this one has involved more personal investment than my academic work generally does. These affective investments, combined with the immersiveness of the process of writing, have fuelled hesitancy to publicly present the ideas as they have been taking shape. Given this, collegial networks of collaboration, support and exchange have been crucial when developing this project from the initial, palpable yet slightly confused enthusiasm to somewhat more articulated questions and ideas. *Many Splendored Things* builds on three articles in particular – "Many Splendored Things: Sexuality, Playfulness and Play", outlining the general theoretical framework for thinking sex through play, in the journal *Sexualities* (Paasonen 2018); the second on *The Incomplete* for a forthcoming collection edited by Thomas Waugh and Brandon Arroyo on confession and sexuality in contemporary media; and a third on Finnish girls' experiences of sexual messaging and sexual play drawing on Silja Nielsen's MA work, co-authored with Sanna Spišák for *Sex Education* (Nielsen et al. 2015) – before I ever knew this would become a larger project. I am grateful to the editors and anonymous peer reviewers of these three publications for the comments, suggestions, criticism and intellectual support. All in all, this book owes much to my fabulous collaborators, so lämpimimmät kiitokseni indeed!

I would also like to thank the participants in the Interdisciplinary Studies in Sexuality seminar at Concordia University, the School of Social and Policy Studies

Seminar Series at Flinders University, the Centre for Research in Media and Cultural Studies research seminar at the University of Sunderland and the School of Art, Centre for Film and Media research seminar at the University of Kent for conversations connected to the talks I gave on my emergent book in 2015–2017. Warmest thanks to Tom Waugh, Monique Mulholland, Clarissa Smith and Sara Janssen for making these visits happen, and for their extremely helpful engagement with the project.

For equally invaluable inspiration, support, feedback, suggestions and dialogue, I would like to thank Kath Albury, Tom Apperley, Feona Attwood, Ricky Barnes, Lauren Berlant, Despina Chronaki, Debbie Ging, Mary Gray, Jamie Hakim, Ken Hillis, Sal Humphries, Ville Hurskainen, Kaisu Hynnä, Kylie Jarrett, Veli-Matti Karhulahti, Anu Koivunen, Katariina Kyrölä, Ben Light, Alan McKee, Laura Helen Marks, John Mercer, Torill Elvira Mortensen, Kaarina Nikunen, Mari Pajala, Michael Petit, Kane Race, Laura Saarenmaa, Olli Sotamaa, Will Straw, Jenny Sundén, Jaakko Suominen, T.L. Taylor, Katrin Tiidenberg, Liza Tsaliki and Annamari Vänskä. Also, many thanks to Samantha Allen for making her unpublished doctoral research available to me.

I remain grateful for the support that my work continues to enjoy at the Department of Media Studies and the School of History, Culture and Art Studies at the University of Turku: I fully realise that this is not always obvious in institutional settings when it comes to studies of sexuality and media. A sabbatical research grant awarded by the Jenny and Antti Wihuri Foundation for the academic year 2015–2016 allowed for the much needed space and time for the project to come about, as well as for doing some of the elementary readings. The recently launched Academy of Finland research project "Sexuality and Play in Media Culture", with Kaisu, Veli-Matti, Kata, Mari, Sanna, Jaakko and our fabulous international network, allows for the further development of some of the strands of thought presented in this book. That is thrilling.

Last, but certainly not least, thanks go to Goldsmiths Press, and Sarah Kember and Michelle Lo in particular, for the smoothest publishing process.

1

Introduction: Sharp Thrills, Sombre Hues

According to sexual therapists, advice columnists and self-help authors alike, one is not supposed to play games, let alone be a player, in one's intimate relationships. When opposed to seriousness and sincerity, the notions of games and play imply deceit, tricks and a range of shifty manoeuvres geared towards the manipulation of potential or current partners. At the same time, the emergence of sex within the markets of leisure runs parallel with its increasing significance and public framing as play (Attwood 2011, 83). This is evident in the abundant uses of the terminology of play in connection with sex, from *Playboy*'s gendered lifestyle branding and playmates of fantastic heterosexual feminine availability to tips on foreplay and afterplay for attuning the more slowly climaxing partners, how-to literature on sexual role-play and the marketing of all kinds of commodities as sex toys. Furthermore, the same sex experts who advise people against acting like players in their relationships are likely to recommend sexual play for additional variation, novelty and experimentation within them.

Play remains the chosen term in diverse sexual cultures to describe how scenes come about, how they evolve and how they are lived out, from sex parties to variations of bondage, age play, pony-play, pup-play or "party and play" sessions combining sex and recreational drug use (e.g. Hale 1997; Lewis 2011; Harviainen and Frank 2016; Wignall and McCormack 2017; Bauer 2018). Kane Race (2015a, 259) points out that, in the context of gay male hook-up cultures, an invitation to play equals an invitation to sex while the notion of play "characterizes that encounter as casual, fun, and obligation free". Sexual pleasures, tied to fantasies and desires alike, can nevertheless be much more cumbersome and complex than the rhetoric of joyful lightness connected to advice literature, play parties, sex toy adverts or the glossy, über-commodified aesthetic of *Playboy* would allow. This book therefore starts from the premise, or claim, that there is more to play and pleasure in the realm of sexuality than joyful and casual lightness. For as the game studies scholar Miquel Sicart suggests, the pleasures that play offers can be deep and dark indeed in their hues: "Play is not necessarily fun. It is pleasurable, but the pleasures it creates are not always submissive to enjoyment, happiness, or positive traits. Play can be pleasurable when it hurts, offends, challenges us and teases us, and even when we are not playing. *Let's not talk about play as fun but as pleasurable, opening us to the immense variations of pleasure in this world*" (Sicart 2014, 3, emphasis added.)

When first coming across Sicart's discussion of play as variations of pleasure that may well be hurtful, serious and difficult, I was struck by its degree of resonance with conceptualisations of sex. For the quest for bodily pleasure – the enchantment of the activity itself – can be seen as the key purpose of, motivation and rationale for both sex and play. As I began to further think through the conceptual conjunctions of sex and play, I was no less struck by the fact that, no matter how self-evident and productive these seemed to be, they had not been extensively conceptualised in feminist and queer studies of sexuality to date. Working through this resonant connection, this book builds on the argument that sex involves experimentation and quest for intensity of sensation and experience where the possibilities of what bodies want and do are never quite set, knowable or stable. I set out to further argue that the openness of variations and options elementary to playfulness and play can help in thinking through the engrossing appeal of sex, the plasticity of desires, appetites and orientations, as well as their congealment in categories of sexual identity.

Playfulness refers here to a mode, capacity and orientation of sensory openness, curiosity and zest for variation that precipitates improvisation in acts of play. *Play* again stands for the actualisations of playfulness: for doing playful things, for acting and carrying out playful scenarios under more or less clearly defined sets of rules and guidelines. The notion of playfulness intermeshes and overlaps with those of improvisation, exploration, curiosity and experimentation, yet it also stands apart from them in foregrounding pleasure and bodily intensity as key motivations for sexual activity. Sexual play, as discussed throughout this book, involves the affective capacities of bodies to move and be moved from one state to another, to sense, to affect and be affected by one another. Sexual play, driven by the quest for pleasure and the intensification of sensation, steadily probes and stretches the horizons of what people may imagine doing, liking and preferring (cf. Cooper 2003). Consequently, play pushes sexual identifications into motions of varying speeds and lengths.

Playful sexuality and sexual play are therefore not antithetical to the felt gravity of sexual selves or identities but means of trying and acting them out, as well as for opening them up to variation and change. As I argue in more detail in the pages to follow, and in the concluding Chapter 6 in particular, a focus on playfulness allows for conceptualising sexual selves as being in constant, more or less subtle transformation. Through sexual play, it is possible to grasp sensations that have remained previously unknown, unimagined or otherwise out of reach and to expand one's ways of being, imagining and acting in doing so. Horizons of bodily possibility are equally opened up by reading, thinking and observation, yet, in the realm of sex, the hands-on, skin-on-skin (or leather-on-rubber, or whatever the preferred combination might be) contact remains elementary to its affective, visceral and transformative force (see also Bollen and McInnes 2006, 110).

Playfulness and play, as laid out in this book, are central to the transformations in sexual desires, fantasies, pleasures and orientations within, in between and even despite the categories of identity across people's lifespans. As sexual desire moves towards different scenes, fantasies, bodies and objects, and becomes attached to them, its forms are reorganized – and so is one's sense of self (Berlant 2012, 65). My general argument is that a focus on play makes it possible to highlight improvisation driven by curiosity, desire for variation and openness towards surprise as things that greatly matter both in sexual lives and in scholarly attentions towards them.

Play and the Hierarchies of Sex

To date, sexual play has been mainly examined in the context of online exchanges and gaming (e.g. Waskul and Vannini 2008; Sundén and Sveningsson 2012; Brown 2015; Shaw and Friesem 2016), in connection with childhood sexual explorations (Lamb and Coakley 1993; Davies et al. 2000; Lamb 2001; Nielsen et al. 2015), and in the context of adult role-play such as in kink and queer communities in particular (e.g. Hale 1997; Beckmann 2001; Barker and Langdridge 2010; Hawkinson and Zamboni 2014). While this book considers both sexual role-play among minors and BDSM (encompassing bondage and discipline, dominance and submission, sadism and masochism), it does not start from the premise that play and playfulness are uniquely characteristic of sexual exchanges on digital media platforms, attributes of childhood sexuality or features of minoritarian sexual cultures. Rather, I propose conceptualising them as dynamics central to sexuality more generally while not limiting my examination to sexual subcultures where appetites divert from the normative routines of vanilla. The key rationale for this book is to make use of play in unravelling the dynamics of sexual fantasy, normativity and pleasure by pushing them beyond any given or clear divisions of straight and queer, yet to do it in such a way that does not erode complexities in how these categories have come about, or in how they continue to be lived and operationalised.

There are two main motivations for doing this. First, like so many other feminist and queer scholars before me, I take my cue from Gayle Rubin's analysis of normative sexual hierarchy in "Thinking Sex", originally published in 1984. Visualised as a circle with inner and outer spheres, Rubin's (1989, 281) model of sexual hierarchy separates "good, normal, natural, blessed sexuality" at its heart from its opposite, namely "bad, abnormal, unnatural, damned sexuality", confined to its outer rim. Like all hierarchies, this one arranges and ranks "bodies, things, and ideas according to levels of power or importance" (Levine 2017, 82). The inner, "charmed circle" of good sex involves heterosexual, married, monogamous, procreative, non-commercial exchanges that are practised in pairs, in a relationship between members of the same generation, in private, without the aid of pornography, props, toys or other paraphernalia. Meanwhile, the outer rim of "bad sex may be homosexual, unmarried, promiscuous, non-procreative, or commercial. It may be masturbatory or take place in orgies, may be casual, may cross generational lines, and may take place in 'public', or at least in the bushes or the baths. It may involve the use of pornography, fetish objects, sex toys, or unusual roles" (Rubin 1989, 281).

Rubin's model has been deployed in tracking the normative value mechanisms through which certain sexual orientations are marginalised while others are firmly embraced and celebrated, as well as the different degrees of mobility and freedom that bodies and desires occupy according to their positioning within the hierarchy (e.g. Warner 2000, 1–5; Kulick 2005, 208). I nevertheless find equal, and possibly even greater, value in how the model, when considered carefully in its circle-shaped incarnation, subtly yet forcefully demonstrates the narrowness, rarity and ultimate impossibility of a sexual life inhabiting the realm of good sex only without ever deviating from its confines. Here, "goodness" comes across as the ultimate form of straight monogamous vanilla sex completely void of unruly fantasy and desire of the kind that might provide it with unpredicted flavour, spark or surprise.

As the very centre point of the circle of sexual value, the norm in fact represents a vanishing point in its narrowness – something that can be approximated and acted out only as more or less offbeat variations. In this sense, Rubin's model unravels the very cohesiveness of the norm it maps out. The circle of sexual hierarchy makes it possible to see how the myriad ways in which sexual tastes, routines and relations fall short of the norm eat away at its seemingly stable centre. As in Judith Butler's (1990) discussion of gender performativity, it becomes impossible to inhabit, enact or live out the norm – as the heart or core of the circle – since attempts to reiterate the ideal unfold as more or less offbeat variations. Meanwhile, the phantom of good sex continues to affect ways in which sexual orientations and desires are approached, marginalised, represented and regulated. Understood in this vein, the ideal of good sex is virtual: it presses upon sexual lives, shapes and orients the ways in which they actualise and become lived out.

This lack of cohesion would not do away with the force that the norm holds, or the hierarchical ways in which bodies and desires become positioned in relation to it, yet it provides analytical openings for considering sexuality as degrees of variation, experimentation and transformation. Thinking about sex through the notion of play is a means of engaging with this phantom-like figure of good sex that is elusive inasmuch as it is normative, the force that it continues to exert in private and public lives, as well as the steady, heavy flow of traffic that occurs across the charmed circle and its outer limits. The project of framing sex through play then focuses on contingency over repetition and sameness, pleasure and change (also Beasley et al. 2015), and does so without a priori distinctions between straight and queer sexuality and the diverse categories of identity that they tap into.

Second, considerations of playfulness and play help to foreground the role of enjoyment and bodily pleasure which, despite their urgency in and for people's lives, critical sexuality studies often leave with surprisingly fleeting theoretical or empirical attention (see Plummer 2003b, 522). While pleasure is a key theme in sexological research examining sexual behaviour, performance, satisfaction and dysfunction, it figures less prominently in theoretical, cultural and critical inquiry connected to sexuality. A focus on play makes it possible to take pleasure, and the quest thereof, as an analytical point of entry without the necessity of attaching it to other purposes, motivations or aims. Writing on the non-instrumentality of affect, namely the experience of affect as valuable in itself, Silvan S. Tomkins (2008, 873) notes that, "It is enjoyable to enjoy. It is exciting to be excited ... Affect is selfvalidating with or without any further referent, as is pain or ... pleasure." The same applies to sex.

For its part, feminist research has long set out to politicise sexuality and the pleasures attached to it, as well as to situate them in historical and sociocultural contexts. Researchers have especially probed the normative hierarchies and social relations of power, the political potentialities of sexual subcultures, and the role that trauma and harm occupy in the emergence of sexual and gender identities (see Holmes et al. 2011, 3-4). As the pioneering feminist anthologies *Powers of Desire: The Politics of Sexuality* (Snitow et al. 1983) and *Pleasure and Danger: Exploring Female Sexuality* (1984; Vance 1989) made evident, the notion of sexual pleasure is not readily detachable from the politics or social operations of power. In their introduction to the former volume, Ann Snitow, Christine Stansell and Sharon Thompson argued for the importance of historicising sex and understanding it as socially constructed rather than as a natural power of any sort: "Certainly there are strong reasons to long for something spontaneous – either sacred, wordless, or romantic – a reliable private pleasure, a refuge from social exhaustion. But ... [t]here is no escaping it: sex as refuge, or sex as sacrament, or sex as wild, natural, dark, and instinctual expression – all these are *ideas* about sex" (Snitow et al. 1983, 10–11, emphasis in the original). To the degree to which feminist studies of sexuality have foregrounded the issues of social construction, power and normativity, the diverse forms and intensities of pleasure have easily been side-tracked as romantic and idealistic notions that position sex as a wild, natural force or "badlands of desire" (Simon and Gagnon 1986, 108), assumed to be pulsating outside the dictates of culture and society. Yet this is certainly not all that can be made of the complex enchantments that sex involves.

In her introduction to *Pleasure and Danger*, the anthology produced from the 1982 Barnard conference that has been seen as the starting point of the sex wars, Carole S. Vance (1989, 1, 6) pointed out how, despite the intermeshing of experiences of pleasure and oppression, happiness and humiliation in sexual lives, violence, vulnerability and the negative range of affect have mostly tinted feminist inquiry. The foregrounding of socio-cultural power has been efficient in addressing the historical transform-ations that have occurred in understanding sex, sexuality and gender. At the same time, this has risked the reduction of sexual desire and plea-sure to the effects of normative scripts and operations of power in ways that downplay the materiality of bodies and the resonances occurring between them. Furthermore, as Chris Beasley, Mary Holmes and Heather Brook (2015, 683) have more recently noted, when feminist research has addressed sexual pleasure, these inquiries have tended to focus on the realm of queer, leaving "heterosexuality in a dark, dull corner, its positive potential for joy and social change virtually unacknowledged and unex-plored" (see also Albury 2002; Beasley 2011, 30–31; Rossi 2011).

On the micro-plane of lived experience, the intensities and orientations of sexual attraction and lust are not, in their paradoxes, contradictions and occasional absurdities, easy to explain through the notions of structure or norm and the levels of fixity that they entail. Writing on black women and pornography, Jennifer C. Nash (2014, 150) points out how sexual "pleasure is often shot through with pain", "desire is often fraught and complicated terrain" and how profound inequalities connected to race, gender and class shape ways of articulating sexuality – just as they push themselves upon other modes and forms of being in the world. Sex can be both hurtful and traumatising, a source of shame as well as one of joy (also Albury 2018, 81). It can be serious and therapeutic, tantalising and absorbing, distracting, boring and dire – as can play. Noting this, Snitow, Stansell and Thompson (1983, 42) address sex as a potentially "peculiar mixture" of contradictory experiences oscillating between objectification and pleasure, degradation and inspiration. Such experiences are however not necessarily mutually contradictory: pleasure can be gained from offering oneself as an object to be appreciated and handled, and degradation surely comes across as inspirational in scenes of power play. In all its ambiguity, sexuality remains "an arena for play, for experimentation, a place to test what the possibilities might be for an erotic life and a social world that would answer our desires" (Snitow et al. 1983, 43).

By zooming in on this experimental openness that the notion – as well as the practice – of play affords within sexuality, *Many Splendored Things* takes on Lauren Berlant's (2008) question: "Who knows what sex could be if people were encouraged to enjoy it as play rather than as a drama?" Conceptualising sex through play rather than framing it as drama makes it possible to foreground both pleasure and the shifts and ruptures that occur in sexual tastes in the course of both improvisation and scripted experimentation. At the same time, the becoming that sexual play allows is by necessity also a process of unbecoming – of both learning and unlearning and, occasionally, of unravelling. The intensities of sexual desire can push people to zones of discomfort in ways that rupture their intimate arrangements and sense of the self while also giving rise to novel attachments and belongings. Sexual play and experimentation, in sum, come with an edge of vulnerability.

All Sorts of Play

As the discussion above already suggests, the concepts of play and playfulness have emerged with some regularity in feminist and queer studies of sexuality. They have not, however, been exhaustively applied in theorising the affective capacities and shifting carnal horizons of possibility that sexual acts, desires and pleasures involve. Within feminist theory, sexuality has been explored as both affective and cognitive, as an issue of both sense and sensibility. Philosopher Elizabeth Grosz (1994, 108) has broadly mapped out sexuality as "a modality of existence, infusing all aspects of the ways we face and act in the world, part of our situation in the world". This understanding of sexuality has some similarity with the more expansive conceptualisations of play in studies of games and play. These have defined play as "a mode of being human" and a "force that pulls us together" (Sicart 2014, 1, 6) and as an exciting frame of action that involves the modulation of experience (Sutton-Smith 1997, 18; Nachamanovitch 2009, 2) and is present in or animates "the essential aspects of all culture" (Caillois 2001, 3). While such characterisations of being and experience may come across as over-arching and transhistorical, they do not foreclose considerations of specificity or variation. Crucially, in terms of this book, both sex and play can be understood as pleasurable activities practised for their own sake (Frey 1991; Abramson and Pinkerton 2002, 5; Waskul and Vannini 2008, 242). There need not be any functional aim, goal or pursuit beyond the enchantment of the activity itself that may give rise to long-standing attachments between individuals, communities and fields of practice.

Following Grosz's typology, sexuality refers to "a drive, and impulse or form of propulsion", to "a series of practices and behaviors involving bodies, organs, and pleasures", to identities as well as to "a set of orientations, positions, and desires, which implies that there are par-ticular ways in which the desires, differences, and bodies of subjects can seek their pleasure" (Grosz 1994, viii). No matter how elusive the pleasures of sexuality may turn out to be, their allure explains much of the interest and attention that the topic of sex holds in private and public lives alike. In studies of games and play, the pleasures of play have been routinely associated with immediate gratification, voluntary participa-tion, fun and spontaneity (e.g. Caillois 2001, 6–7). Defined in this vein, the frame of play may seem to knowingly divert attention away from the risks and harms caused by forms of sexual harassment, coerced intimacies and acts bordering on or qualifying as violence. If such dynamics are to be conceptualised in terms of play, then it would be obvious that the sexual games that some people play impact others in ways that are far from vol-untary, pleasurable or joyful.

According to thesaurus definitions of the term, to play means to "engage in activity for enjoyment and recreation rather than a serious or practical purpose"; to take part or compete in sports; to "represent (a character) in a theatrical performance or a film"; to perform a musical instrument; as well as to "move lightly and quickly, so as to appear and disappear; flicker". In these definitions, play is distinctly separate from seriousness of purpose or understanding, fast and fickle in its rhythms and speeds, as well as laced with degrees of pretence. Play is connected to the skills, techniques and practices of sport, theatre and music as fundamentally an issue of performance. While not exactly identical, a similar range of meanings is connected to the French term "jouer" and the German "spielen" referring to play of the musical, athletic, wagering and theatrical kind. There is an unmistakeable sense of theatrical drama to this vocabulary of performance and display foregrounding a sense of lightness, non-seriousness or even fickleness.

The notion of play may therefore come across as shades too light, or happy, in ways that help to downplay the range of vulnerabilities and anxieties at the heart of sexual lives. Entangled in relations of trust, love and desire, sex can involve a visceral need to be wanted. There are emotional risks involved in one's investments and desires not being returned, in one's interests and advances being rebutted, and in acute sensations of insecurity, insufficiency, failure and embarrassment haunting moments of physical proximity. For some, the mere act of getting naked in front of others can be a painfully strenuous experience. When desires and needs between partners are not symmetrical – as they regularly are not – or when their intensities remain incompatible, tensions and anxieties may haunt sexual interactions in ways that postpone or block access to enjoyment, pleasure and physical abandon (see Tomkins 2008, 228–230).

The Judeo-Christian legacy of sexual shame alone tints sexual lives, articulations of desire and explorations of pleasure on scales both individual and collective, while pressing most tightly on those whose proclivities are deemed abnormal, deviant or plain bad within the sexual hierarchy (e.g. Califia 1999, 139). When having sex, people "fear dependency and possible loss of control as well as our own greedy aggression, our wishes to incorporate body parts, even entire persons" (Vance 1989, 5). The more negative affective registers, from shame to disgust and guilt, can intensify and amplify sexual desire by adding an edge of transgression and frisson to the encounters at hand. Yet they can equally bar access to pleasure by simply rendering the encounter awkward, strained or pained.

Sex can be an object of duty, a cause of pressure and a source of stress, and the promises of release and gratification connected to it may well fall short.

It is therefore crucial to re-emphasise that play – be it sexual or other – need not be understood as fully free, voluntary, egalitarian and exclusively connected to positive affect. This would in fact be key to understanding the gravity of sexual desires, expressions and pleasures that this book sets out to examine in the context of media culture. Like human actions in general, play can be asymmetrical, risky, hurtful, violent and damaging in its reverberations and the pleasures it offers – or curbs. During sexual play, we may "become dumb actors in one another's charades" (Simon and Gagnon 1986, 118; see also Sicart 2014, 2; Stenros 2015, 72–76). Since sex is not merely a personal affair but equally an issue of social operations of power, of civic liberties and public agency, it carries a range of meanings exceeding the instantaneity of any physical engagements themselves. As Feona Attwood and Clarissa Smith (2013, 329) point out, while playful, entertaining and stimulating, "even the avowedly hedonistic pursuit of sex may be more than *just* frivolous, . . . it might, like forms of 'serious leisure' have significant benefits (and costs) for individuals and society".

Sexual play fuelled by desire can be light or heavy, cumbersome or casual, spectacular in its props or focused on the nuanced particularities of skin. It can take the form of role-play or tentative tickling. Play may enter surprising routes that are neither casual nor serious by definition and that test out bodily boundaries of comfort – that which feels good, surprising, interesting, uncomfortable or merely unpleasant. The meandering bodily explorations opened up in sex and the tensions and investments involved in bodies coming together can involve mixed pleasures, acquired tastes and ambivalent feelings. And, as the recent work on the so-called dark side of play in game studies illustrates, all this can well involve disrespect and disregard towards established rules, such as the comfort zones of one's partner (e.g. Brown 2015; Mortensen et al. 2015).

Examples of sexual play gone awry are certainly abundant, from acts leading to physical injury to soft and hard boundaries being ignored, safe words disrespected, intimate arrangements turned oppressive, acts enforced, partners not wanting to play along or playing with different sets of rules even within mutually pre-agreed scenes (e.g. Barker 2013, 902–903). One can knowingly set out to play, even without much desire to do so. Not everyone plays nice and not everyone plays at all. Sex can certainly be fun, ludic and ludicrous (Waskul and Vannini 2008), yet framing sex in terms of play does not equal its reduction to free, recreational exploration. In contrast, I suggest that a foregrounding of practices of pleasure allows for a nuanced understanding of the affective intensities and investments involved in sex precisely since it does not presume the default presence of either playful lightness or the viscerally felt heaviness of trauma in sexual lives. Furthermore, thinking sex through play affords the conceptual openness necessary for examining the force and contingency of sexual desire as that which both binds identities and sets them in motion.

Things to Follow

All this may seem abstract or, even worse, convoluted. My project in the ensuing chapters is both to lay out these ideas in more detail and to render them more concrete through contemporary media examples addressing sexuality and play on online platforms, in bestselling novels, tabloid television and independent documentary cinema. In fact it should be noted that while the core rationale of this book involves a theoretical argument for framing sex through the notions of playfulness and play, as briefly sketched out above, it stems from markedly empirical, rather than exclusively conceptual or philosophical interest. *Many Splendored Things* draws especially from my long-term engagement with studies of pornography and affect theory, as it does from a collaborative project on girls' online practices of sexual messaging (Nielsen et al. 2015) and from my interest in Jan Soldat's documentary films on German kink communities. I return to many of these films in chapters 4 and 5 in order to unravel some of the dynamics of sex, play and sexual play and their connections with notions of identity, even though this would not be a cinema studies book in any recognizable shape or form.

Chapter 2, *Magic Circles and Magical Circuits of Play*, digs into theoretical discussions central to this book in studies of games, play, sexuality and affect in order both to map out existing work done at their intersections, and to more carefully contextualise and situate the project at hand. The chapter engages with the so-called classic conceptualisations of play in order to see what productive avenues they may open up. Studies of games and play have largely separated sexuality from their line of inquiry by arguing that sex involves other goals and aims than the pleasurable autotelic pursuit itself – such as procreation or orgasm. Questioning the viability and necessity of such instrumental claims and conceptual divides, the chapter makes an argument for taking play seriously in theorisations of sexuality. Its latter part explores the role of material bodies in studies of sexuality that have been preoccupied with the notion of the sexual drive ever since Sigmund Freud's discussion of the libido. Moving from sexual scripts to affect theory, the chapter makes an argument for the value of affect in addressing the capacities of bodies in studies of sexuality. All in all, Chapter 2 weaves through a heterogeneous range of scholarship on play and sex with the key aim of finding paths to bring the two concepts productively together without conflating them or positioning them as either distinct or mutually exclusive.

This discussion paves the way for Chapter 3, *"Raising the Ordinary to the Extraordinary"*, which looks into the mainstreaming and commodification of play in sexual role-playing guidelines and in the ambivalent international cross-media spectacle of E L James' *Fifty Shades of Grey* series. The chapter starts out by examining the gendered scripts, positions and dynamics of sexual play that circulate on online platforms and in popular advice literature, as well as the ways in which the terminology of play is deployed in framing sex as a leisure activity connected to commodity markets. Looking into the narrative patterns of romance, it then tackles the dynamics of instrumentality, pleasure and kink play in *Fifty Shades*. Rather than focusing on critiques of the series and its depiction of BDSM – as well-founded as these may be – the chapter foregrounds the productivity and value of sexual fantasy in terms of both capitalist logics of monetization and the carnal intensities that it affords. Linking sexual play with discussions on the experiences of enchantment, the chapter then explores the pleasures of *Fifty Shades* in terms of bodily capacities and intensifications.

Digging into the dynamics of childhood, sexuality and play, Chapter 4, *Pervy Minors and Adult Babies*, takes something of an unorthodox route. By drawing on a survey of more than 1,200 Finnish female respondents under the age of nineteen, it first explores the motivations of young people to engage in online sexual messaging and role-play connected to learning but, even more centrally, as driven by curiosity, fun and the quest for pleasure.

Reading the survey results in relation to extant literature on childhood sexual play, the chapter foregrounds the edge of play not as one of risk, harm or trauma so much as one of possibility, openness and pleasure. The chapter's second line of inquiry examines media depictions of age-play through tabloid television coverage of littles and Soldat's documentary films on adult baby play among adult gay men, *Coming of Age* (2016) and *Happy Happy Baby* (2016). By addressing the joys of playing a child and the potential sexual frissons that this entails, the chapter seeks to broaden and complicate the conceptual interrelations of age, sex and play. Rather than separating childhood explorations from adult sexuality either conceptually or empirically, it argues for understanding their differences as ones of degree rather than ones in kind, and as driven by the affective dynamics of pleasure and excitement. Furthermore, by moving from commercial television to independent documentary film, it inquires after the different spaces that media open up and close down for understanding age-play.

In Chapter 5, *Slaves, Prisoners and the Edge of Play*, I examine Soldat's films on BDSM play: *Der Unfertige/The Incomplete* (2013), *Haftanlage 4614/Prison System 4614* (2015), *Hotel Straussberg* (2014), *Die sechste Jahreszeit/The Sixth Season* (2015), *Der Besuch/The Visit,* (2015), *Zucht und Ordnung/Law and Order* (2012), *Ein Wochenende in Deutschland/A Weekend in Germany* (2013) and *Protokolle/Protocols* (2017). Sexual role-play emerges in these films as creative and productive activity that is seriously ludic, detached from the mandates of rationality and driven by the quest for bodily intensity. Rather than presenting sexual play as a functional solution to the problem caused by trauma – and hence articulating sexual tastes as something "curable", should harm and trauma eventually be overcome (Barker and Langdridge 2010) – Soldat's films foreground the centrality of bodily pleasure as a key motivation for play in ways that are productive in thinking about sexual orientations more generally. Discussing the films in relation to scholarship on BDSM, trauma and desire, as well as considering the ethics involved in the cinematic depiction of sexual cultures and likes of the more extreme kind, the chapter also examines motion and flow between different scenes, spaces and roles of play, as well as the very edges, or limits, of the notion of play itself.

The concluding Chapter 6, *Ripples across Identities*, moves further away from discussion of media to address the relations of sexuality, play and identity in the frameworks of feminist and queer theory. Summing up the book's key theoretical argument, it examines play as facilitating new forms and patterns of sensation through improvisation, and as disturbing the seeming stability of sexual identities. In foregrounding contingency, intensity and pleasure, the chapter argues for the centrality of fluidity in the realm of the sexual, as well as for the importance of conceptualising bodily desires, orientations and attachments outside clearly defined and mutually exclusive categories of sexual identity.

Rather than trying to force variations of sexual play into any fixed definitions or categories – to map out the rules of the game, so to speak – my interests throughout this book lie in the productive resonance that conceptualisations of play and playfulness allow in thinking about sex and sexuality. I ask how the concepts of play and playfulness can be used in eroding some of the tenacious norms and dualisms through which sexual lives continue to be labelled and understood – be these ones separating the straight from the queer, childhood from adulthood, normality from deviancy, work from play or fantasy from reality. It then follows that gender is, similarly to sexuality, figured as variations in ways of being, rather than through any clear – let alone binary – distinctions.

While the separation may come across as artificial or unproductive to some, this book is about sex rather than about gender: the "sex" I am addressing is not that of the sex–gender divide, and my examination of sexual play does not extend to the intersectional intermeshing and overlapping categories of identity at any length. This risks the caveat of both white and masculinist bias of the kind that Corie Hammers (2015) identifies in anti-social queer investigations of sexuality detached from the notion of gender. This risk is amplified in my engagement with Soldat's films focusing on the sexual lives of white German men. In asking what play brings into theorisations of sex, my attempt is not to efface any differences that matter but to explore lines of thinking that do not necessitate fixing these differences in, or approaching them as, pre-set taxonomies. This orientation of openness involves problematising identity as a default category for analysis.

As with any book, the list of things *not* covered would be long and undoubtedly boring to read. My final disclaimer therefore concerns the concepts used. While discussing romance in Chapter 3 as a narrative genre, there is little mention in this book of eroticism, love or relationships. To compensate, there are myriad discussions on sex. Instead of making use of the notions of play and playfulness in order to describe certain kinds of relationships, or "love styles" (see Waskul and Vannini 2008, 242), and hence isolating them as issues pertaining to specific platforms, personalities, identities or life arrangements, this book sets out to explore what these concepts, in their foregrounding of experimentation, openness and pleasure, can do in and for studies of sex and sexuality, as well as how sex and sexuality appear when considered through this particular analytical lens. In doing so, *Many Splendored Things* argues for the value of thinking sex through play in feminist and queer knowledge production.

2

Magic Circles and Magical Circuits of Play

Exploring the topic of sex as play some decades ago, Nelson E. Foote (1954, 159) noted that "The view that sex is fun can ... hardly be called the invention of immoralists; it is everyman's discovery." During the years to follow, sex has increasingly been conceived of as pleasurable, fun and recreational activity. Feona Attwood connects this to transformations in how sex is perceived as "a cultural pursuit, an exercise of taste, a set of skills, a communicative practice, a performance, a form of self-care, and a type of leisure in which media are produced and consumed" (Attwood 2011, 88; also Attwood and Smith 2013). Following Attwood, sex cuts through all kinds of fields of action without being reducible to any single one of them. According to one prevalent frame of understanding, sex signifies hedonistic and leisurely exploration of possibilities:

Although increasingly mainstream, this new sexual hedonism draws on some previously quite marginal sexual sensibilities. The first of these is derived from sex-positive and sex-radical writing and practice devoted to the reclaiming of sexual pleasure and to a revaluation of reviled practices such as masturbation, S/M, the use of pornography and sex work. The second is drawn from gay cultures, emphasizing the celebration of diversity and the creation of communities based around sexuality. The third is a "playboy" sensibility, embodied in the men's lifestyle magazine of the same name and in the development of clubs focused on leisure, straight men's entertainment and the availability of female "playmates". (Attwood 2011, 86)

In gay hook-up cultures, an invitation to play signifies an invitation to sex with no strings attached (Race 2015a, 2015b), while in the United States, casual hook-up culture has been identified as characteristic of the social and sexual relationships among college students (Kalish and

Kimmel 2011). The ubiquity of sexual encounters involving no expectation of relationships to follow is indicative of a redefinition of sex as a leisure activity that can be casual, serious or anything in between. All this is further supported and fuelled by the broad use of hook-up apps such as Tinder or Grindr. Hooking up allows for expansions of sexual repertoires and explorations of desire, yet Rachel Kalish and Michael Kimmel (2011, 138) argue that "as the new normative sexual experience … it structures that very erotic exploration into definable and normative constructs, constraining the very impulses it enables". Kath Albury (2018, 81) nevertheless further points out that "casual sex between heterosexuals is not a recent innovation, nor is the 'gamification' of dating a purely digital phenomenon", but rather something championed by feminists and other activists at least since the nineteenth century. What may be novel in this is the mainstreaming and increasing public visibility of such engagements.

The term play has long been used in sex parties of all kinds, be the context one of BDSM, age-play or a swingers' event where other participants are potential playmates for its duration (Frank 2013). Understood in this vein, sex is play in the thesaurus senses of the term: a site for acquiring physical skill and for displaying technical mastery in improvised encounters practised for the sake of enjoyment (see also Attwood 2011, 89). In parties, sex may also gain an additional performative dimension if other people participate as an audience (Harviainen and Frank 2016, 12). Kane Race (2015b, 506), however, argues that although gay male hook-up parties are "ostensibly organised around sex, group play actually comprises a number of linked activities, including chatting and chilling, filming sex, watching porn, collective browsing, various forms of consumption and the exchange of information about other individuals and encounters". These play scenes unfold as exchanges where sex is both fuelled by and feeds into engagements with screen-based media in ways allowing for a range of sociability and pleasure, from the casual to the intense.

Writing on the spaces of play, Johan Huizinga famously coined the notion of a "magic circle" to describe their separation from other realms of everyday life, the suspension of mundane rules and codes, as well as the specific spaces, rituals and codes that play entails:

Play is distinct from "ordinary life" both as to locality and duration. It is "played out" within certain limits of time and place …

All play moves and has its being within a play-ground marked off beforehand either materially or ideally, deliberately or as a matter of course ... The arena, the card-table, the magic circle, the temple, the stage, the screen, the tennis court, the court of justice, etc., are all in form and function play-grounds, i.e. forbidden spots, isolated, hedged round, hallowed, within which special rules obtain. All are temporary worlds within the ordinary world, dedicated to the performance of an act apart. (Huizinga 1949, 9, 10)

According to a logic attached to spaces of sexual play – from BDSM dungeons to adult baby cribs and fields set for pony-play – when entering the domain, participants adapt to pre-agreed roles, rules and codes of conduct, and act accordingly (e.g. Hale 1997, 233; Fernbach 2002, 197; Wignall and McCormack 2017, 807). For a submissive partner, entry into a scene of play may also involve moving into a sensory, cognitive and affective "headspace" of altered experience intensified by transformations in the body's chemical balance. Headspace can be specified as a subspace, drop, little space, pony space, pup space, etc., according to the scenes and roles involved. The norms governing appropriate ways of doing gender, sexuality or even species can be suspended in scenes of play where impro-visation remains constant, yet their rules may allow for little flexibility in terms of what physical activities are expected and accepted (Cooper 2003; Harviainen and Frank 2016, 11).

In a play party, casual sex with novel partners in different constellations is merely to be expected, not to mention sought after, even if the same people would not tolerate such errant behaviour from their partners in other settings. As J. Tuomas Harviainen and Katherine Frank (2016, 4) note, "At lifestyle events, participants engage in activities that would be sanctioned or disapproved of in other realms; despite local variation, then, the rules, norms, and expectations of events allow participants to exper-iment with physical and emotional transgressions in situations where safety and danger are balanced." This magic circle is not self-contained but "the membrane between worlds is porous": "participants remain cog-nizant of the social, psychological, and physical consequences that their actions would have outside of that circle" (Harviainen and Frank 2016, 3, 16; see also Denfeld and Gordon 1970; James and Smith 1970).

The detachment of spaces of play from those of everyday life, as implied in the notion of a magic circle, may echo and find support from a puritan fencing off of sex from other mundane surroundings and attachments. John H. Simon and William Gagnon (1986, 109) see such "disjunctive experience" manifesting in routines like turning off the lights before having sex in order "not to be seen, not to see, not to be seen seeing". A more mundane and ephemeral sort of entry to a space of sexual play can occur without there being any change in physical location, or without this space being in any way separable from the other rhythms and routines of life. Sex does not necessitate any disconnection between scenes of play and other modes of experiencing the world and engaging with the bodies in it. Rather, sex can be seen as involving bodily transformations in the intensities and qualities of relation, attachment and interaction.

As improvisation and creative adaptation, play within and outside sexuality has the potential to transform everyday meanings and to expand the boundaries of what people may desire and do, how and with whom (Adelman 1992, 72). Rather than being confined in any specific magic circles per se, magical circuits of sexual play emerge and unfold across mundane spaces and locations, in all sorts of instances and occasions. Within these circuits, not all social rules and conventions apply. Dirty talk, for example, may come about as a means to both express and amplify sexual desire when the terminology of fucking replaces the vocabulary of making love and a beloved metamorphoses into a nasty slut. The language that functions as amplifier of sexual desire is unlikely to be deployed outside the frame of play without the context being a confrontational and possibly aggressive one. The same would apply to the motions of slapping, biting, pinching, tugging and pulling hair that can express, fuel and amplify the intensities of sexual arousal but most likely would, in a different context, come across as abusive (also Ryan and Mohr 2005).

Sexual play may come about spontaneously and through improvisation when a touch, sense of physical proximity or a frisson of desire turns a moment into one of sexual experimentation without any specific planning or set-up involved. In other instances, sexual play may emerge in realms not intended for the purpose – for example, when people shoot videos of themselves exposing their genitalia and pleasuring themselves in spaces of work and share them online for the purposes of shared entertainment (Paasonen et al. forthcoming). One may well force one's play on to others, as when masturbating in windows, streets or parks. Alternatively, one can play with oneself without any sociability being involved, given the frequency with which autotelic practices geared towards sexual pleasure, fantasy and exploration are also autoerotic in character. This goes against an understanding of play as fundamentally a social activity, as in sociologist Georg Simmel's definition of play as a non-instrumental, pleasurable form of association based on the exchange of stimulus where more serious purposes, pursuits or ends are suspended. For Simmel (1949, 255), play is accompanied, or driven, "by a feeling for, by a satisfaction in, the very fact that one is associated with others and that the solitariness of the individual is resolved into togetherness, a union with others". As Race (2015a, 259) notes, adapted to discussions of sex, this definition "foregrounds a role for sex in the assembly of affective associations that Simmel would term 'sociability'". Seen in this vein, sexual play is a means of building affective associations disconnected from emotional ties or extended intimacies, yet it should be emphasised that these associations do not emerge within human interactions alone. Sexual fantasies both open up towards the world and work inwards within bodies as resonant associations. Autoerotic play fuelled by fantasy is not necessarily solitary inasmuch as it can be inhabited by non-human actors from sex toys and other paraphernalia to erotic literature or the abundantly available scenarios harvested from online pornography, themselves resulting from complex networks of performers, producers, distributors; cameras, software, hardware and server farms; bodies of flesh as well as those of silicone, plastic and metal (see Paasonen 2011, 104–105). In such circuits of play, affective reverberations cut through human and non-human actors that can occupy equally pivotal roles in the mise-en-scène of desire.

In a more social setting, a shift towards sexual play can be communicated by dressing up in the props or uniforms of a role-play scenario, by "changing into something more comfortable" or merely by stripping off one's garments. The gestures involved can be dramatic or subtle in their nuances, depending on the nature of the encounter about to unfold and the established relationships between the play participants. Some accessories adorn the body in ways that accentuate its characteristic features while others erode personal traits and yet others assemble them in novel ways. Uniforms and costumes are broadly used to indicate status, skill, desired roles and acts within play, as well as to locate the play participants in relation to one another (Hale 1997, 224; Weiss 2011, 112). Costuming allows for people to be subsumed by roles and their respective, regularly polarised positions of power within the play scene (Steele 1996, 180). Dressing up can be a means to indicate dominant or submissive position, to arouse one's partner(s) or to experience more solitary thrills.

The props involved in play, from sexy underwear to more specific paraphernalia, are nevertheless not mere communication devices or instruments for attracting attention. Following Maurizia Boscagli's (2014, 52) discussion of materiality, such props can be seen as "torn between competing forces, animated by a traffic between meaning and libidinal volatility". In other words, the object-world connected to and integrated in sexual play is an active element in the networks of actors – both human and non-human – that comprises the scene of desire and its circuits of bodily excitement (also Wignall and McCormack 2017, 805). Props and fetishes function as objects of sexual desire and fantasy animated by the affective intensities attached to them. They animate people in return through a "complex energetic charge to act on the matter that is subjectivity itself" (Boscagli 2014, 53).

In her study of San Francisco BDSM culture, Margot Weiss conceptualises kink paraphernalia as technological prostheses allowing for transformations in the forms of embodiment and bodily technique. These "produce *a body in play*: a body that is simultaneously divided into parts and extended through objects, both produced and transformed through consumption" (Weiss 2011, 104, emphasis in the original). Play paraphernalia reorganises bodily zones, contours and extensions as well as the capacities of what these bodies can do and sense in accordance with the objects' surface feel, material density, flexibility and impact. The tactile capacities of toys then craft, expand and reconfigure connections and exchanges between human and non-human bodies and make "novel sensations and relations possible. SM toys are carefully designed to amp-lify, prolong, or expand bodily sensations; toys are catalogued as stingy, thuddy, sharp, soft, cutting, surface, deep, intense" (Weiss 2011, 114).

In the case of fetishes, seeing, caressing, smelling or dressing in one's particular inanimate object of attraction affectively re-attunes the body by moving it from one state to another in immediate and possibly forceful ways (compare Steele 1996, 144; Califia 1999, 177). Such objects prime and cue the body for sexual play much like seeing and touching a human partner might, with the notable exception of the sense of control that fetishes allow for (see Kaplan 2006, 3, 7). To a degree, fetishism "bridges the gap between subjects and objects by disregarding the injunction that relations to objects should be rational and unclouded by emotion while only relations to subjects can be passionate or loving" (McCallum 1999, 109). The complex sexual dynamics revolving around an object of desire, whether it be human or not, are both affective and cognitive, and magnetic in the force with which they impress themselves on those properly attuned.

Mapping out Play, Framing out Sex

Huizinga (1949) saw play as fundamentally meaningful activity intrinsic to all animal life. Play has since been examined in similar terms as non-human category, modality and instinct crossing the dividing lines between species and possibly creating connections between their respective members (e.g. Sutton-Smith 1997; Caillois 2001, 25, 28; Nachamanovitch 2009; Wirman 2014). Among human participants, play has been defined as markedly social activity that binds people together in more or less public – and occasionally clandestine – arrangements (Simmel 1949; Weiss 2011 Stenros 2015, 57). For Huizinga, play was elementary in and for human lives, voluntary in its participation, non-utilitarian in its orientation and absorbingly intense in its forms. Play offers "rapture and enthusiasm": "A feeling of exaltation and tension accompanies the action, mirth and relaxation follow" (Huizinga 1949, 132). As Huizinga (1949, 43) himself noted, many of these characteristics are also "illustrative of the sexual act".

These definitions would indeed seem applicable to sex: to the thrills and impossibilities of sexual desire and to the interlacing of pleasure and pain involved in bodies opening up towards and impacting one another. Nevertheless Huizinga did not see many of the formal and functional characteristics of play as "really illustrative of the sexual act. It is not the act as such that the spirit of language tends to conceive as play; rather the road theretho, the preparation for and introduction to 'love', which is often made enticing by all sorts of playing" (Huizinga 1949, 42.) For Huizinga, foms of courtship, flirtation and wooing, as additions and preliminaries to sex – addressed as love – may match the criteria set for play while sex as such would not. It would therefore be "erroneous to incorporate the sexual act itself, as love-play, in the play category. The biological process of pairing does not answer to the formal characteristics of play as we postulated them. Language also normally distinguishes between love-play and copulation. The term 'play' is specially or even exclusively reserved for erotic relationships falling outside the social norm" (Huizinga 1949, 43).

Bonnie Ruberg (2010) points out that, for Huizinga, only reproductive heterosex serves a purpose while other sexual practices "might even be classified as 'perverse.' This perversion, it seems, is inextricably bound up with playfulness." The conflation of sex with heterosexual copulation – "the biological process of pairing" – is hardly surprising in a book originally published in 1938. Two decades later, Roger Caillois made a similar rhetorical gesture in his formal taxonomy of play. Caillois (2001, 13, 27, 31) divided ways of playing into two mutually opposing modes: *paedia* as tumultuous, exuberant, frolicsome and connected to the "primary power of improvisation and joy" and *ludus* as a "taste for gratuitous difficulty" involving skill and effort. Within the mode of paedia, Caillois (2001, 27, 34) evokes the Sanskrit term *kredati* and the Chinese term *wan* to designate "the sudden and capricious movements provoked by superabundance of gaiety and vitality ... illicit sex relationships, the rise and fall of waves, and anything that undulates with the wind", as well as "casual, abnormal, or strange sex practices". Both kredati and wan refer to play driven by improvisation and joy of the kind that he does not extend to other kinds of sexual encounters or engagements.

Within the modes of paedia and ludus, Caillois categorises play into four distinct groups or types. Of these, *mimicry* is connected to taking on the figure or persona of something or someone while *ilinx* entails momentary bodily ecstasy sought out in play (Caillois 2001, 129). As fantasy play, mimicry would be applicable to sexual role-play while ilinx, as unruly "voluptuous panic upon an otherwise lucid mind" where one surrenders "to a kind of spasm, seizure, or shock which destroys reality with sovereign brusqueness", would seem descriptive of the thrills of sex more broadly (Caillois 2001, 19–21, 23). Caillois nevertheless draws no such connections between sex and modes of play while leaving the category of "illicit, abnormal and strange sex" fitting the mode of paedia equally vague. Writing on fairground rides and the play category of ilinx, he notes that their "effects of dizziness and terror are joined to produce an added diffuse and insidious anguish and delight, that of seeking a sexual liaison. At this point one leaves the realm of play as such" (Caillois 2001, 136). Why precisely this would be the case, he chooses not to explain or elaborate.

Like Huizinga, Caillois associates practices belonging to Rubin's vast terrain of "bad sex" with playfulness. By implication, sex following more normative identifications, relationships and routines is framed outside play proper. According to this line of thinking, the bulk of straight sex, whether revolving around penile-vaginal intercourse or not, has little to do with playful explorations of any sort. Writing some eight decades after Huizinga and six after Caillois, Sicart (2014, 21, 26), despite offering a highly useful definition of play as bound up with diverse shades of plea-sure, as addressed in the previous chapter, is equally agile to detach play from sex. Sicart argues that sex can be *playful* but not *play* since it involves other purposes and therefore conflicts with the autotelic character of play as an end in itself. Meanwhile, other realms of human action can inter-mesh with play – for example, when creative play takes over or occupies a political context and balances the autotelic aspects of play with social aims, goals and purposes (Sicart 2014, 71, 81).

The strained yet tenacious conceptual distinction between play and sex, of which there would be multiple additional examples on offer, may speak of the enduring legacy of what Harviainen, Ashley Brown and Jaakko Suominen (2014), in their extensive game studies literature overview, identify as the field's general reluctance to address sexuality, and as a lin-gering sense of awkwardness when doing so. They associate such aversion with potential puritan prudishness, awareness of the stigma connected to the topic of sexuality in academic research, as well as with something of a paradigmatic puberty mentality within game studies. Consequently, "Instead of engagement with the theme of sexuality itself, and what it may represent to players and play in a larger context, researchers are happy to settle for analyzing titillating case examples" (Harviainen et al. 2016, 14). In other words, sex is picked up as an accent separate from the broader patterns in which sexual lives are organised, lived, sensed, made sense of or theorised.

This, of course, is not to say that sexuality would have remained absent in studies of games and play: as Evan W. Lauteria and Matthew Wysocki (2015, 1) note, "sex and play are intricately tied together". These interconnections have been examined in terms of sexual gaming content and game characters, representations, tasks, goals and plotlines connected to, or making use of, sexuality (e.g. Osborne 2012; Wysocki and Lauretia 2015; Shaw and Friesem 2016). In addition, videogames, massively multiplayer online role-playing games (MMORPGs) and other online platforms have been explored in terms of the forms of exchange and desire that they facilitate between the bodies of participants and those of players, pixels and imagination (e.g. Waskul and Vannini 2008; Sundén 2009; Ruberg 2010; Brown 2012; Sundén and Sveningsson 2012). All in all, scholarly focus has been mainly on in-game sexual dynamics, on variations of sexual play, on play with sexuality in game environments, as well as on the economies of desire, forms of intimacy, bodily intensity, queer and unruly gender performativity that all these afford.

Despite such notable, and by now multiple, efforts, a separation of sex from play has a tendency to re-emerge in game studies literature, especially when it zooms in on the notion of play itself. In her research on sexuality in role-playing games, Brown (2015, 11–12) notes how sex and sexuality have been used in game studies to define "the boundaries of what may be considered ludic" and hence to reach some kind of definition of games through negation. Brian Sutton-Smith (1997, 63), for example, in evoking the vintage Cartesian mind–body dualism, suggests that "Dreams and play are perhaps as appetitive for the mind as food and sex for the body." This dualism frames both dreams and play out from the realm of carnal passions, cravings and orientations in ways that flatten out the complexities of imagination and fantasy, from playful sex scenes to erotic dreams and gourmet fantasies. At the same time, the dualism paradoxically pairs dreams with the mind, and play with sex, and hence suggests their intimate cohabitations and possible intermeshings. Associated with both food and sex, play then becomes lodged in the bodily terrain of physical desires and actions.

The default separation of sex from play remains problematic for a number of reasons. First, considering how Sicart (2014, 16) elsewhere argues that the autotelic nature of play "is always being discussed and negotiated", it would seem to follow that the key criterion of play as being an end in itself would in fact not be altogether clear, stable or set as such. In other words, the analytical power of ludic autotely in separating play from sex would be questionable for the simple reason that play may easily indeed leak towards functional, performative and instrumental purposes. One only needs to think of the bourgeoning field of gamification, namely the application of game design elements in other contexts spanning from education to marketing, journalism, health, work productivity and politics, to illustrate the diverse realms of instrumentality connected to play.

Second, the separation of sex from play, in Huizinga, Caillois and Sicart alike, frames play as a highly specific realm of action – or even as an object of sorts – while still defining it in broad strokes as a form of being in the world, as a mode of being human, as elementary to culture and as something bridging divides between different species. This considered, the exclusion of sex from the realm of play simply comes across as counterintuitive. Third, and most crucially in terms of this book, the prising apart of sex and play presumes and frames sex as a clearly outlined set of activities, orientations and attachments. It therefore presumes that sex comes with a definite and shared set of aims, and that sex is productive and purposeful by default. While scholars of games and play do not necessarily define what purposes they are referring to, it is fair to assume that they are connected to the goals of orgasm, procreation and relationships.

Rather than boxing in either play or sex as separable from other fields of human action, or setting out to answer the question of whether sex can be play or not (yes? no? maybe? depending on the context?), it is notably more productive to consider what conceptualisations of play and playfulness may bring to, and afford in, examinations of sex and sexuality. This necessitates thinking of sex and play parallel to, or alongside, one another without fully equating them – and certainly without positioning them as mutually incompatible to start with.

Procreation, Pleasure and Play

To state the obvious, neither orgasm nor procreation is the key aim or purpose of sexual play. All sorts of playful experimentation with the feel, touch and scent of bodies can be categorised as sexual without it being reducible to orgasm as a teleological goal. While this would be most pronounced in practices such as tantric sex where the techniques practised involve prolonging orgasm and sexually retuning the body towards broader sensory receptivity, allowing for extended peak experiences without climax, this would not be the only available example. As practices of bodily intensification, sexual play, from bondage to role-playing and beyond, need not revolve around orgasm or be genital in its focus – a point also discussed below in chapters 4 and 5.

The overwhelming majority of sexual encounters would in fact fall outside any narrow definitions of purposefulness or usefulness. Sexual play is not necessarily instrumental or productive except for the bodily intensities, thrills and pleasures it offers. Meanwhile, these can be pressing and considerable in themselves. Measured in terms of material outcomes, sex is fundamentally unproductive. Similarly, for Caillois, play "creates no wealth or goods, thus differing from work or art. At the end of the game, all can and must start over again at the same point. Nothing has been harvested or manufactured, no masterpiece has been created, no capital has accrued. Play is an occasion of pure waste: waste of time, energy, ingenuity, skill, and often of money" (Caillois 2001, 5–6; also Waskul and Vannini 2008, 242.) While meaningless, these activities are nevertheless not senseless, for "there is a sensation to be understood" (Karhulahti 2013). This sensation matters and is purposeful as such, as well as productive in the sense of giving rise to both fleeting and more lingering bodily intensities and attachments.

Given the massive concern with avoiding procreation rather than advancing it in heterosexual relations, reproductive purposes for coitus represent an exception rather than the rule. Sex practised for reproductive purposes is differently purposeful and involves the monitoring of ovulation cycles, bodily temperatures and the scheduling of opportune timing for ejaculate to enter the womb. It does not necessitate penetrative sex or any physical interaction between partners. And should such carnal contact occur, other interests, foci and purpose easily eclipse sexual pleasure and experimentation. Furthermore, reproduction is not exactly a pressing concern in any variations of oral and anal sex, licking, sucking, fingering, probing, slapping or stroking, irrespective of the partners' genders. The key question then is what is meant with sex in the first place when framing it out from the realm of play.

Attempts to define sex through reproductive purposes obscure the range of enjoyable practices that people engage in while also staging sex in exclusively, narrowly and problematically heteronormative terms. By doing so, they fail to grasp the degrees to which sex is connected to and driven by the pursuit of pleasure. Suggesting something of this sort, sex researchers Paul Abramson and Steven Pinkerton (2002, 6) note that "Even penile-vaginal intercourse is practiced far more often than necessary to ensure the continuation of the species." This assessment is undoubtedly correct, yet also something of a stark understatement. It would also be a highly unremarkable remark to make, given that the detachment of coitus as a possible source of pleasure from the purposes of reproduction in het-erosexual arrangements was pointed out in the Kinsey report data some seven decades ago (see Foote 1954, 159–160).

Despite all this, procreation continues to play a key role in sex research as a premised innate need and motivator for sexual encounters that is not necessarily easy to balance with the purposes of pleasure. This is already evident in how the publisher heralded Abramson and Pinkerton's trea-tise, *With Pleasure*, as presenting "a controversial new theory about sex-uality that proclaims the importance of pleasure over reproduction". That an emphasis on sexual pleasure over reproduction was presented as both novel and controversial in the year 2002 seems to me remarkable, as well as disappointing. It gestures towards the weight of the puritan legacy in North American sex research, the shadow of which continues to loom large not only on the sexual politics of that particular continent but on the dynamics of scholarly exchange internationally. It further speaks of the persistent ways in which sexuality continues to be framed "as a biolog-ical function rooted in evolutionary imperatives which are then translated straightforwardly into social institutions and cultural norms" (Epstein 1994, 189) – a view that sociological, feminist and queer sexuality scholars have tackled for several decades.

Examining the notion of sexual play in a more interdisciplinary framing, it has notably often been evoked in studies of species other than human. Scientific articles on sexual play among mammals have routinely taken a functionalist angle by zooming in on its role in mating behaviour, in facilitating copulation, in social bonding and in reciprocal interactions. Consequently, studies exist, for example, on sexual play among squirrel monkeys (Latta et al. 1967), bonobo chimpanzees (Enomoto 1990), domestic sheep (Orgeur and Signoret 1984) and rhesus monkeys (Harlow and Lauersdorf 1974). In ways not entirely different from Huizinga's (1949, 56, 129) association of courtship but not sex with play, such studies emphasise playful exploration and learning preceding but not occurring during penile-vaginal intercourse (see also Sutton-Smith 1997, 103; Ryan and Mohr 2005). It is perhaps needless to point out that the notion of sex is, in these studies, firmly rooted in, and confined to, reproductive purposes.

The outcomes of primate studies have also been adopted in addressing binary gender differences in human "passion and play" as ones that "begin at birth and encompass all developmental stages, from early sex reflexes through early sex behavior, personal characteristics, juvenile play, the subsequent maturation of aggression, and then into adulthood and the roles of parenthood", manifesting as male aggression and female passiveness in the realm of heterosex (Harlow and Lauersdorf 1974, 348–349, 352; also DeLamater and Friedrich 2002). For their part, researchers zooming in on human sexual play have focused on its role in the formation and maintenance of intimate relations in the fields of sexology, family and sex therapy, and in frameworks which, while allowing for degrees of variation in such behaviours, tend to be firmly and steadily heterosexual in their samples, bent, orientation and foci. Consequently, scholars have mapped out playfulness as a personality trait that facilitates the emergence of positive emotions, effects relationship satisfaction, "signals nonaggressiveness in men and youth and health as signs of fecundity in women", and associates positively with love, sexuality, seduction and attachment (Proyer 2014, 502, 509).

Psychologist Kurt Frey's (1991) account of sexual behaviour as adult play remains rare as an extended consideration of pleasure, sexuality and play (see also Apter 1991). It has also been resisted for conceptual confusion: guarding the separateness of play and sex, Sutton-Smith (1997, 103) sees Frey's discussion as exemplary of "letting the sexual identity rhetoric run away with itself". Frey (1991, 56) argues that sexual play can only be defined phenomenologically, in terms of the experiences involved in the play activity itself. For Frey (1991, 56–57), writing within the framework of reversal theory, sex involves a paratelic state characteristic of play that lays "emphasis on immediate gratification, focus on heightened

emotionality and sensuality, effort to become 'worked up' and emotionally charged, and activity which is freely chosen, spontaneous, and experimental". Without such a state of mind, sex will feel much more like work
and become void of pleasure (also Stenros 2015, 68). And if one is not in
the right mood, sexual activity becomes drained of the enchantment and
gratification that otherwise motivate and characterise it.

The separation of playfulness from other moods nevertheless involves
the caveat of simplifying the contexts of and motivations for sex. One may,
for example, professionally offer and sell sexual services so that play is literally work – possibly pleasurable and possibly not – to at least one participant, and a source of titillation and gratification for others. Clients can
seek out such services for the lack of a suitable partner, for the excitement
of paying for them, or because they want to keep their inclinations secret
from the people close to them (Califia 1999, 237): in any case, the enterprise
requires non-spontaneous planning and scheduling. All this fits uneasily
in the conceptual confines set by Frey. In any arrangement, one partner
may be "in the mood" and another not. While Caillois (2001, 45) identifies
this as the corruption of play by the real world, it is more fitting to conceptualise it as one of the modes in which play unfolds, moves into and out. At
the same time, play remains attuned to the world in which it is set, independent of whether its affective charge is high or low, and whether there
is much or little spontaneity to the scene and the experimentations taking
place within it.

Importantly, the moods of work and play need not be seen as mutually
exclusive binary opposites. Despite the broad use of the dualistic terminology of being turned either "on" or "off" – similarly to electronic gadgets
made operable through electric current – moods are more of an issue of
gradations in bodily affectation ranging from flatness to heightened intensity and back again, with all the nuances, amplifications, complications
and paradoxes that such a contingent scale entails. A fleeting tingle of
desire may be motivation enough for casual sex for some, while others
only feel inclined to touch another person's body with guarantees of emotional commitment and a firm sense of being specifically sought out and
desired. It is possible to discover pleasure in scenarios that come about
without much volition or initiative of one's own, and to not arrive at any
in scenes of one's own meticulous crafting. The issue is also one of more

sustained attunements and orientations where some feel the intensities of sexual desire only all too acutely whereas others do not register them as central, meaningful or pleasurable in their own lives (see Flore 2014). Rather than conceptualising asexuality as the opposite of sexuality, or as a problem to be somehow solved, the issue can then be considered one of different bodily intensities and qualities that contribute to the specific hue and rhythm of a person's life.

Frey's discussion of sex as adult play finds some resonance in James P. Carse's (2012) broad discussion of the centrality of play for human interaction and creativity, which also extends to sexuality. Carse builds a binary conceptual division between finite and infinite play. The former is defined through set rules and clear roles and results in winners and losers once the game is through. In contrast, the joyful openness of infinite games is motivated by the sheer desire to keep on playing. The creativity, improvisation and openness of horizons of possibility characteristic of infinite play are then juxtaposed with the fixity and formulaic nature of finite play. Like all binary oppositions, Carse's orders the world it describes into two assumedly distinct and mutually contradicting modes of being, operating and thinking. These paradoxically flatten out much of the complexity that different forms and styles of play allow for thinking about pleasure and bodily intensity. Infinite play within sexuality involves the probing of possible pleasures and options without the goals of reproduction or orgasm as "embodied play" and "the drama of touching" (Carse 2012, 85). In infinite play, players "prepare themselves to be surprised by the future" and this openness entails an understanding of the self as contingent and emergent in its horizons of possibility (Carse 2012, 18, 58). In contrast, finite play entails the staged, scripted and costumed theatre of seduction where one wins and the other is defeated (Carse 2012, 82).

Despite examples such as Neil Strauss' bestselling *The Game: Penetrating the Secret Society of Pickup Artists* (2005) that provides guidelines for straight men to gain the upper hand in the game of courtship in ways illustrative of finite play, these two modes and forms of play can be pitted against one another only at the expense of analytical richness. As argued in some detail above in the context of props and paraphernalia, scripting, staging and costuming of all kinds can play a central role in sexual play geared towards the affective registers of surprise and excitement.

Independent of any discrepancies between the partners' interests, future plans or access to pleasure, sex can be conceptualised as a game resulting in winners and losers only with some difficulty. As improvisation occupies a central position in all kinds of sexual play, its rules can be notably lax or ephemeral. (Brown 2015, 13; Stenros 2015, 70, 94.) Independent of pre-established agreements between partners, the forms and possibilities of sexual encounters are never fully set or knowable from the outset, nor fully theirs to foresee or to control. Knowing decisions are elementary in setting up scenes of play, yet there is rawness, immediacy and fickleness to sexual fantasy, desire and the routes within which play unfolds.

As a sense – or at least as an imminent possibility – of openness and experimentation, playfulness cuts across all kinds of sexual arrangements. To separate play and playfulness from other moods and intensities that animate bodies ultimately means operating with a partial and norma-tive understanding of sexuality that frames out a broad range of practices, routines and experiences – or, alternatively, supports hierarchies of value and normality between them. This may then lead to vigilant patrolling at the boundaries of the concept of play in terms of what qualifies or fails to qualify as such, what it may or may not entail.

Scripts and Performances

Sexual play takes place within, and derives a large part of its dynamics from, social organization, identity categories, normative operations, power relations, gendered images and tropes. In studies of gender and sexuality, sex has been extensively examined as a matter of acquired and enforced hierarchies, scripts and rules that provide gendered guidelines of action while also separating the acceptable from the unacceptable, the so-called normal from the deviant, vanilla from kink and the private from the public (e.g. Warner 2000; Hoppe 2011).

In their sexual script theory, first outlined in the 1970s, Simon and Gagnon (1986, 100) argue that the illusion of a self, autonomous in its desires and "distinct from the roles it may be required to play", emerges within the webs of internalised and improvised cultural norms. Script theory conceptualises sexuality in terms of learned imageries, routines, appetites and interactions that follow gendered outlines (see also

Richardson 2007, 461; Vörös 2015). These scripts are played out on the levels of *cultural scenarios*, namely normative guidelines that proscribe certain roles for individuals to perform; *interpersonal scripts* that emerge as "patterned improvisation" through which "appropriate identities are made congruent with desired expectations"; as well as *intrapsychic scripts* involving the fantastic reorganisation of reality that links individual desires to social meanings (Simon and Gagnon 1986, 98–99; Irvine 2003; Vörös 2015, 125–127). Unpacking the function of scripts, Simon and Gagnon make broad use of theatrical terminology. In staging the self in accordance with interpersonal scripts, "the actor ultimately must submit to the playwright, while both nervously anticipate the responses of overlapping but not always harmonious panels of internal and external critics ... The concept of scripting, then, can take on a very literal meaning: not the creation and performance of a role but the creation and staging of a drama" (Simon and Gagnon 1986, 110). In this framework, sexual encounters solicit improvisation by the play participants (Vörös 2015, 126).

Also writing in the 1970s, Michel Foucault (1990,156–157) mapped out the deployment of sexuality as acts of transforming desire into discourse – as scripting that is based on, and reproduces, an understanding of "sex" as precondition for individual intelligibility. Such scripting has both allowed for and necessitated a grouping together of "anatomical elements, biological functions, conducts, sensations, and pleasures, and enabled one to make use of this fictitious unity as a causal principle, an omnipresent meaning" (Foucault 1990, 154). Developing this line of thinking, Judith Butler further conceptualised gender as "an identity tenuously constituted in time ... instituted through a *stylized repetition of acts*" where actors become seduced by the gender fictions they enact (Butler 1988, 519, 522, emphasis in the original). The illusion of an abiding gendered self emerges, for Butler, "through the stylization of the body" and the mundane repetition of "gestures, movements, and enactments" that render individuals culturally intelligible (Butler 1988, 519–520). These normative scripts and templates precede the individual: "The act that one does, the act that one performs, is, in a sense, an act that has been going on before one arrived on the scene" (Butler 1988, 526). The compulsory repetition of norms entails openness for transformation as re-enactments always differ both from the norm and from one another to some degree. The reiteration of cultural scripts and proscriptions therefore also tests out their boundaries (Butler 1988, 531).

While drastically different in many respects, sexual script theory and the performative theory of gender have more in common than their use of theatrical metaphors. Both explore the operation of norms as sociocultural dictates, or templates of intelligibility, as well as their repetition on the micro-level of everyday gestures and encounters. In a firmly constructionist vein, both take critical distance from biological accounts of gender and sexuality by framing them as products of language and discourse always in the making, the former placing greater emphasis on individual agency than the latter (Jackson and Scott 2007, 96–97). Stevi Jackson and Sue Scott (2007, 109) point out that sexual scripts need to be understood not as locking people into predictable roles but as "fluid and open, offering opportunities to improvise. Scripts are played with, not simply played out; they are open to renegotiation as we take cues from partners and make sense of what is happening to them, to us and between us." As "active compositions" (Jackson and Scott 2007, 111), sexual scripts are under constant renegotiation and open to play. For sexologist Osmo Kontula (2009, 24), they "constitute a method with which people are able to organize their sexual behaviour" that "amounts to a kind of role play". There may seem to be default lightness – and perhaps even an edge of frivolity – to the notion of play when applied to sex, with all its theatrical connotations of performances, acts, scenes and scripts. This is, however, only one available interpretation, and one not foregrounded in either theories of sexual scripts or those of performative gender. Arguing against interpretations of her own work that see subjects as free to perform whatever identity they happen to choose, Butler proposes that constraint be rethought as the very condition of performativity that is "neither free play nor theatrical self-presentation" (Butler 1993, 94).

Sexual script theory and performative gender theory remain two key contexts in which the vocabulary of play has entered studies of sexuality, yet this book does not build on either one of them. My focus is not on the social or discursive construction of sexuality, on the psychoanalytical underpinnings of subjectivation connected to the orientation of desires, or on the formation of sexual identities. Rather, my interests lie in exploring sex in terms of physical intensities of arousal and pleasure that transpire as people play with themselves, with objects, ideas or other people. While addressing the constraints within which sexual tastes and preferences become forged, my attention focuses on the thick materiality and humming desires of bodies, their carnal capacities and potentialities that are irreducible to language, signification, discourse or categories of identity.

According to the main argument of this book, playfulness, as curiosity towards possible ways of being and acting out in the world, and play, as the realizations of playful acts and actions, open up conceptual means to explain how the ways of doing sex, relating to other bodies and making sense of one's own corporeal capacities come to vary. Such contingency is much more difficult to map out if approaching the issue in terms of normative operations of social power that push bodies in line and confine desires into clearly contoured identity categories. Furthermore, the pursuit and motivation of sexual pleasure explain something of how acts and motions solidify into routines in the course of their repetition. Simon and Gagnon observe that "Few individuals, like few novelists or dramatists, wander far from the formulas of their most predictable successes. Once finding a formula that works, i.e., the realization of sexual pleasure as well as the realization of sociosexual competence, there is an obvious tendency to on some levels 'fix' or pararitualize the formula" (Simon and Gagnon 1986, 111). When mapping out the features of play, Huizinga similarly addressed both its inner variation and repeatability:

While it is in progress all is movement, change, alteration, succession, association, separation. But immediately connected with its limitation as to time there is a further curious feature of play ... Once played, it endures as a new-found creation of the mind, a treasure to be retained by the memory. It can be repeated at any time ... In this faculty of repetition lies one of the most essential qualities of play ... In nearly all the higher forms of play the elements of repetition and alternation (as in *refrain*), are like the warp and woof of a fabric. (Huizinga 1949, 9, emphasis in the original)

Following this line of thinking, sexual play is generic and tied to repeatable patterns, yet equally primed towards variation, improvisation and change. Huizinga's characterisation helps to conceptualise sex as exploration, discovery, as well as the repetition of formulas and patterns that may, over time, solidify into routines short of intensity. There would, however, be no complete repeatability to any scene of play, even if the settings, partners, props and the choreographies performed were as identical as possible. The moment in time will be different, as will be the bodies involved, the previous motions and sensations accumulated in their somatic archives as "treasures retained", as well as the degrees of their mutual attunement and resonance. The choreography of sex itself always unfolds with a distinct rhythm, speed, sensation and intensity, independent of how closely the partners stick to a previously rehearsed script. Any template remains impossible to fully replicate, should someone so attempt, for things just play out differently, with another mood and rhythm.

Even when choreographies become routine, their repetition remains tied to pleasure as the key aim and motivation. In order for motions or scenes to become repeated, they need to promise pleasure at least to one participant, or to have facilitated some in the past. The pleasure may remain elusive and out of reach, as when people try to find enjoyment in acts they feel they should enjoy – be it penile-vaginal penetration, oral or anal sex, a position or a stylisation of the body preferred or insisted upon by a partner. Some may not feel like having sex without some dressing up involved; for others, additional accessories completely ruin the mood.

What Bodies Can Do

Sexual script theory, which has been highly influential in social constructivist approaches to sexuality, emerged from a process of writing against the functionalist and behaviouristic currents in sex research. In fact, it "rejected the whole apparatus of biology that located the explanations of sexuality as internal to the body". For Simon and Gagnon, "the phenomenological experience of either sexual desire or the desire for sex was a learned way to label ... interests within the context of specific interpersonal and intrapsychic conditions. *In our view there is no sexual wisdom that derives from the relatively constant physical body*" (Simon and Gagnon 2003, 492, emphasis added). This understanding of sexuality as detached from the capacities, desires and affordances of bodies comes with the effect of hollowing out their experiential range and visceral force. Identifying this dilemma, Florian Vörös (2015, 129) argues that encountering sexual script theory through the lens of affect nevertheless makes it possible to inquire

after the "carnal thickness" of scripts and the dynamics of sensory intensification in which they take place.

Contra the statement that there is no sexual wisdom to be derived from
the physical body – understood as constant, passive and inert materiality –
it is productive to recall Baruch Spinoza's (1992, 105) famous point that
"nobody as yet has determined the limits of the body's capabilities: that is,
nobody as yet has learned from experience what the body can and cannot
do." Despite advances in studies of human physiology since Spinoza com-
posed his *Ethics* in the seventeenth century, to a great extent the limits
and shapes of bodily capacities remain uncharted and unknown. This is
partly due to the complexity of bodily operations, as well as to the inter-
mingling of affect, cognition and sensation in how we feel our bodies and
how we feel out the world that makes generalisations over these capacities
so strenuous (e.g. Cervero 2012, 4, 53, 88). Sexual play presents one means
of testing out bodily capacities, and of pushing their perceived limits.
Meanwhile, social norms, as operations of power, affect what bodies can
do and what they cannot do. In doing so, they separate individuals from
their potentiality (Agamben 2011, 43).

Simon and Gagnon are certainly not alone in turning scholarly
attention away from the pulsations, exertions and excretions of sexual
bodies. Theirs is indicative of a broader tendency within studies of sexuality to overlook "the sexed body and its lustful desires" (Plummer 2003b,
522). Addressing this paradox of "vanishing sexuality" within sex research,
Ken Plummer (2003b, 525) inquires after the inclusion of the "sweating
and pumping, sensuous and feeling world of the emotional, fleshy body"
instead:

"Sexualities" involve social acts through which we "gaze" at bodies, desire bodies,
taste (even eat) bodies, smell bodies, fashion and adorn bodies, touch bodies,
hear bodies, penetrate bodies and orgasm bodies. These bodies can be our own
or those of others. "Doing sex" means "doing erotic body work." Sex body projects
entail, at the very least, presenting and representing bodies (as sexy, non-sexy, on
the street, in the gym, in the pornomovie); interpreting bodies and body parts (the
"gaze" and the "turn-ons" and "turn-offs" – sexual excitements of different kinds
from voyeurism to stripping); manipulating bodies (through the use of fashion,
cosmetics, prosthetics); penetrating bodies (all kinds of intercourses from body
parts like fingers and penises to "sex toy objects"); transforming bodies (stages of
erotic embodiment, movements towards orgasms); commodifying bodies (in sex

work, live sex acts, stripping, pornography and the like ...); ejecting and ejaculating bodies as all kinds of bodily fluids – semen, blood, sweat, saliva – even urine and fecal matter – start to commingle; possessing bodies (as we come to own or dominate others' bodies); exploiting bodies (as we come to abuse or terrorize them); and transgressing bodies (as we go to extremes in the use of our erotic bodies). (Plummer 2003b, 527)

Following this line of thought, all kinds of sexual wisdom can be derived from bodies that are, in fact, far from being constant or fixed in their intensities, attachments and affectations. In their aversion to biology, Simon and Gagnon turned away from the capacities and phenomenological experiences of bodies, just as they turned away from accounts of sexual desire as other than a product of society. Sexual script theory was, from the first, resistant to Freud's influential discussion of the libido which, like much early sex research, framed sex as an instinctual drive, need and instinct similar to thirst or hunger – even as *the* driving force of human action. For Freud, libido was a central element of the id, the unconscious mental energy that forms the basis of life, and is therefore primary. As the basis for emotional ties with other people, the world and one's self, sexual instinct "holds together everything in the world" (Freud 2011, 18):

We call by that name the energy (regarded as a quantitative magnitude, though not at present actually measurable) of those instincts which have to do with all that may be comprised under the word "love". The nucleus of what we mean by love naturally consists (and this is what is commonly called love, and what the poets sing of) in sexual love with sexual union as its aim. But we do not separate from this – what in any case has a share in the name of "love" – on the one hand, self-love, and on the other, love for parents and children, friendship and love for humanity in general, and also devotion to concrete objects and to abstract ideas. Our justification lies in the fact that psycho-analytic research has taught us that all these tendencies are an expression of the same instinctive activities. (Freud 2011, 17)

While the issue is too broad to properly unpack here, this centring of sexual desire as an engine driving people's lives and their multiple attachments involved a radical edge, yet it came with ample regulatory impulses delegating the proper routes that normal sexual development should take, what its gendered patterns and object-choices should be, and in what

kinds of intensities it should unfold. Framed in terms of health and healthiness, the normative notion of normality remains influential in much sex
research. Consequently, both the excessive intensity of sexual desire and
the shortage thereof are seen as issues requiring intervention or fixing, be
it through medication – such as the ever-elusive "women's Viagra" – or
therapy.

While Simon and Gagnon wrote against Freud's notion of the sexual
drive, Silvan S. Tomkins both revised and strongly critiqued it. Tomkins
conceptualised the intensities of sexual desire in terms of affective amplification: if sexual desire remains disconnected from the affect of excitement, there may be little to it that is compelling, interesting or worthwhile.
Similarly to Frey's conceptualisation of the necessity of "being in the
mood" in order for sexual play to take place, Tomkins saw the affective
amplifier of excitement as a prerequisite for sexual desire to push through
the events, intensities, obligations and frictions that occupy everyday lives.
In doing so, he argued for the centrality of affect for sexuality, cognition,
perception and sensation alike: "Excitement, rather than being a deriva-
tive of drives, is the major source of drive amplification. But if excitement
lends its magic to the drive system it is no less compelling as a support of
sensory input, of memory, of thought and of action." (Tomkins 2008, 188.)
Furthermore,

The excitement of sexuality is the same excitement as to poetry or mathematics'
beauty bare, or the possibility of good food. Although mathematics and sexuality
are different, the excitement that amplifies either cognitive capacity or drive is
identical. Sexuality without the affective amplification of excitement, however,
makes a paper tiger out of the penis. The id is not very imperious or pushy without
affect. The affect amplifies by increasing the urgency of anything with which it is
co-assembled. (Tomkins 1995, 53; also Tomkins 2008, 619–620)

Samantha Allen (2015, 56–57) points out that Tomkins' take on the sexual
drive "bears a scarce resemblance to Freud's 'sexual instinct' – a strong,
river-like force that must be channelled or diverted in its flow through
human development; rather, for Tomkins, the drive is more like a flick-
ering pilot light on a furnace with affect primarily responsible for the com-
bustion". Affect is aroused in ways and through factors that individuals can
scarcely control, yet without it "nothing else matters – and with its amplification, anything else *can* matter. It thus combines *urgency* and *generality*.

It lends power to memory, to perception, to thought, and to action no less than to the drives" (Tomkins 2008, 620, emphasis in the original). For Freud, the sex drive is central to emotional connections with the world, whereas for Tomkins, the affective capacities of human bodies orient their actions, interactions and relations. Excitement, in particular, is that which invests motions with a sense of magic: at the same time, it remains fickle, waxes and wanes, and weakens in the course of repetition and familiarity (Tomkins 2008, 193).

Tomkins' discussion of affect was rooted in experimental psychology. His key aim was to map out and explain the affect system as hardwired capacities of the human body divided into nine basic registers of interest-excitement, enjoyment-joy, surprise-startle, distress-anguish, anger-rage, fear-terror, shame-humiliation, disgust and dissmell (see Tomkins 2008, 627). This affective range expands from the positive to the negative through the neutral register of surprise-startle as interruption and reorganisation of attention fuelled by novelty that can tip towards either negative or positive intensities and provides drives with different qualities of experience. Tomkins (2008, 77, 180) postulated a general human goal and tendency to minimise and reduce negative affects and to maximise positive ones. There is a certain connection here to Spinoza's (1992) theorisation of "affectus" as an emotional and bodily state of affecting and being affected. For Spinoza, emotions, or affectations, emerging in encounters with the world can either increase or diminish the body's force of existence and powers of acting.

While Tomkins identified eight basic affects, Spinoza operated with three emotions: pleasure, pain and desire – the last of these being nothing less than "the very essence of man", the tendency to persist in one's own being (Spinoza 1992, 110, 163). Desire then translates as desire to persist but also to increase one's capacities to act: as such, it involves certain optimism, or openness, in terms of that which is to become. In experiences of pleasure "the body's power of activity is increased or assisted", while in pain these capacities become truncated (Spinoza 1992, 177–178). Consequently, Spinoza defined pleasure as good and pain as bad in ways not altogether dissimilar to Tomkins' broad division between negative and positive affects. At the same time, Spinoza noted that the goodness and badness of things are themselves about modes of thinking and comparison, and therefore "one and the same thing can be at the same time good and bad, and also indifferent" (Spinoza 1992, 153). Furthermore, affective capacities are contingent as such: "the human body can be affected now in one way, now in another, and consequently ... it can be affected in different times by one and the same object" (Spinoza 1992, 133). Affectations vary from one person to another, as they do within one person's realm of experience: "it is possible that what one man loves, another hates, what one man fears, another fears not, and that one and the same man may now love what he previously hated and may now dare what he previously feared, and so on". Meanwhile, for Tomkins,

There is literally no kind of object which has not historically been linked to one or another of the affects. Positive affect has been invested in pain and every kind of human misery, and negative affect has been experienced as a consequence of pleasure and every kind of triumph of the human spirit. Masochism and puritanism are possible only for an animal capable of using his reason to govern his feelings ... The same mechanisms enable him to invest any and every aspect of existence with the magic of excitement and joy or with the dread of fear or shame or distress. (Tomkins 2008, 74)

This certainly applies to sexual play where degrees of pain can be sought after as sources of pleasure and as amplifiers of desire through the touch of a slash, a sudden bite or a violent sensation of an orifice stretched open. Paying careful attention to the capacities of physical bodies, Tomkins examined the qualities in which affect becomes registered and the ways in which these qualities then organise relations and interactions between different bodies. Herein lie crucial differences in respect to new materialist theorisations of sexuality drawing on Spinoza via Gilles Deleuze and Félix Guattari that frame affect as a pre-human and non-human force generating the capacities of individual and social bodies (e.g. Massumi 2002; Fox and Alldred 2013, 770). Writing on sex and affect, Nick Fox and Pam Alldred (2013) foreground the openness of bodily capacities, even as these are modulated and closed down by social operations of power that seek to organise and categorise them. For Alldred and Fox, bodily capacities of acting and sensing are products of affective flows occurring in relations with other bodies: "Desire affects other bodies and things, but above all, it produces the sexual body and all its anatomical, physiological and cognitive capacities: this body is not pre-existing, but entirely produced (territorialized) out of materials in the sexuality-assemblage" (Fox and Alldred 2013, 776). Like Tomkins, Fox and Alldred identify affect as key to the qualities and forms of experience, yet, perhaps paradoxically, their formulation of desire as producing all bodily capacities positions the body, in its anatomy and mass of bones, nerves, fluids and tissue, as passive, inert matter waiting to be assembled.

Considerations of the material affordances of bodies – that which they can physiologically do – need not be conflated with determinism of any kind: the issue is rather one of understanding their qualities, the ways in which these intersect with and impact on one another, as well as how bodies become as they move from one state to another. A focus on affect within sexuality provides a means of accounting for the vitality and the visceral gravity of bodies alongside the longstanding, and by now stale, nature/nurture debate, and the adjunct framing of sexuality as either a natural force connected to reproduction or a social construct resulting from the repetitive internalisation of expectations and norms (see also Allen 2015, 35). This certainly does not necessitate or justify the romanticisation of sexuality as somehow external to society or culture. Rather, it allows for a shifting focus on carnal intensities and reverberations and treating them as complex dynamics irreducible to either the teleology of procreation or the operations of ideology and social power.

As a "ballistic response of the body" (Tomkins 2008, 720), affect, as understood here, is not antithetical to language or cognition but a force that weaves in and out of human action and experience in different intensities, providing them with specific textures and qualities. Sexual excitement and desire animate bodies, intensify the encounters between them, and transform these bodies, their affective capacities and desires in the process (Bollen and McInnes 2006, 109). Sex involves an edge of openness, of potentiality, that orients bodies to seek their pleasures – independent of how light, strained or pained their hues may occasionally be.

3

"Raising the Ordinary to the Extraordinary"

Sex advisers of all kinds routinely suggest variations of play – such as new routines of foreplay, the introduction of sex toys and sessions of role-play – for spicing up long-term relationships where habitual motions have solidified and dulled any dizzying sense of lust and opportunity there may initially have been. Sexual play, then, comes across as a means of setting congealed desires and palates back into motion. Lionel S. Lewis and Dennis Brissett noted something of this kind in their 1967 analysis of popular marriage manuals depicting sexual play as a form of work. Portraying orgasm as product of the labour of marital sex, these manuals highlighted the role of work schedules, special techniques and equipment in and for successful performance. According to the authors' summary, "Depicting sex as work is probably the consequence of the need of Americans to justify and dignify play and to resolve the contradictory values of work for work's sake and pleasure for pleasure's sake" (Lewis and Brissett 1967, 8).

Seen in this vein, the framing of sex as work, rather than as play, or the framing of sexual play as work, is a means of legitimising it through motives other than those clustered around the pursuit of bodily pleasure. At the same time, the authors argue that this may render such pursuits somewhat grim as ones resembling an achievement or duty. Furthermore, "The female is particularly cautioned to work at sex, for being naturally sexual seems a trait ascribed only to the male" (Lewis and Brissett 1967, 11). The marriage manuals that Lewis and Brissett examined compared the skill of sex to the mastery of domestic work such as cooking and laundry as a performance requiring some strain: "To the house-wife's burden is added yet another chore", one that produces the highly valuable product of orgasm as fuel and proof for marital happiness (Lewis and Brissett 1967, 11). As

Attwood (2011, 88) notes, guidebooks have long framed sex in this vein as a matter of domestic skill within the framework of self-help.

Guidelines and tips on sexual play continue to balance its instrumental roles in improving relationships, on the one hand, and the pursuit of pleasure as an end in itself, on the other. These two pursuits are not necessarily easy to combine. Consider, for example, the ubiquitous concept of "foreplay" where play is that which precedes the so-called real thing as an appetizer of sorts. In the framework of straight sex in particular, foreplay is recurrently allocated an instrumental role as stimulation for penile-vaginal intercourse (often identified as sex proper). When penetrative sex remains the assumed key goal and culmination of sexual activity, foreplay – serving both instrumental and functional aims – no longer belongs to the realm of play as such. The notion of foreplay therefore both roots play into the heart of sexual practices and displaces it as means to an end, given that "sex" is that which comes after yet does not precisely result from play.

Similar instrumentality emerges in guidelines on sexual role-play. Charting the importance of sexual fantasy with the aid of sex and relationship experts, Lelo, the Swedish producer of high-end sex toys, concludes that "Creating a fantasy can provide the fake-it-til-you-make it inspiration and erotic energy that you may be missing as your relationship becomes more stable and long term. From dress up to seduction, to exploring more different roles that are adopted only in the bedroom; it's just a matter of building that fantasy with your partner!" (Thorn, n.d.) In an interconnected article, Lelo provides tips and advice for sexual role-playing in the scenarios of the boss and his secretary, the hitchhiker, teacher and pupil, home delivery, doctor and nurse, as well as "man maid action". Many of these scenarios are familiar from the stock materials of commercial American pornography, while the accessories for acting out others are readily available from fantasy costume stores selling uniforms of naughty nurses, school girls, nuns and French maids for Halloween and bachelorette parties.

Women's lifestyle news site *Bustle* similarly starts its how-to tips on sexual role-play by listing available stock roles, such as personal trainer and client; doctor and patient; masseuse and client; repairman and homeowner; delivery man and homeowner; teacher and student (Marin 2014). *Cosmopolitan* equally reiterates the stock fantasy scenarios of strangers picking each other up in a bar and "classic power dynamics" such as those between the cop and the criminal, the doctor and the patient. If these play patterns and roles seem familiar, this would be due to their reiteration across decades (Harviainen 2011, 60). Venturing beyond the readily available off-the-shelf scenarios, *Cosmo* further suggests exploring one's personal fantasy, sharing it with one's partner and then establishing limits for the scenes of play. The tips progress from possible preparations such as dressing up and setting the stage to the importance of fun and the possibility of doing things that one would not be comfortable doing outside a scene of play (Clark-Flory 2013). Here, sexual play literally forms a magic circle allowing for diverse experimentations with bodily motions, encounters, pleasures, zones of comfort and discomfort, acceptability and the lack thereof.

These tips and guidelines all frame role-play as an instrumental means towards both better sex and better relationships. In fact the scenes of play they propose are to be acted out exclusively in the context of committed, monogamous relationships where partners communicate openly, trust one another, and respect one another's boundaries of comfort. There is generally no space for additional sexual partners, casual or anonymous sex since emotional safety and commitment remains the prerequisite for play to take place. It is advised for couples to spice up their interaction by pretending to be strangers hooking up in a bar, but certainly not to hook up with an actual stranger – despite the regularity with which such encounters occur, not least with the aid of hook-up apps. Without the couple in question moving from their mundane routines to the magic circle of play operating under a different set of rules, there might perhaps not be much exceptionality to these scenarios to start with. And without the safety boundaries associated with the couple format, sexual play would be too risky for experts to recommend. In order to be playful or understood in terms of play, sex is seen to require a proper context embedded in the normative social fantasy where intimacy within the couple format translates as having a life (Berlant 2000, 5–6). Having *a sex life* worth disclosing then is assumed to require, and is dependent on, one's investment in monogamy.

Sexual role-play guidelines aim to teach people how to play, with the implicit premise that they are not prone to or skilled in sexual play to start with. The straight women and couples forming the target audience for the tips in question are assumed to be in acute need of help in tapping into their fantasy lives and sexual desires grown tepid. The scripts, lines and scenes of play on offer are a mix borrowed from popular fiction and sampled from guidebooks and other expert advice. The website MarriedGames.org is among the many resources to offer ready-made scripts of sexual role-play for settled couples to rehearse and reiterate. In the script for *Dominatrix*, "A domineering woman holds no restraints in commanding and abusing her male subject until he fulfils her every sexual whim", whereas in *Eroticon*, a Star Trek/scifi-themed space adventure, "an erotic power has taken over the minds (and sexual appetites) of the crew. In order to overcome this dark force, the captain and lieutenant must release their secret passions." In *Naughty Babysitter*, "With no parents in sight, a teenage beauty fulfils a boy's every desire, taking sex education to a whole new level" and *Princess and Servant* unfolds as a "gentle and romantic fantasy about arranged marriage and a forbidden passion between a lonely princess and her adoring servant".

For those interested in further exploring such templates, a range of more detailed guidebooks is on offer, from Emily Rizor's *Sexual Role Playing Scripts for Couples: Volume 1* (2010), Elizabeth Cramer's *131 Dirty Talk Examples: Learn How To Talk Dirty with These Simple Phrases That Drive Your Lover Wild & Beg You For Sex Tonight* (2013), and Michael and Barbara Kortekaas' *123 Frisky Sexual Fantasies & Erotic Roleplay Ideas: Dare to Play Naughty Sexy Scenarios for Couples* (2013). In all these instances, sexual play becomes a form of working at relationships while playfulness grows inseparable from constant reskilling of the kind that *Cosmopolitan* has long guided women in. Women are advised on giving better oral sex; on exploring and exceeding their sexual boundaries of comfort; on seducing, surprising and keeping a man. It is therefore hardly exaggeration to state that these kinds of guidelines tend to follow the contours of normative scripts operating within predictable, prefabricated gendered positions (see Harvey and Gill 2011, 56; also Attwood 2005, 2011; Attwood and Smith 2013, 331).

Digging into this landscape of commodified sexual advice, play scripts and rules, this chapter explores the pleasures they afford in the context of E L James' *Fifty Shades of Grey* series. *Fifty Shades* may be a highly predictable example to evoke in this context, yet its global success and broad recognisability make it an apt case to address the circulation of cultural scripts on an international scale while targeting heterosexual female consumers in particular. As the current prime example of mainstream and extensively commodified depiction of kink play, *Fifty Shades* speaks of the pleasures of sexual fantasies, as well as the various constraints and templates that they come in. Rather than setting out to critique the series for either its shortage of aesthetic merit or the viability of its depiction of BDSM, my interests lie in the appeal that its fantasy scenarios of sexual play, desire and pleasure hold.

Generically Kinky

Initially written as fan fiction online, then published as e-books through The Writers' Coffee Shop in 2011–2012, the *Fifty Shades* trilogy gained viral popularity and was published through Vintage as *Fifty Shades of Grey* (James 2012a), *Fifty Shades Darker* (James 2012b) and *Fifty Shades Freed* (James 2012c). Despite the notably and unequivocally negative critical reception that the series continues to enjoy, it has been translated into more than forty languages and has sold over 125 million copies worldwide (Deller et al. 2013; Grigoriadis 2015). *Fifty Shades* has since spawned a film trilogy as well as a literary spin-off trilogy, *Grey* (James 2015), *Darker* (James 2017) and the forthcoming *Freed* recounting the narrative from the male protagonist's perspective (see Flood 2015). All this points to extensive and sustained consumer interest in the fiction in question.

The first volume introduces the main couple – Anastasia Steele, a 21-year-old English literature undergraduate student, and Christian Grey, a 27-year-old billionaire businessman CEO – the blossoming of their mutual passion, Anastasia's introduction to sexual pleasure, Christian's kinky tendencies, his playroom setup, childhood traumas and desire for control that haunt the couple's newly acquired bliss. At the end of the first book, Anastasia leaves after too hard a BDSM session only for the couple to be reunited in the beginning of the next book. Following the classic popular romance narrative formula of "boy meets girl, boy loses girl, boy gets girl", the two latter books focus on the couple's growth haunted by past shadows, external intervention and violence. In the second volume, the couple are stalked by Christian's former submissive partner and, in the third, by Anastasia's former boss, who manages to nearly kill her. These events intersect with Christian's initiation to intimate cohabitation, his gradual recovery from trauma and his ensuing sexual transformation where some "kinky fuckery" remains but does not dominate the couple's relationship as it adapts to the normative pattern of loving vanilla sex, monogamous matrimony and parenthood (also Pääkkölä 2016, 14). It is nevertheless the BDSM scenes and their gendered sexual dynamics that have remained key to public debates and commentaries on the series.

First of all, *Fifty Shades* illustrates the circulation of sexual fantasies from the products of popular media to commodity production and play guidelines. The success of the books, like the high public visibility of the first film, has fuelled a range of themed commodities from beginner's BDSM kits to spankers, blindfolds, whips, collars, ropes, handcuffs and other restraints for trying out some of the sexual scenarios depicted, including "*Fifty Shades of Grey:* The Official Pleasure Collection", a line of sex toys approved by James (see Comella 2013; Deller et al. 2013, 860; Dymock 2013, 889). In a move of literal domestication, the *Fifty Shades* brand has helped to reposition BDSM from something marginal and extreme into stuff that is fashionable and acceptable enough for non-kink-identifying straight couples to experiment with (Martin 2013, 980). A plethora of additional guidelines and tips for appropriating elements from the books into private moments of play remain readily available on online clickbait sites. A *Huffington Post* interview with James addresses the reader feedback she has received, describing how the novels "really helped bring some passion back into their marriages, and into their relationships". James continues: "Yes, and isn't it nice to be dominated now and again, or dominating somebody else, or doing a little role-playing – if it's all in fun?" (Thomas 2012.) Framed in this vein, the books are inspirational and serve a directly functional purpose in helping people to improve their sexual lives.

Second, *Fifty Shades* exemplifies the force and appeal of cultural scripts connected to gender and sexuality, as well as the scale of their international distribution. The roles of the main characters – the virgin of modest means and the ultra-rich, all-powerful yet haunted white cis-gendered male BDSM top – and the power dynamics between them are the stuff of generic sexual role-play scenarios. Anastasia is highly feminine, yet also

Fig. 3.1
Google Image search for "Fifty Shades of Grey toys"

awkward and insecure, whereas Christian radiates masculine strength, decisiveness and desire for control, even if regularly crumbling into sweaty pieces in his solitary existence. There is no room for the reversal of or play with roles within their sexual scenes where the dynamics of domination and submission become mapped on to a binary relationship dynamic of unequal wealth, stature and agency.

Third, *Fifty Shades* speaks of the appeal of genre fiction built as variations on a theme. James started out by writing *Twilight* fan fiction on an online forum involving active member interaction. The first story version, "Master of the Universe", appeared under the pen name Snowqueens Icedragon:

James published her stories online in forums filled with a very specific fan group: the Twihards, or, specifically, the slice of Twihards who are obsessed with not only the interactions of Stephenie Meyer's two main characters, human girl Bella and vampire Edward, in the four *Twilight* novels, but also their erotic peregrinations. *Twilight* was the bible, but Snowqueens Icedragon and her fellow fan-fiction writers spun their tales in many different directions. James had the clever idea of remaking Bella as Anastasia Steele, a Brontë-loving virgin finishing college in the Pacific Northwest, and transforming Edward into Christian Grey, a bondage-loving, emotionally stunted Seattle billionaire. (Grigoriadis 2015)

Fifty Shades is essentially a sexed-up variation of romantic genre fiction that borrows from familiar tropes, scenes and characters, as outlined in Janice A. Radway's classic 1984 study of Harlequin romance. Both exploring popular romance novels and interviewing their avid readers, Radway mapped out their ideal format and characters:

The typical romantic narrative need not provide a logical explanation for the personality transformation it observes so carefully, because it is prepared for by the hero's first introduction. The hero of the romantic fantasy is always characterized by spectacular masculinity. Indeed, it is insufficient for the author to remark in passing that the romantic hero has a muscular physique. The reader must be told, instead, that every aspect of his being, whether his body, his face, or his general demeanor, is informed by the purity of his maleness. Almost everything about him is hard, angular, and dark. It is, however, essential to add the qualifying "almost" here because, in descriptions of the ideal romantic hero, the terrorizing effect of his exemplary masculinity is always tempered by the presence of a small feature that introduces an important element of softness into the overall picture. (Radway 1984, 128)

In *Twilight*, the dark hero is literally a vampire – an immortal, pale teenager whose passion, should it be unleashed, would be the romantic heroine's undoing. In *Fifty Shades*, the hero is a young white businessman firmly representative of the one per cent, an avid kickboxer and runner repeatedly described as a physical joy to behold. Anastasia is frequently lost in visual contemplation of Christian's overpowering, magnetic good looks: "My mouth goes dry as he casually strolls around the piano toward me. He has broad shoulders, narrow hips, and his abdominal muscles ripple as he walks" (James 2012a, 112).

Christian looks cool and calm – actually, he looks heavenly. He's in a loose white linen shirt and jeans, no shoes or socks. His hair is tousled and unkempt, and his gray eyes twinkle wickedly at me. He is jaw-droppingly handsome. He rises and strolls towards me, an amused appraising smile on his beautiful sculptured lips. I stand immobilized at the entrance of the room, paralyzed by his beauty and the sweet anticipation of what's to come. The familiar charge between us is there, sparking slowly in my belly, drawing me to him. (James 2012a, 311)

Despite being the object of a desiring female gaze, this "elegant, beautiful, Greek god" (James 2012b, 183) is unfailingly in control, whether this be in matters of his business empire or in his sexual arrangements. Given

Christian's "unruly dark copper colored hair and intense, bright gray eyes" (James 2012a, 7), his darkness – central as such to the romantic hero – remains more metaphorically embedded in the shadows of trauma, deep secrets and kinky sexual preferences (Harrison and Holm 2013). In a fully Gothic vein, Christian, filled with self-doubt and self-hate, thinks of himself as nothing short of a monster with a "dark, twisted", "ugly, torn" soul and can only feel relieved that Anastasia does not know the depths of the depravity that lurks beneath his handsome surface (James 2015, 43, 501, 504–505, 545). His inner softness, or even squishiness, opens up ever broader and soggier as his love for Anastasia blooms, revealing childhood experiences of hunger, violence, hurt, death, abandonment and neglect necessitating therapeutic healing.

The stuff of trauma emerges as a key explanation to both Christian's BDSM interest and his discomfort with physical intimacy. Anastasia, the only woman allowed to touch the burn scars on his muscular, sculpted torso, finds herself thinking of them as "stark physical embodiment of a horrific childhood and a sickening reminder of what mental scars he must bear" (James 2012b, 125). Figuring out the routes of trauma, Anastasia soon charts their connections with "his control freakery, his possessiveness, his jealousy, his overprotectiveness ... I can even understand why he doesn't like to be touched – I've seen the physical scars. I can only imagine the mental ones, and I've only glimpsed his nightmares once" (James 2012b, 422).

In an interview, James defines Christian as "the ultimate fantasy guy. And that's the point: As long as you accept that fantasy guy – fantasy sex, fantasy lifestyle, a broken man who needs fixing through love – what woman could resist that?" (Thomas 2012). In other words, the hero's hidden vulnerability and softness is presented as the key component of the overall fantasy scenario. It would be the heroine's task to rescue the hero who, despite his spectacular masculinity, power and domination, is in acute need of healing through romantic love. According to the romance formula that is here dutifully followed, the heroine, younger and preferably virginal, is the one with the special capacity to soften, tame and heal the hero. Romantic narrative closure then aims to dispel the "mystification, unreadable looks, 'hints of cruelty' and wordless coldness" in the hero's menacing behaviour with the aid of the heroine's virtues and her skills in feminine care (Snitow 1983, 249). All this forms a specific, exclusive bond between the couple. The heroine's capacity to make the man open up means that she has been chosen from among all other women – even if she preferably fails to register her own exceptionality, beauty and attractiveness (Radway 1984, 54–55). In Radway's (1984, 128–129) analysis, female heroines are able to "translate male reticence and cruelty into tenderness and devotion" by bringing "to the surface traits and propensities that are part of the hero's most basic nature". Closely following this script, Anastasia – "good and innocent and courageous" (James 2015, 511) – is able to save Christian from his nightmares of torment and abuse.

The Workings of Sexual Fantasy

The committed female readers in Radway's study were not drawn to explicit depictions of sex. Rather, they were "interested in the verbal working out of a romance, that is, in the reinterpretation of misunderstood actions and in declarations of mutual love rather than in the portrayal of sexual contact through visual imagery" (Radway 1984, 66). In her contemporaneous analysis of Harlequin fiction, Ann Snitow (1983) identified virginity as one of the heroine's key characteristics and the narrative formula as being both fuelled and saturated by shivers of arousal, erotic touches, suggestive glances and carnal quivering paving way for the concluding scene of marital sex. Written a quarter of a century after these studies, *Fifty Shades* both details the resolution of the couple's mutual tensions and dwells on the details of their sexual coupling. Anastasia's enthusiastic engagement in premarital sex in no way destroys her characteristic purity, which runs deeper than the skin.

While not unique in romantic erotica, the scenes of BDSM play marked *Fifty Shades* apart from competing titles and afforded it a specific edge. *Fifty Shades* is naughty but the transgressions it offers occur safely within the confines of heterosexual romance, commitment and passion (see also Dymock 2013). Like Ann Summers parties promoting sexual paraphernalia to women, the novels chart out the boundaries of "the acceptably kinky" within the marshes of the "plain perverted" while foregrounding female experience and pleasure throughout (Storr 2003, 208–211). In fact, it is the separation between the two that guides the series' narrative as negotiation concerning the two partners' preferences, expectations and boundaries of comfort.

In her analysis of *Fifty Shades*, Eva Illouz (2014) identifies it as a genre hybrid combining Gothic romance with self-help. She argues that the books represent a primarily social fantasy, rather than a sexual one, in that they provide guidelines for navigating the tensions of heterosexual gender relations in late capitalist culture through the formulas of self-help (Illouz 2014, 30). BDSM scenes then come across as means to translate relations of power and their various instabilities into scenes of sexual play through the "elaborate erotic drama" that its rituals afford (Steele 1996, 163, 171). For Illouz, the success of bestsellers is indicative of them providing solutions to social tensions and guidelines towards a happier life – a point previously made by both Radway and Snitow who interpreted romance as negotiating and possibly compensating for the discrepancies and unresolvable tensions within heterosexual relationships. While improving sexual lives through the practical tips it offers, *Fifty Shades*, according to Illouz, also promises guidelines for happier relationships and self-discovery.

Illouz sees *Fifty Shades* as speaking to women in relationships, rather than functioning as pornographic stimulation as such, yet it remains unclear as to why these two modes of reading – that of advice and that of sexual arousal – should be seen as mutually exclusive and whether the books comprise a social fantasy rather than a sexual one by default. People, female consumers included, clearly get something from these fictions, yet this something is unlikely to be one single thing. Alternatively, this "something" can be conceptualised as pleasures generated by the circulation of sexual fantasies that intensify and animate bodies through mind play irreducible to the kind of functionality or instrumentality implied by the framework of self-help. For, as compelling as Illouz's argument is, it ultimately downplays the centrality of sexual titillation and pleasure connected to the fantasy scenarios in the remarkable success of *Fifty Shades*. The novels do provide practical how-to tips on sexual play and pleasure as they narrate Anastasia's journey from complete sexual inexperience – she initially has no sexual history even in masturbation – to a diverse and gratifying sexual life, as well as Christian's route from scripted kink to marital happiness. The core story, or fantasy, is nevertheless that of exclusively monogamous, possessive and even monomaniac sexual and romantic desire.

Illouz explains the appeal of *Fifty Shades* through the Freudian notion of fantasy as both a representation and distortion of reality: "Fantasy works around reality, incorporates it, defends the self *against* reality, and yet helps one to live *with* it. In this view, fantasy is a mediation between different systems, it includes that which it denies, and it offers a transition between different aspects of consciousness" (Illouz 2014, 28, emphasis in the original). Understood in this vein, fantasies make lives more liveable. Since Illouz examines *Fifty Shades* as a social fantasy, she does not discuss the Freudian overtones of the books themselves. Meanwhile, Christian's journey of self-discovery and healing, as narrated by James, faithfully follows a pop-Freudian route of interpretation where sexual preferences and behaviours are rooted in childhood events, relationships and traumas.

The Freudian model of sexual desire is rooted in primary trauma as the child comes to realise her separateness from "the caretaking environment/mother/breast that she relies on for nurturance and pleasure" (Berlant 2012, 27). The mother's body, and the lost breast in particular, is the object of both desire and trauma: connection to and unity with the mother's breast is forever sought in future sexual liaisons and activities without this fullness ever being possible to achieve. This is a narrative of loss, lack and melancholy within which "to love an object is to attempt to master it, to seek to destroy its alterity or Otherness" (Berlant 2012, 25). Love is therefore not antithetical to aggressiveness, but sadism and masochism are integral to human attachment, while "Love enables the pressure of desire's aggression to be discharged within a frame of propriety" (Berlant 2012, 25). Christian dominates young, white, brown-haired women, having witnessed the death of his young and brown-haired drug-addict mother whose pimp abused both of them. Childhood trauma – recounted in several flashback snippets of nightmare regression – explains Christian's compulsion to control and punish Anastasia, as well as to keep her safe. All these aspects fold into his BDSM play as DIY therapy, but only romance suffices to transform his painful dreams to happy ones as the smell of the lost mother blends into the sweet scent of his new girlfriend (see James 2015, 321).

Christian's desire for control extends beyond his "red room of pain" to the details of Anastasia's diet, exercise, birth control and social life. The couple's gendered, unequal power dynamic finds resonance in the lack of power switches in their scenes of play. Meanwhile, possessiveness and jealousy translate as love, care and commitment, and Christian's tendencies for stalking and jealousy are depicted as being in Anastasia's best interest. The frame of propriety is highlighted and eroticised through repetitive declarations of ownership that fuel desire for both parties involved: " 'You are mine,' he whispers. 'Only mine. Don't forget it.' His voice is intoxicating, his words heady, seductive. I feel his growing erection against my thigh" (James 2012a, 119). In the state of matrimony, the wedding ring, as a symbol of possession, becomes an arousing fetish object in its own right: "I reach for his left hand and plant a kiss on his wedding ring, a plain platinum band matching my own. 'Mine,' I whisper." (James 2012c, 119) "His wedding ring clinks against the glass as he takes another sip of wine. Now that is a sexy sound" (James 2012c, 240).

"And this." My nail traces his ring finger. "Definitely this." My finger stops at his wedding ring. "This is very sexy."
"Is it, now?"
"It sure is. It says this man is mine." And I skim the small callus that has already formed on his palm beneath the ring. (James 2012c, 394)

In these gestures and declarations, sexual desire, ownership and romantic love are glued together into a fantasy figure intended to appeal and arouse. On the one hand, the books' scenes of sexual play broaden the boundaries of the terrain of "good sex" by accommodating all kinds of props, scripts, techniques and power play into heterosexual romantic coupledom. In its more spontaneous and reciprocal forms, sexual play is firmly posed as an issue of pleasure. On the other hand, this is indeed a normative, conventional narrative of both desire and love firmly "bound up in institutions like marriage and family, property relations, and stock phrases and plots" (Berlant 2012, 7). All in all, *Fifty Shades* unfolds as a markedly Freudian account of love, trauma, sex, gender and desire.

In his discussion of sexual fantasies, Martin Barker (2014, 145) takes critical distance from Freudian and post-Freudian psychoanalytical theories that treat fantasies as compensatory "playback for real traumatic experiences" and "distorted management of childhood problems and traumas, almost always family generated". For Barker, such compensatory understandings of sexual fantasy reduce them to origin stories of childhood and family life in ways that efface from view the experiences of later life, relationships, communities, bodies and sexual cultures. Instead of seeking the roots of sexual fantasy in early trauma, Barker is interested in the diverse work that fantasies do in people's lives. This means conceptualising them as productive means for trying "out versions of self-in-sexual-society, reimagining themselves through others' reimaginings" (Barker 2014, 146). Drawing on empirical research on porn audiences, he offers an insightful five-fold conceptualisation of sexual fantasy as "a conscious accentuation of desire"; "a means to look at our responses to things"; "a world of possibilities to be explored and thought about"; "a visitation to a distant realm of desires and fantasies"; and an imagining of "what I might or might not be" (Barker 2014, 155). Understood in this vein, fantasies contribute to the creation of novel connections, the imagining of play scenarios and the build-up of desire.

Such unpacking of what sexual fantasies may do, what trajectories they may take and what people may do with them foregrounds contingency, experimentation and imagination as core features of sexual lives. Rather than instrumentally helping people to cope with various frictions and discrepancies, fantasies play an active part in how these arrangements and feelings unfold and develop. Following Barker, fantasies are a means of exploring the world and its possibilities, playing with scenarios that one might wish to experience or enjoy at a distance, as well as for intensifying sexual desire.

E L James describes how, in the feedback she receives, women write of having discovered previously unknown aspects of themselves: "They're quite freaked out by it, but in a good way. They're thinking, 'Wow, this is amazing. Why has it taken me so long to discover this?'" (Thomas 2012). Such discovery can be understood through any one of Barker's five conceptualisations of the productivity of sexual fantasies, or any combination thereof. The zones of intensity engendered in acts of reading are resonant points of contact between personal sexual fantasies and those rendered public through their publication and circulation. In these resonant points of contact, scenarios of sexual play on the pages of a book push and open up the perceived horizons of bodily possibility as that which readers can imagine doing, experimenting with or enjoying. It is through such shifts, as diverse as they may be in their speeds and lengths, that sexual likes and practices continue to change – a point returned to and further elaborated in Chapter 6.

Resonant Corporeal Intensification

Illouz deploys the term resonance to describe how books that become bestsellers encapsulate some of that which Raymond Williams (1977) identified as structures of feeling. For Williams (1977, 133–134), structures of feeling were common qualities and experiences of life characteristic to specific generations, contexts and locations. Given the partly emergent quality of these formations, they are ephemeral and possibly difficult to translate into language while nevertheless being acutely felt. For a bestseller to resonate with structures of feelings therefore "means that a narrative is able not only to address a social experience that is not adequately understood, named, or categorized but also to 'frame' it in adequately explanatory ways" (Illouz 2014, 23). Following this line of thinking, that which resonates strikes a chord in its familiarity but also articulates something that people have not quite found the means to express.

Framed through affect theory, the notion of resonance can be seen as descriptive of relations and contact between bodies, be those bodies human or representational ones. Here, resonance refers to moments and experiences of being moved, touched and affected by that which is tuned to "the right frequency": to instances of attunement or harmony discovered by accident as certain bodies, images, texts or figures of fantasy fascinate, linger and stick. Such resonance presumes no similarity between the different bodies involved. Rather, it describes momentary connections between them that alter in intensity and shape over time. Memories of such encounters may reverberate long after the bodies have ceased to be in contact with one another (see Paasonen 2011, 16–18, 2013). Understood in terms of such resonance, the appeal of *Fifty Shades* is due not only to its power to address the complexities and tensions of heterosexual coupling but also to its very visceral force to capture both individual and public attention. In order for the play scenarios of *Fifty Shades* to resonate, its readers need not share any kink interest or identify with the main characters and their inner lives. The pleasures taken can be much more fleeting, attached to singular instances and scenes, and intercepted by diverse misgivings concerning the fictions in question.

In accordance with the conventions of romance (Snitow 1983, 247), Anastasia's perspective is emphasised through the use of the first person singular and the description of sensory intensities that it affords. The books describe in minute detail what is happening to Anastasia's body, how she and Christian respond to one another and how all this feels. And, as Ruth Deller and Clarissa Smith (2013, 937) point out, since *Fifty Shades* is "Written by a woman, from a woman's point of view and for a female audience", the books have been "discursively fabricated as potentially revelatory so that to read them was to engage in public debate about female sexuality". As a media phenomenon, *Fifty Shades* is tightly entangled with the notion of "mummy porn" as its perhaps most iconic example. As in pornography more generally, the accounts of physical intensity, of bodies moving and being moved aim to move the bodies of those reading through instances and connections of resonance (see Paasonen 2011). Writing on masochistic erotica, Smith (2009, 29) points out how its reader "engages in an empathetic relation with the narration – this is how sex can feel, how it works on the body. It is a relation of co-animation." The pleasures of *Fifty Shades* can be associated with "corporeal intensification which requires going beyond the limits of 'ordinary, nice, well-behaved sex'; submitting to feeling, letting go; letting oneself experience sexual desire" (Smith 2009, 30). Love and desire, as they play out in the books, can be understood as "intensified zones of attachment" (Berlant 2012, 18) allowing for resonant reader encounters.

Fifty Shades offers fantasy scenarios of youth, whiteness, physical beauty and abundant wealth manifesting in lavish apartments, private planes, helicopters and yachts, new cars, expensive jewellery, designer fashions, fine dining and exclusive holidays. This fantasy is unburdened by scarcity or need other than that of the emotional and physical kind, the gradual yet constant fulfilment of which comprises the main narrative dynamic. *Fifty Shades* can be interpreted as a story about fulfilment through sexual learning and intimacy that is played out through and within scenes of play fuelled by sexual and romantic desire. Berlant (2012, 6) maps out desire as "a state of attachment to something or someone, and the cloud of possibility that is generated by the gap between an object's specificity and the needs and promises projected onto it". Love, again, is "the embracing dream in which desire is reciprocated": "In the idealized image of their relation, desire will lead to love, which will make a world for desire's endurance" (Berlant 2012, 6, 7). In *Fifty Shades*, desire paves the way to love: their combined force drives the main characters into scenes of sexual play beyond their previous boundaries of comfort.

The arrangement between the main characters is initially one of contractual submission and control, scripted by Christian:

"And I want you to know that as soon as you cross my threshold as my submissive, I will do what I like to you. You have to accept that and willingly. That's why you have to trust me. I will fuck you, any time, any way, I want – anywhere I want. I will discipline you, because you will screw up. I will train you to please me. But I know you've not done this before. Initially, we'll take it slowly, and I will help you. We'll build up to various scenarios. I want you to trust me, but I know I have to earn your trust, and I will." ...

He's so passionate, mesmerizing. This is obviously his obsession, the way he is ... I can't take my eyes off him. (James 2012b, 221)

While these dynamics evolve towards more reciprocal ones involving no punishment, Christian remains in control and knowledgeable about carnal pleasures. As the resident sex expert, he knows Anastasia's body and desire far better than she does, and guides her through experimentations of all kinds. As Meg Barker (2013, 898) notes, "Anastasia rarely communicates any desires of her own but rather Christian orchestrates their scenes completely." Consent is "inevitably complicated under such conditions wherein one person does not know their desires and is restricted from articulating some possibilities, whilst the other automatically knows what they both want" (Barker 2013, 890). In her psychoanalytical reflection on female masochism and heterosexual pornography, Elizabeth Cowie (1993, 142–143) points out the fundamentally passive character of pleasures offered by fantasies of submission and non-consent. Projecting sexual aggressiveness and activity on the male heterosexual partner, such fantasies express a will to be pleasured while relieving the female subject from feelings of guilt or responsibility. Considered in this vein, *Fifty Shades* caters to and reframes the fantasy of submission as pathway to sexual pleasure and intimacy. Sexual play does not, for the most part, involve much activity from Anastasia. It is Christian who sets the scene, coins and unpacks its rules according to his own preferences, while also mastering the secrets of Anastasia's pleasure – which, consequently, turn out not to be secrets at all.

Singing the Body Electric, in Different Terms

The relationship between Anastasia and Christian is rife with trauma and friction, yet these do not, for the most part, extend to their scenes of sexual play. There is no lack or incommensurability of desire. Anastasia's learning curves are steep while joint orgasms regularly drive the couple into bodily pleasures of previously unknown intensity. These scenes may be haunted by the shadows of Christian's trauma and Anastasia's insecurity, yet they are even more marked by the easy availability of physical ecstasy. With the exception of two BDSM scenes ending in tears owing to Anastasia's sense of her boundaries being violated, scenes of play work out to a spectacular degree. The first time they have sex, Anastasia reaches orgasm from nipple play and, very soon after, through coitus. She embraces these newly acquired insights into her embodied affordances and that which her body can do: "I can't stop grinning. Now I know what all the fuss is about. Two orgasms ... coming apart at the seams, like the spin cycle on a washing machine, wow. I had no idea what my body was capable of, could be wound so tightly and released so violently, so gratifyingly. The pleasure was indescribable" (James 2012a, 118). And as Anastasia first experiments with fellatio, she instinctively masters deep throating and swallows Christian's semen with ease and mutual pleasure:

Hmm... he's soft and hard at once, like steel encased in velvet and surprisingly tasty – salty and smooth ...

Hmm ... I pull him deeper into my mouth so I can feel him at the back of my throat and then to the front again. My tongue swirls around the end. He's my very own Christian Grey flavor popsicle. I suck harder and harder, pushing him deeper and deeper, swirling my tongue round and round. *Hmm* ... I had no idea giving pleasure could be such a turn-on, watching him writhe subtly with carnal longing. My inner goddess is doing the merengue with some salsa moves ...

Holy crap. His hands are really gripping my hair. I can do this. I push even harder and, in a moment of extraordinary confidence, I bare my teeth. It tips him over the edge. He cries out and stills, and I can feel warm, salty liquid oozing down my throat. I swallow quickly. Ugh... I'm not sure about this. But one look at him, and he's come apart in the bath because of me, and I don't care. I sit back and watch him, a triumphant, gloating smile tugging at the corners of my lips. His breathing is ragged. Opening his eyes, he glares at me.

"Don't you have a gag reflex?" he asks, astonished. (James 2012a, 136–137)

As may be evident at this point, the novels' style is far from artful. Their trash-iness has certainly been broadly and vocally declared (Deller and Smith 2013, 941; Harman and Jones 2013). The train of Anastasia's inner thought is dotted with exclamations such as "holy fuck", "holy crap" and "double crap", as well as descriptions of her "inner goddess" sulking, nodding, dancing samba and doing triple axels in response to life events. Descriptions of sex, the books' key attraction, are variations on a theme that make consistent use of chosen expressions, metaphors and phrases, from sensory explosions to a temporary, unworldly sense of disorientation, contractions of inner muscles, visceral feelings of being all sensation and being consumed by it:

"Come for me, Ana," he whispers breathlessly, and I unravel at his words, exploding around him as I climax and splinter into a million pieces underneath him. And as he comes, he calls out my name, thrusting hard, then stilling as he empties himself into me.

I am still panting, trying to slow my breathing, my thumping heart, and my thoughts are in riotous disarray. *Wow ... that was astounding.* (James 2012a, 118, emphasis in the original)

Ahhh! I tip my head back and concentrate on the invading, punishing, heavenly sensation ... pushing me, pushing me ... onward, higher, up ... and when I can take no more, I explode around him, spiraling into an intense, all-consuming orgasm. (James 2012a, 480)

And that's it – I'm gone. I explode around him, crying out an incoherent rendition of his name as my intense orgasm arches my back off the bed. I think I see stars, it's such a visceral primal feeling. (James 2012c, 261)

The reverberation of "raising the ordinary to the extraordinary" (James 2015, 16) cuts through the books from the couple's first encounter, during which Anastasia makes the remark about an artwork hanging on the wall of Christian's office, to the novels' events where Anastasia's orgasms unfold as similar to the spin cycles of a washing machine. The extraordi-nariness of everyday life equally reveals itself when the mundane act of cooking chicken fry-up becomes foreplay for a sexual scene. The couple's sexual play is absorbing and exhausting and, like play for Caillois (2001, 6), it affords escape from mundane responsibilities and routines.

Immersive and possibly disturbing, the intensities of sexual pleasure so closely depicted in the books are kin to Jane Bennett's (2001, 4) definition of enchantment as experiences of being "struck and shaken by the extraordinary that lives amid the familiar and the everyday". Enchantment refers to sensations of intense pleasure, attraction, wonder and magic. Tomkins (2008, 681) saw enchantment as connected to drastic changes in one's life and as partitioning "the life space *firmly* between life as it has been and as it now promises in vidious contrast". Moments of enchantment then involve transformations in one's immediate experience as well as their radical review as sensations of magnified potentiality (Tomkins 2008, 919). Making the world come alive, enchantment is, for Bennett (2001, 5), a sense of wonder entailing a "temporary suspension of chronological time", a sense of being transfixed and spellbound by something encountered. As such, enchantment involves "a condition of exhilaration or acute sensory activity. To be simultaneously transfixed in wonder and transported by sense, to be both caught up and carried away – enchantment is marked by this odd combination of somatic effects" (Bennett 2001, 5).

Wrapped together in intensities of enchantment, romantic and sexual desire transforms Christian's sombre moods from "flat and grey as the weather" into ones of heightened intensity and aliveness, and shifts his world from monotonous monochrome "into one rich with color" (James 2015, 4, 518), as if illustrating Tomkins' notion of "vidious contrast" between life as it was before and as it now appears in its newly enchanted form. Anastasia is able to bring both Christian and his heart "back to life" (James 2017, 231) and has herself "never felt so alive, so vital" (James 2012b, 359, 375). According to the generic defaults of romance fiction, "The body of the heroine is alive and singing in every fiber, she is overrun by sexuality that wells up inside her and that she cannot control" (Snitow 1983, 254). This all results from the immediate attraction between the main couple, registered as an affective charge. The overwhelming attraction that Anastasia and Christian feel towards one another truncates their capacities to act in the world as their energies and focus flow into their mutual connection bordering on obsessiveness. This attraction galvanises their bodies, makes them flourish, and fills their lives with a sense of purpose largely detached from the surrounding world as they, in Walt Whitman's phrasing, sing the body electric.

Snitow (1983, 256) associates the sex-saturated liveliness of romance fiction with the generic features of pornography exploring "the explosion of the boundaries of the self" where "social constraints are overwhelmed by a flood of sexual energy". What is particular to romance fiction in comparison with, say, hardcore pornography, is the negotiation, or balancing, of this visceral force with both emotional attachment and domestic security (Snitow 1983, 259; also Smith 2007, 201). In contrast to the plenitude of bodies and desires, abundant satiation and "enjoyment in sensuous material reality" that in Steven Marcus' (1964, 22) analysis of Victorian pornography form the quintessence of this narrative realm, *Fifty Shades* narrows down the availability of bodies to just one partner while tying sexual attraction together with monogamous commitment. Both the echoes of transgression connected to Christian's kinky bent and Anastasia's continuing and increasing curiosity about her bodily capacities, combined with the couple's insatiable lust for one another, revolve in the registers of excess characteristic to pornographic fiction. This flood of sexual desire comes across as a visceral force that fills their lives with enchantment, liveliness and meaning. Sexual play further transforms the everyday into scenes of magical, abundant intensity: "I am just sensation. This is what he does to me – takes my body and possesses it wholly so that I think of nothing but him. His magic is powerful, intoxicating. I'm a butterfly caught in his net, unable and unwilling to escape. I'm his ... totally his" (James 2012b, 79).

Ill Effects and Poor Quality

It remains more than easy to mock products of popular media culture such as *Fifty Shades* for their quality or their formulaic predictability of events, characters and scripts. Snark abounds in social media, clickbait and online news coverage of the books and films, from "17 Dumbest, Most Disturbing Aspects of '50 Shades of Grey'" (Sager 2015) to "50 Laughably Bad Fifty Shades Darker Quotes: Prepare to Have Your Insides Melted and Unfurled" (Armitage 2017), "Fifty Terrible Lines from *Fifty Shades of Grey*"

(Humphrey 2015) and that the writing involved is "absolutely batshit" (Bryan 2015). The poor quality of the writing remains the most routine source of complaint, possibly matched only by the disenchantment felt owing to the misguiding portrayals of BDSM play or the films' lukewarm, non-explicit coverage thereof, as encapsulated in Jack Halberstam's (2015) gleefully smarting critique: "The movie version of *Fifty Shades of Grey* promised dynamic sex, the subjugation of a feisty if inexperienced woman, the allure of a dominant man, but it delivers only a series of pre-queer theory lectures on BDSM and has less effect, I am willing to bet, on the libidinal urges of its audience than an episode of *The Golden Girls* – and I mean no disrespect here to that glorious and lusty project of octogenarian girl power."

The novels have been heavily critiqued for their depiction of BDSM that misunderstands and misrepresents both consent and desire while also contributing to the subculture's broader pathologisation as symptomatic of things gone wrong, whether these involve childhood trauma, experiences of violence or abuse. As discussed below in Chapter 5, BDSM can function as trauma play but this would hardly be the only available, let alone the most pressing of motivations. *Fifty Shades* has equally been accused of coining scenes bordering on sexual abuse under the guise of romance while falling dramatically short of conveying the lived experiences of sexual domination and submission (Morgan 2012; Tripodi 2017, 104). Especially since the first film premiered, journalistic accounts drawing on interviews with kink practitioners have listed the errors and irritations connected to James' treatment of BDSM. In many instances, these accounts set out to correct its depictions of kink practice in terms of how true, untrue or plain wrong they may be, from the dynamics of consent to the types of rope and constraint used (e.g. Picardo and Reilly 2015; Smith 2015; Steel 2015).

It should come as no surprise that *Fifty Shades* allows ample room for critique and errata, considering that the franchise results not from engagement with or participation in BDSM culture, its conventions or codes, but from a more distanced fascination and interest concerning them, embedded in the fantasy templates of romantic fiction. Complaints over the depiction of consent in *Fifty Shades* are connected to how it has become an internationally circulating cultural fantasy template, while the commodity production connected to it offers women play props and devices for exploring its scenarios. If the novels misunderstand and misconstrue the very basis of a BDSM scene, then these play templates are skewed in ways that feed into gendered dynamics of domination and violence in hetero-sexual relationships (e.g. Barker 2013; Tripodi 2017). Rather than facilitating female sexual pleasure, such templates would literally bring about pain.

Some critics have framed *Fifty Shades* as unequivocally harmful – having landed people in hospitals after experimentation goes wrong (see Deller and Smith 2013, 936). Evoking the perennial discourse of ill media effects, commentators have raised concerns over the fiction's impact on women and young people. Emma Green (2015) critiques *Fifty Shades* for casually associating hot sex with violence outside the context of BDSM that foregrounds communication skills, self-knowledge and emotional maturity as requirements for sexual gratification. By doing so, the series allegedly feeds American rape culture: "As images of Ana being beaten by Christian become the new normal for what's considered erotic, they raise questions about what it means to 'consent' to sex" (Green 2015). For their part, Andrew Adesman and Alexis Tchaconas (2015) raise concern over the first film's harmful impact on teens, despite the fact that, in the United States, the film's age limit was set at seventeen – in contrast to that of twelve in France, for example. The authors argue that its cinematic depiction of kink, much like the viewing of violence and pornography (both categories left with no further description or explanation), feeds aggression, risky sexual behaviour and date violence. If these concerns sound familiar, this would not be altogether surprising, considering that similar views of mass-market romance trying to "convert rape into love" have been voiced for a number of decades (see Snitow 1983, 255).

Studies focusing on the series' harmful effects and its promotion of violence against women have also garnered social media attention. In a study mapping out such effects, Amy Bonomi, Lauren Altenburger and Nicole Walton (2013) each read the first *Fifty Shades* novel and compared their summaries with the US Center for Disease Control and Prevention's definitions of emotional abuse and sexual violence. Their study found abuse and violence to run rife in the novel, which therefore presents a dangerous cultural influence: "While Anastasia is depicted as experiencing 'pleasure' during some of the couple's sexual interactions, our analysis shows she is simultaneously confused and terrified that she will be hurt in such interactions, and she yearns for a 'normal' relationship; in addition, Anastasia's consent in the sexual activities is coerced through the use of alcohol and intimidation/pressure" (Bonomi et al. 2013, 741).

Summing up the argument, the anti-pornography advocate Gail Dines (2014, i) argues that the books "eroticize violence against women and render invisible the predatory tactics the 'hero' (Christian Grey) uses to groom, seduce, and abuse a much younger woman (Anastasia Steele)" and, in doing so, undermine "the health and emotional well-being of its female readers". Dines goes on to explain the resonance that the books have found among female readers by indicating how "the misogyny inherent in porn has filtered into mainstream pop culture and been internalized by both women and men. Whereas 'old-fashioned' feminists argued that real power is about changing the structures that deny women economic, legal, and political equality, the newer wave of feminism, informed in large part by postmodernism, voided itself of any institutional analysis, arguing instead for individual empowerment rooted in a sexuality that is fun, hot, and edgy" (Dines 2014, ii). Reading *Fifty Shades* as emblematic of the violence, debasement and dehumanisation targeted against women that she finds characteristic of contemporary pornography, Dines explains its popularity with a media-illiterate (female) population which, through the manipulation of cultural industry professionals, is buying into the fantasy, to detrimental effects.

In a subsequent study, Bonomi et al. (2014) engaged in an empirical study of female readers and non-readers of *Fifty Shades*. Summarising the findings, they state that women who had read the first novel

were more likely than nonreaders to have had, during their lifetime, a partner who shouted, yelled, or swore at them (relative risk [RR] = 1.25) and who delivered unwanted calls/text messages (RR = 1.34); they were also more likely to report fasting (RR = 1.80) and using diet aids (RR = 1.77) at some point during their lifetime. Compared with nonreaders, females who read all three novels were more likely to report binge drinking in the last month (RR = 1.65) and to report using diet aids (RR = 1.65) and having five or more intercourse partners during their lifetime (RR = 1.63). (Bonomi et al. 2014, 720)

The authors then report correlations – although no causalities – between eating disorders, experiences of abuse, active sexuality and the consumption of *Fifty Shades*. Notably, having five or more sexual partners is, for reasons left unspecified, equated with potential health risks and unhealthy behaviours. The authors continue to speculate on the books both aggravating existing trauma and influencing the onset of risk and harm "by creating an underlying context for the behaviors" (Bonomi et al. 2014, 725). In yet another study, the research team found correlations between women reading *Fifty Shades* and their "higher levels of ambivalent, benevolent, and hostile sexism" (Altenburger et al. 2017, 455). This series of studies both generalises and speculates on the relationship between this particular series of fiction and the ways in which the participating women make sense of their lives, experiences, bodies and sexualities in order to prove and isolate the harmful effects of singular cultural products. No greater degrees of nuance are evident in the popular coverage of these studies, according to which " 'Fifty Shades of Grey' Might Be Bad For Your Health" (Jacobs 2014), encourages young boys to violent behaviour, disempowers young girls and skews their relationship expectations, even if – perhaps counterintuitively – they would not even be readers of the said novels (Grossman-Scott n.d.).

In sum, *Fifty Shades* has been accused of achieving the ills of the sort that earlier feminist critics identified as patriarchy's doing on a much more expansive and totalising scale. As an ill media effect, the series has been invested with the potential of rendering heterosexual women promiscuous and vulnerable to male violence, of keeping adolescents from figuring out the difference between sex and abuse, and for obstructing parents from teaching the distinction between the two. James would then have much indeed to answer for, for penning and promoting her fantasy scenarios. The female readers presumed in these discourses of concern are prone to the effects of fiction, passively absorbing the fantasy scenarios on offer and applying them to their own sex lives without sufficient reflection and at the very risk of their sexual health. There figures bear similarity to eighteenth-century visions of the female romantic fiction readers prone to arousing fantasies and their harmful, escapist allure (Laqueur 2003, 203–204). They are also close kin to behaviourist "magic bullet" and "hypodermic needle" media effects models developed around the Second World War, according to which effects are injected into fundamentally passive audiences in order to manipulate them to act towards desired ideological goals. The

Fifty Shades series is quintessentially a product of popular – or mass – culture and its consumers have been accordingly addressed as a feminised, uncritical, vulnerable and passive mass played by the fantasy scenarios that the books feed them with.

Meanwhile, the interests, motivations and pleasures described by readers themselves are complex and mixed, ranging from general interest towards the phenomenon to enjoyment taken in the depictions of sex and the thrills of the romance narrative, as well as the pleasures of mocking the novels' style and quality (Deller and Smith 2013; Click 2015). As Sarah Harman and Bethan Jones (2013, 952) note, the novels have "generated an ironic, even guilty, fandom in which readers and viewers bemoan the series' flaws, while enjoying (sometimes furtively) the texts". Such "snark fandom", as routinely performed and shared on social media platforms from Tumblr to Twitter, Facebook and YouTube, takes joy in both the books' content and their aesthetic shortcomings in ways far removed from the figure of readerly passiveness implied in the accounts addressed just above.

Some of the respondents to Deller and Smith's (2013, 944–946) study on *Fifty Shades* readers complained of the sex scenes being repetitive to the point of boredom. It may nevertheless also be that the novels' widely critiqued prosaic language translates as accessibility *precisely* due to it being so repetitive, hyperbolic and straightforward in its delivery. There are no convoluted sentence structures or obscure cultural allusions in how James translates Anastasia's bodily intensities into textual guise. That which is considered bad, simple or unskilled in literary terms may also come across as guileless in that the chosen means and forms of expression do not overshadow that which is being communicated. Should stylistic trickery be deployed, there might be less credibility to claims of authenticity, namely to the series being put on paper by an amateur author for the sheer pleasure of writing and sharing the outcome with others. The rationale and motive of *Fifty Shades* revolves around sexual fantasy rolled into textual pleasure, rather than around poetic ambition or literary experimentation. Part of the appeal of *Fifty Shades* is then rooted in its home-cooked characteristics. A particular, accessible and, by the looks of it, compelling DIY aesthetic is at play.

The broad resonance that *Fifty Shades* has found among audiences is centrally tied in with its explorations of sexual yearning and ecstasy through play. Although this point may appear obvious, it has been downplayed in many analyses, feminist and other. Such resonances are aided by, and possibly amplified through, the familiarity and accessibility of the characters, dynamics and plotlines drawing on the templates of romantic erotica. The series' popularity indicates that there is something enchanting in its particular combination of romance formula, sex and BDSM and the visions of bodily intensification that it so idiosyncratically offers. Much remains to be said of the enchanting, tortuous dynamics and manifold pleasures of sexual desire and play that erotic fiction aims to probe.

4

Pervy Minors and Adult Babies

Thinking of sex in terms of play means both crossing and bringing together notions often considered mutually exclusive, or at least positioned as being in persistent friction with one another. For if sex is understood as the stuff of adult experience, and not that of minors, then adults are similarly excluded from the realm of play, seen as "a child's work" (see Paley 2004). Scholars have distinguished between childhood sexual play and adult activities by contrasting the former's characteristic "curiosity and playfulness" with the latter as "marked by an understanding of sexual behaviour and its consequences. In addition, children's normal sexual behaviors are spontaneous and open, in contrast to adult behaviour, which is private" (Essa and Murray 1999, 232). Such boundary work, revolving around the ever-elusive trope of normalcy, separates childhood play from adult work and childhood asexuality – or innocence – from adult sexuality in ways that do not allow for much flexibility within, let alone in between, the categories.

Such boundary work in fact crafts out ontological distinctions between childhood sexual play and adult sexuality defined by seriousness: the curious, playful, spontaneous and open character of the former would not extend to the latter. In a reverberation of Rubin's virtuous inner circle of good sex, adult sexuality is defined as a decidedly private affair heavy with awareness of causes and consequences. The distinction between childhood and adulthood is then crafted out as one in kind in ways implying that as children grow up, they become different creatures while their playful tendencies gradually atrophy. According to Henri Bergson's well-known distinction, differences in kind, as opposed to those in degree, involve the determination to reduce quality to quantity (Bergson 2007,

299; Deleuze 1991, 20–21). When differences (of any sort) are mapped out as ones in kind, it becomes difficult to identify continuities and variations in quality across the different things or phenomena examined.

Play bleeds into work just as fantasy constantly tints and orients experiences of reality. For its part, sexuality can be understood as embodied capacities and intensities that play a key role throughout people's lives, rather than as something emerging as if from thin air with the hormonal surges of puberty – a point already raised by Freud in his discussion on the sex drive and the polymorphous perverse child. In order to unravel some of this, this chapter explores age, sexuality and play from two different angles: the first looks at sexual play among young people while the second explores adult age-play. The chapter first moves into a discussion of Finnish girls' experiences of online sexual role-play as driven by curiosity, learning, fun and the quest for pleasure. The second line of inquiry examines adult age-play and its depictions in television talk-shows and documentaries, on YouTube channels and in Jan Soldat's documentary films, *Coming of Age* (2016) and *Happy Happy Baby* (2016), which highlight the pleasures – sexual and other – of playing a baby or a toddler, as well as the broader processes of bodily learning and the testing out of boundaries that sexual play enables. This line of inquiry makes it possible to tease out some of the dynamics of childhood and adulthood, asexuality and sexuality in connection with play as experimental openness connected to bodily pleasure.

Pervy Role-Play

Late in 2013, Silja Nielsen set up a survey for her media studies MA thesis on the Finnish-speaking version of the then highly popular online community for girls, goSupermodel (2006–2016). The purpose of the study – consisting of both multiple-choice questions and free-form replies – was to inquire after girls' experiences of sending and receiving sexual messages in different social media services and apps. Rather than focusing on the interactions taking place on goSupermodel alone, the survey set out to chart how common sexual messaging was, how girls felt about it and who they were communicating with. The key aim was to look at girls as active participants in and contributors to online sexual practices, rather than as passive and only unwilling recipients of unsolicited come-ons, proposals or other forms of harassment.

The 1,269 responses analysed, submitted by girls aged from 11 to 18, revealed a range of experiences from having received no messages to having been harassed by adult men and enjoying sexual exchanges among one's friends, as well as many things in between. Some messaging was described as distressing, disgusting and scary whereas other exchanges revolved around the registers of amusement, interest, fun and pleasure in ways speaking not only of differences among the respondents but of the diversity of sexual messaging practices. The survey participants drew clear distinctions between solicited and unsolicited exchanges, as well as between those involving different communication partners. Messages from older people were largely dismissed as unpleasant and creepy whereas those received from friends and attractive peers could be very much desired and reciprocated. Mapped out in terms of play, the incidents experienced as distressing or yucky involved a sense of being played against one's own volition by unknown people, assumed to be ones of a different generation. In the more pleasurable instances, the exchanges were driven by mutual playful interest, curiosity and desire.

We have addressed the study's research design, ethical concerns, cultural context and key findings elsewhere (see Nielsen et al. 2015), and I will not repeat these here. Rather, I want to explore one specific strand emerging from the survey, namely that of sexual role-play. On goSupermodel, users commonly engaged in textual role-playing games with a sexual theme, plot or bent, ironically referred to as "pervy role-play" (in Finnish, *pervo roolipeli*). As many as 43 per cent of the respondents reported playing reciprocal, pervy role-playing games together with their friends through private messaging. This pervy role-play involved pre-agreed characters and an overall framing within which a collaboratively developed plotline began to emerge: sex may have been the main object of focus or something of a subplot in terms of core action. In this sense, pervy play represents a continuum of "cybersex", aka textual-sexual role-playing, as it has been practised on online platforms since bulletin boards, IRC, Multi-User Domains and Usenet, well before the ubiquity of social media.

Since the sexual role-play in Nielsen's survey was dialogical, it was described as solicited, as a source of pleasure and as a realm of diverse explorations. Like sexual messaging among young people more broadly, pervy play involved experimentations with gender and sexuality, as well as negotiations over what is considered playful in the first place (see Tsaliki 2016, 108). Many survey participants spontaneously defended their role-play – possibly assuming that a study inquiring after these routines came from an angle of concern or condemnation characteristic of much public discourse on young people's sexting practices: "No pervy role-play, a stupid term. But as such a role-playing game including basic smut but sex wasn't the main point" (girl, 13). "I played a role-playing game that was realistic and tried to convey the whole relationship without prettifying any of it. So it wasn't just a 'pervy' role-play since sex was a neutral thing and I'm old enough to understand" (girl, 16). As Nielsen (2014, 36) notes, despite "pervy" being the chosen term among the young people themselves, it gained a somewhat pejorative resonance when taken up by an unfamiliar adult.

Communications on the site – as on numerous other virtual communities designed for girls – took place with the aid of modifiable avatars and thus involved a form of role-play to start with. On such platforms, it is common for the play characters to take on, alter and discard accessories, hairstyles and fashions and, in doing so, to experiment with and to negotiate the available palettes of body aesthetics and techniques of sexiness (also Tsaliki 2016, 175–199). The sexual role-play scenarios described nevertheless took place through private messaging and chat, and hence unfolded in textual form. Role-play facilitates examinations of sexuality through characters and settings chosen according to preference: it is possible to play a character much older and more experienced than oneself; to be a vampire, a rock star, of any gender or sexual bent, and to alter the narrative trajectory at will (Nielsen et al. 2015, 477). Like fan-generated slash fiction envisioning queer encounters between film and television characters, pervy role-play on goSupermodel allowed for experimentation outside normative sexual scripts (e.g. Tosenberger 2008; Brown 2012). In the open-ended answers, one 17-year-old described her play experiences as "gay erotica" and a 14-year-old as "love between two people" where "neither of the story characters was in any way dominated". The improvised scripts of sexual role-play drew from diverse media materials and interests – if not necessarily knowledge – concerning sexual bents and routines. They also remained unruly in relation to any instantly recogniz-able norms of "good sex".

Role-playing games are between fictitious characters. I started playing them when I was 14. Mostly these games include gay relationships, and sex is described in detail. (Although that's not the main point.) When it comes to sex, the topics range from hardcore submission to oral sex, rape, etc. There are no real limits. (girl, 18)

Messages in role-playing games have been very detailed and realistic but not disturbing. Some might consider the messages too crude or lewd but I think it's a matter of attitude. (girl, 17)

In a study conducted in the 1990s, Finns recounted their early experiences of "playing house, touching, playing doctor, playing at being animals, and actual sex play, closely resembling adult sexual experiences" – in fact half of the contributors had experiences of adolescent sexual play (Kontula 2009, 81–82). They recalled emulating the behaviour of adults and domestic animals, as witnessed in their immediate surroundings. These surroundings were largely agrarian and the media environments in question limited to national broadcast radio and television, cinema, newspapers and magazines. Nielsen's adolescent survey participants, who were clearly older at the time than the retrospectively reminisced pre-pubescent children in the 1990s study, similarly borrowed and appro-priated pervy role-play characters from their immediate surroundings, yet these were media-saturated, rich in literary and screen-based fiction, user-generated content and celebrity culture. In addition to books, films and television, play characters were harvested from among celebrities and members of popular pop bands. Even more drastic differences vis-à-vis agrarian childhood play, as recounted in the 1990s, involved the play scripts themselves, which tapped into explorations of gay sex, "hardcore submission", "oral sex, rape, etc."

For some, such disclosures might function as proof of the corrosive powers of the sexualisation and pornification of culture to create bias in young people's – and especially girls' – understandings of their sexual selves and the range of bodily activities available to them in increas-ingly pornographic and violent manners. The scenario of "hardcore submission" undoubtedly has a different ring to it than that of playing house, doctor or animal. I would nevertheless suggest that, rather than

emulating scripts found elsewhere in culture, within and outside pornography, sexual role-play makes use of such materials in a reflexive
manner through and with characters other than oneself. The Finnish
teens participating in Nielsen's survey lived amidst an increased visibility of all kinds of sexual cultures, tastes and attachments, as well as
the media narratives covering them. From queer and trans YouTube
vloggers to sexually experimental Instagram celebrities and confessional autobiographers, the contemporary mediasphere remains
expansive in the sexual images it shows and the stories it tells (see also
Duguay 2016; Hall 2016; Raun 2016; McAlister 2017). Online pornography, provided in carefully indexed subcategories and with a plethora
of tags indicating distinctions between different preferences and styles,
would be only one easily available resource for testing out the possible
range of one's sexual interests and disinterests. The transformations
in the materials and resources of sexual play across generations then
primarily speak of notable expansions in the increased diversification
in sexual and intimate citizenship – that is, in the publicly recognised,
represented and debated ways of acting out sexual lives (Weeks 1998;
also Plummer 2003a).

Pervy role-play, as depicted in the survey, remixes cultural images
and texts in ways that make it possible to examine how sexual lives are
lived, how pleasures may be found and what risks all this may entail.
Through online play, young people can further explore sexual narratives,
identifications and resources with little regard as to how the bodies, acts,
encounters and interactions played out may be situated within normative sexual hierarchies. Things improvised in play need not in any direct
or literal way translate into scripts for trying out sexual identities or for
expressing personal desires. Play, after all, is largely about the pursuit of
fun, and this fun can well be sarcastic and cruel in its tones: one 13-year-
girl, for example, described the pleasures offered by a play script placing
unpopular teachers in a cleaning cupboard having sex. As social play and
improvisation, pervy role-play facilitates – but does not necessitate – forms
of learning and explorations of fantasy in the registers of interest, fascination and repulsion. A play script can be engrossing in its grossness or in its
exaggerated dynamics bleeding into humour. Sex need not be a primary
theme in such exchanges.

Returning to Martin Barker's (2014, 155) discussion of sexual fantasies addressed in the previous chapter, pervy role-play can function as a means of trying out "versions of self-in-sexual-society" – of exploring a world of possibilities, distant realms of desires and fantasies and possibly imagining "what I might or might not be". Role-play can be detached from one's personal desires inasmuch as it can be viscerally felt. It can be acted out through crafted characters and facilitate the probing of sexual dynamics and boundaries of one's own potential interests. Independent of the specific exchanges in question, the pursuit would centrally be one of pleasure connected to sexual interaction, sharing, learning, imagining, humour and fantasy.

The Tricky Topic of Childhood Play

Incorporating and working through both personal likes and social norms, sexual play – whether practised by adolescents or adults – can be serious or anything but, follow normative cultural scripts or elaborately break against them. In studies to date, childhood sexual play has nevertheless been conceptualised primarily as the exploration of embodiment, sexuality and appropriate gendered roles and routines. Understood as a form of learning fuelled by curiosity, it has been framed as a negotiation of expectations and orientations concerning both embodiment and the surrounding world. Children up to seven years old have been observed to "form the concept of marriage and or long-term relationships: they practice adult roles as they 'play house' ... engage in heterosexual play, including 'playing doctor'" (DeLamater and Friedrich 2002, 10). Furthermore, "through play, children act out communication skills necessary in adult interaction and test out emotions that are associated with different situations" (Kontula 2009, 81; also Essa and Murray 1999; Lamb 2001).

Among younger children, sexual play may, for instance, involve simulated sex, explorations of one's own genitalia or those of others, or verbally exploring sexual terminology, possibly with little understanding of its meaning (Davies et al. 2000, 1334). For educators, "Sexualized behavior in younger children is often the starting point for suspicion of sexual abuse", even though "some sexualized behaviors are common" and there is in fact "no consensus regarding what constitutes 'normal' sexual behavior over the developmental stages of childhood" (Davies et al. 2000, 1330). Consequently, scholars have examined correlations between childhood experiences of sexual play (both consensual and not) and later experiences of abuse and trauma, while disclosures of sexual play have been studied as indicators of abuse (e.g. Essa and Murray 1999; Davies et al. 2000; Larsson and Svedin 2002). More broadly, sexual play has been approached as indicative of inappropriate adult influences, such as sexually explicit media, breaching the boundaries of childhood (Essa and Murray 1999, 231). Despite its acknowledged ubiquity, childhood sexual play is easily identified as harmful effects of adult culture and society, or even as signs of sexual violence against children. Chosen and pleasurable sexual play among young people has been of considerably less scholarly interest.

As is the case with all kinds of play, sexual experimentations among young people can involve "teasing, bribing, and manipulation" (Larsson and Svedin 2002, 272). Children can persuade, manipulate and coerce one another to play but also enter the scenes of play freely, knowingly and gleefully (see Lamb and Coakley 1993). The degree to which studies on the topic to date have revolved around the risks of coercion and abuse is noteworthy, even if not precisely surprising. All this speaks of the ambivalent position that sexual pleasure holds in sex research more generally. On the one hand, sexual pleasure remains perpetually present in explorations of its shortage and lack; on the other hand, the intensities of sexual pleasure are seldom taken seriously enough to exclusively focus on, conceptualize and foreground as an end in themselves (see Spišák 2016a). Further strain is caused by the reluctance to account for sexual pleasure, desire and curiosity among young people below the age of consent.

According to the somewhat ubiquitous discourse of sexualisation, sex-saturated media culture pushes into the lives of children, and into those of girls in particular, and exposes them to things that they are too immature to process (see Mulholland 2013; Spišák 2016b; Tsaliki 2016). By doing so, the notion of sexualisation frames sexuality as a force external to childhood that then makes a forced entry of sorts. This flattens out the circuits of exploration, curiosity and pleasure connected to sexual play as they cut through people's lives in different intensities and with diverse outcomes. Addressing British reports on children and sexualisation, Barker comments on the frequent use of the term "exposure". For Barker, this speaks of a dismissive attitude towards young people's motivations for exploring sexually explicit content – including the motivations of " 'masturbation', 'wanting to know more about sex', 'curiosity' and 'boredom' " – by presuming "cumulative effect, corrupting influence, and slippery slope to doom, all of which is set in motion by that word 'exposed' " (Barker 2014, 143). Contra the abstract figure of a young person at risk, passively and unwillingly exposed to pornographic imagery, empirical research points to young people foregrounding their media literacy, displaying resilience in terms of disturbing content and disclosing a range of reasons for consuming sexually explicit material to start with (e.g. Bragg and Buckingham 2009; Buckingham and Chronaki 2014; Albury 2014; Spišák 2016a).

When asked, adolescents frame the pleasures afforded by online sexual play as escapes from boredom, as forms of social bonding, bullying and flirtation, as well as the riskier testing out of bodily possibilities (Nielsen et al. 2015; Tsaliki 2016, 108). Through play, it is possible to learn what bodies can do, what they are supposed to do and what not, as well as what the bodies of other people may enjoy doing. Following Tomkins' (2008, 226) conceptualisation of sexuality as amplified by the affective charges of interest and excitement, activities ranging from bodily self-exploration to investigations into pornography, sexting and sexual role-play are driven by a quest for bodily pleasure, the shapes and trajectories of which alter according to age and life-stage. Bodily experiences of all kinds layer as people discover more of the sexual cultures and practices that they are surrounded by. It then follows that the horizons of bodily possibility connected to sexuality remain in constant transformation. Sexual scripts and fantasy scenarios continue to vary, and possibly to expand, as do the shapes of curiosity concerning orientations, intensities and desires. Pervy role-play at the age of sixteen is unlikely to be all that similar to the play in which the same person was immersed at the age of six, or that which she may experiment with at fifty-six, yet these would not be completely unconnected either.

Those Finns who, in the 1990s' study, recalled their childhood experiences of sexual play in negative terms of shame and harm had been caught out and punished by parents or other adults (Kontula 2009, 82).

It was therefore the regulatory interference of educators, rather than the fumbling routines of play among children as such, that had tinted memories in painful hues. Those whose games were not found out reminisced with fondness about the sexual thrills – and even orgasms – afforded by play routines. This finding resonates with that of a memory-work project that my research team conducted together with the Folklore Archives of the Finnish Literature Society in 2012 on the memories and experiences of pornography (see Paasonen et al. 2015). The notions of risk and harm central to public debates on childhood, sexuality and media did not play a central role in the respondents' accounts of their early experiences of pornography. While these same people may have had concerns about the negative effects that sexual imageries currently have for minors, such as their own children, or for other people more generally, our forty-five respondents did not see themselves as having been harmed by pornography in their youth. When mentioned, negative sensations were connected to memories of adults introducing sexually explicit materials against the young person's own volition, or to having been coerced to watch these together with people of their own age. When porn encounters were knowingly sought out, as they for the most part were, memories remained notably nostalgic and warm, detailing the trials endured in order to access such materials. All in all, there were no accounts of trauma connected to porn encounters during adolescence (Spišák and Paasonen 2017).

Peer review feedback on the collaborative projects discussed above – on teenage girls' sexual messaging online and on memories of childhood porn encounters – has pointed out that the absence of trauma in the respondents' accounts does not translate as the absence of trauma as such. This would be accurate, given that both the memory-work essays and survey responses are strategic, selected and planned and therefore allow for no access to the complexities of people's thoughts or inner lives. The question nevertheless remains as to why trauma should be postulated as the self-evident outcome of adolescent sexual exploration even when the people recounting such routines remain silent on the topic – or when they explicitly deny the presence of traumatic harm in their own memories. To assume that repressed trauma is nevertheless present, always already there albeit not disclosed or admitted to, may be a means of further stigmatising early sexual exploration as innately harmful and problematic (cf. Barker and Langdridge 2010; Harrison and Holm 2013). In cases where such assumptions do not find support in empirical research, the foregrounding of trauma is likely to speak primarily of scholarly premises concerning sexuality, and of theoretical frameworks drawing on Freud.

While I will return to the theme of trauma and its connections to sexual play in Chapter 5, the remainder of this chapter looks further into the pleasures and dynamics of age and play in the context of adult age-play and its diverse media coverage. And why might this be? For the simple reason that I want to rethink the divide that is recurrently postulated and operationalised in sex research between play and playfulness in childhood and adulthood. According to the broader assumption lodged in this distinction, play is natural for children and indicative of overall openness towards the world, yet closes down and congeals as people age: there would therefore be no room or need left for playful experimentation once people learn appropriate ways of being sexual. Sexuality is often considered the end of adulthood and play alike (see Bauer 2018, 145). Adults, then, are assumed not to play – and if they do, theirs is play of an altogether different kind, learned from expert guidelines for spicing up routines, or guided by the social principles of specific sexual subcultures far detached from the heterosexual mainstream. Playfulness would otherwise be a capacity gradually lost, along with the motivation, drive and ability for play.

If one understands playfulness as a mood and orientation of openness and play as acts of exploration motivated by pleasure, then the question would be one of variations rather than ruptures – of differences in degree rather than ones in kind. Following this line of thinking, both children and adults play: children play adults and adults play at being children in ways that are sexual, defined by the participants as non-sexual, and many things in between (also Bauer 2018, 147). This would not mean that these play practices are either similar or ontologically distinct from one another. The forms that playfulness and play take, and the roles that they serve in people's lives – sexual and other – simply change. The same would apply to sexuality as the exploration of bodily pleasures and intensities, attachments and identifications.

Deviant, Sordid and Safe

The category of so-called paraphilic infantilism is connected to the dynamics of dominance, submission and care in age-play relations between daddy doms/little girls (DDLG), mommy doms/little boys (MDLB), daddy doms/little boys (DDLB) and mommy doms/little girls (MDLG), as well as a range of queer bois, grrrls, daddis and mommis (Bauer 2018). The relations between caregivers and littles of different ages broaden into myriad variations of lesbian dads, cross-dressing toddlers, intergenerational relations, sexual likes and aversions. In the case of Adult Baby/Diaper Lovers (ABDL), age-play involves "wearing, urinating, and defecating in diapers . . . using baby toys, sucking on pacifiers, crawling, using bottles, sleeping with blankets, and expressing desires to become a baby, be treated like a baby, and have their diapers changed", both in connection with masturbation and other sexual activity and not (Hawkinson and Zamboni 2014, 864). ABDL has recently given rise to a range of advice literature and information resources, from the website littlespaceonline.com to e-books such as Brian M.F. Burch's 2014 *The Adult Baby Guidebook: The Life Struggles of the Perpetually Diapered*, guiding its readers in understanding the adult baby phenomenon and in dealing with the multiple difficulties that it may give rise to, Penny Barber's 2016 *The Big Book for Littles: Tips & Tricks for Age Players & Their Partners*, which, true to its title, is a practical guide for finding and expanding "Little Space" – aka age-play headspace – and Evelyn Hughes, Rosalie Bent and Michael Bent's 2017 *Diaper Discipline and Dominance... a Journey into Upending the Traditional*, targeted at couples who may desire initiation into diaper play.

Paul Rulof's *Ageplay: From Diapers to Diplomas* (2011) covers much of the same ground but also sets out to describe and chart the phenomenon in its different manifestations, from the first age-play diagnoses of the 1950s to the ensuing development of aficionado networks and cultures. Rulof (2011, 7) maps out age-play as variations on the intensity spectrum from casual exploration to committed, immersive lifestyle, while emphasising that the notion of play, as deployed here, would not be "connotative of something trivial or frivolous. Rather, many people take ageplay very seriously. Although most people engage in age-related role-playing, others insist that they are not role-playing and feel that they are engaging their personality in a literal way." As if echoing Sicart's (2014) definition of play as pleasurable activity irreducible to fun and connected to a more sombre range of affective hues, Rulof defines age-play as seriously ludic – as both casual exploration and an issue of identity-work (see also Richards 2015, 61).

A further, possibly divisive spectrum involves sexual and non-sexual age-play. Drawing on data from a survey conducted among members of the kinky social networking site Fetlife, Rulof (2011, 19–33) charts age-play from reliving childhood, rewriting it, practising care, exploring different gendered childhoods and options, performing innocence and experiencing relaxation and enjoyment through regression, to the more explicitly sexually driven motivations of fetishes and taboos. These role-play dynamics draw some of their appeal from the broad conceptual separation of childhood, as a realm of sexual inexperience, from adult sexuality. Here, at least three figures of the child emerge: the *autobiographical, recollected child* who once was one's own self and with whom one can reconnect through role-play; the child as a *play role* played without it being directly connected to one's embodied memories while allowing for explorations of other ways of being in the world (Bauer 2018, 141); and the symbolic, *cultural figure of the child* of the kind that Lee Edelman (2004) identifies as a compulsory symbol of reproductive futurism.

This third figure of the child, distinct from empirical children, has been articulated as one of fragile innocence from Jean-Jacques Rousseau's eighteenth-century *Emile* to Edelman's symbolic encapsulation of hetero-conservative cultural tendencies. Contra the curiosity and resilience expressed by empirical young people in their practices of sexual play, this figure operates with the ideological notion of innocence that confuses relative ignorance with purity and cleanliness connoting asexuality (e.g. Higonnet 1998). The notion of sexual innocence and purity central to the modern figure of childhood is in fact one of emptiness, passiveness and blankness: "a coordinate set of *have nots*, of negations" (Kincaid 1998, 15, emphasis in the original). Emerging with Romanticism, this figure was, in James R. Kincaid's (1998, 53) terms, "strangely hollow right from the start: *un*corrupted, *un*sophisticated, *un*enlightened". At the same time, as Kincaid extensively argues, this figure has been eroticised as a highly valuable, as well as malleable, object of adult desire precisely owing to these properties – or the lack thereof. Playing child in ways that feed in and out of sexual titillation, arousal and climax for the scene participants very much rubs against this figure of innocence even when these scenes derive some of their force from the frissons of transgression. Meanwhile, other age-play aficionados are drawn to less sexually charged physical proximities, dependencies and care that age-play affords them, while many others enjoy the dynamics of domination, submission and humiliation of age-play as a BDSM practice.

If childhood sexual play evokes tensions and concerns due to its inappropriate approximations of the adult world, then adult age-play evokes a different range of concerns about the motivations of playing baby, toddler or pre-teen, or to act as a nurse, parent or carer for one. The shadow of paedophilia never seems to loom too far away, just as people engaging in pup-play may need to constantly ward off suspicions of zoophilia as the driving passion for their activities (Wignall and McCormack 2017; Bauer 2018, 140). Although acted out by willing adults among themselves, the playful crossing of the boundaries of childhood and adulthood, with the limits of consent and the ideological and moral concerns that these entail, remains rife with tension.

Adult baby play involving diapers is a marginal niche in the gamut of sexual likes. Like many other forms of sexual role-play, it has been taken up as a titillating, shocking and amusing – or possibly bemusing – theme in popular media. Probably the most widely circulated and recognised example involves the 2005 *CSI* television series episode "King Baby", where the crime scene investigation team discovers the age-play practices of a deceased sixty-something casino owner. The first tell-tale signs of kink include a mysterious diaper rash and signs of rectal penetration on the dead man's body whose stomach contents include only milk. Following these clues to the casino owner's mansion, the team uncovers bloodied adult-sized diapers and a nursery playroom painted in shades of powder blue, fitted with toys, an adult-sized crib and playpen. As the team begins to educate itself on adult age-play, the case further evolves with the discovery of baby bottles filled with human breast milk and diapers featuring LSD.

The unabashed sensationalism of the episode, as encapsulated in the flashback-like re-enactments of adult baby play featuring the ageing, heavy "King Baby" sucking on his thumb in a white bonnet when waiting to get changed, echoes the coverage of the topic elsewhere on US television, from the shock and awe "freak show" entertainment of the *Jerry Springer Show* in the 1990s (Gamson 1998a) to the seemingly therapeutic yet equally scandalised treatment of adult babies on *Doctor Phil* some years later. As Joshua Gamson (1998b; 1999) points out, the emotional publics of talk shows have facilitated increased visibility for minoritarian sexual cultures while simultaneously giving rise to hierarchies within them drawn according to the axes of class, respectability, freakiness and kinkiness. In the tabloid talk shows that Gamson studied, sexual nonconformity served the purpose of "funny pieces" that encouraged viewers to separate between "bad" and "good" nonconformists, as well as between socially acceptable and deviant carnal appetites (Gamson 1998b, 14). In such labour of distinction, adult babies are more likely to inhabit the realm of bad sex than that of good.

Rulof (2011, 16) notes that early and mid-1990s American talk shows first afforded adult babies broader publicity while a Usenet alt.fetish.diapers newsgroup and bulletin boards were beginning to establish networked connections among age-players. In addition, the specialised newsletter *Diaper Pail Fraternity* (later more gender inclusively titled *Diaper Pail Friends*) was first put in circulation in 1980 (Allen 2015, 83–90). In other words, gradually growing media attention, both mainstream and less so, was supported by the self-organisation of, and media production within, the sexual culture itself. Confessions of unusual sexual tastes and deeds – more often brushing shoulders with the titillations of sensationalism than not – abound in contemporary media culture that tirelessly zooms in on and details sexual styles, likes and experiences of people more or less famous, on scales both local and global, in veins both spectacular and not (Plummer 1995, 3–5, 9; Attwood 2006, 78–79). Adult babies and other littles fit only too well into this landscape as objects of wonder and aversion.

"My Husband is an Adult Baby!"

The 2015 episode "My Husband is an Adult Baby!" of the British TV tabloid *Jeremy Kyle Show* encapsulates much of this dynamic. Interviewing Maxine, a woman who has been married to a man wearing diapers for over three decades, Kyle expresses a spectrum of astonishment and bemusement, beginning with his introduction: "when I started this job ten years ago, I knew I'd speak to all sorts of people from different walks of life. And if one approaches it like that, you have an open mind. However, when I read this this morning, 'my husband is an adult baby', I'm going to be absolutely honest with you, as honest as I know the people at home and in the studio would want. It just seems a bit leftward to me." As Maxine explains her husband's diaper habit springing from his life-long bedwetting and incontinence as something that provides him with a sense of safety and comfort, Kyle nods empathetically. He then continues to summarise some of the exchange, with his interviewee shortly intercepting: "So the point that you guys wanted to make to us is that this isn't some sordid sexual [*no, no*] experience for him [*no*]. It's about comfort, it's about going back and trying to deal with something that's obviously important to him." Detaching diaper play from things sexual, Kyle continues to probe the boundaries of normality: "But you seem to have taken this some much further ... I'm not gonna lie to you, I just thought, that's a bit strange, you run an ... I don't even find it funny ... an adult baby [*it isn't funny*] nursery [*it's serious*]."

The exchange involves offbeat normalisation where the sexual is prised apart from play and the sordid from the regular while age-play is rendered understandable by framing it as a functional solution to a problem and as beneficial to personal wellbeing under challenging, chronic circumstances. According to this line of thinking, age-play may make sense when disconnected from sex and when serving instrumental purposes: were such play an end in itself, detached from therapeutic purpose and carried out for the sole purposes of sexual gratification, there would be no apparent escape from sordidness. This, of course, necessitates turning a blind eye to age-play as a BDSM practice deeply tied in with its codes of conduct and consent, as well as with its overall power dynamics. The de-sexualisation of age-play is in stark contrast with the long-term presence of infantilised participants in scenes of kink play where they are "mocked, bottle-fed, lightly punished and made to sing nursery rhymes" (Fernbach 2002, 205; Weiss 2011, 16). Kink baby roles may be randomly assigned or purposely sought out; they may be experiments in submission or a personal sexual fantasy lived out.

Meanwhile, the sexual scenarios and likes connected to age-play, in and out of BDSM play spaces, remain notably diverse (see Rulof 2011). In sum, a de-sexualisation of age-play involves its detachment from BDSM in ways that do no justice to the diverse interests and attachments of the littles and their carers themselves.

As Maxine explains their nursery concept, Kyle leans forward in an apparent state of acute curiosity, his approach growing aggressive in contrast to his interviewee's defensive and guarded manner: "people come to us ... and they become a child [*are they booking for a day or a night or what do they do?*]. They're booking for a day or a week ... and they may bake with mummy or daddy or they may play crayoning." Here, Kyle not only shifts restlessly about but faces the studio audience in exaggerated astonishment, turning his head from left to right, and back again. These shots are met with counter-shots of the audience laughing in bewildered amusement that echoes the host's affective register. Maxine grows increasingly animated and faces the audience: "Lots of people crayoning! I've got aunties that crayon. They just crayon, you know, with the children."

A photo of Maxine's husband in his daddy role appears on a studio screen as Kyle seems to struggle with the notion of role reversal and perches forward while dropping his voice: "What do you get from that, 'cause a lot of women wouldn't... [*Privilege! It's a privilege, because I*] Do you have kids? [*No, unfortunately we weren't able to, emm...*] Is that part of it?" As Maxine begins to grow visibly uncomfortable and to play with her necklace, Kyle presses on: "For you and for him, it's a very serious thing [*Yeah! It is!*] It fulfils many roles, for you both, it answers many questions: not any kids of your own, he's had problems since childhood, answers and ticks every box, yeah?" This seems to solve the basic mystery to Kyle's liking: while the incontinence issue would explain the husband's preference in non-sordid terms, the lack of children would cover Maxine's mothering and care habits in an equally acceptable vein. Failing to live out the normative model of reproductive family life, the couple are assumed to perform parenthood in the guise of play. This line of reasoning exemplifies what Samantha Allen (2015, 68) identifies as "the fight to maintain sexuality as its own independent province ... in lay reactions to psychoanalytic theories of sexuality". Age-play "answers and ticks every box" in Kyle's instant stint of psychotherapy, affording a sense of closure.

This state of balance would nevertheless only be momentary as Maxine's husband, Derek, soon comes into the studio. The couple nervously hold hands on stage as Kyle, now sided with the audience, meanders into a kneeling-perching position resembling that of Copenhagen's fabled Little Mermaid statue, thrusts his body forward and continues with his chosen line of inquiry:

Kyle: Do you have a physical relationship with your wife?

Derek: Yes! It's like any other –

Kyle: Do you wear a nappy all the time?

Derek: I have to. 'Cause I suffer with incontinence –

Kyle: Now just take again this in the right way because I, I'm completely and utterly – not confused – I don't know about this ... Would you be doing this, with full respect, if there hadn't been those *physical* problems in your life do you think?

Derek: Yes.

Kyle: Why?

Derek: Yes. This was a – a liking I had when I was seven. I had a fascination for nappies.

Kyle: It's not a sexual thing at all?

Derek: No, not sexual at all.

Kyle: Because you would understand, and again we talk about educating so would you understand that some people perhaps would feel that it is – at the best will in the world, let me say that in front of – a *deviant* thing if you want me to be honest but you've *stressed* to us all morning that it's not that. You're in a loving relationship with your wife, you've got problems, but you – you just – do this – and you'd do this whether you had these problems or not. Do you think that, do you understand that people find it a bit – leftward?

At this point, Maxine has all but stopped looking at Kyle or visually responding to anything he says. Pictures of a nursery cot follow while Kyle inquires after their clientele:

Kyle: Is it all shapes and sizes, ages?

Derek: Yes. Yeah, everybody. Boy, girl, different ages – our youngest is, em, just over eighteen, our oldest is eighty-one.

Kyle: Explain this to me because everyone when this story started they would think as I was trying to say to you, em, this is – slightly deviant, I only use that word, that's not my judgement – each to his own as you're not breaking the law, as I would say, in this country, but you're saying there are people out here – and this benefits a lot of them.

Maxine: Well I hope so.

Kyle: Do you feel it's normal, for the want of a better phrase, do you feel...

Maxine: What's normal?

Kyle: Yeah, completely agree.

The exchange is rife with references to deviancy and normality, some with scare quotes around them and others – such as the vintage *leftward* – without. Kyle gestures towards both respect and honesty in justifying his style of inquiry while evoking the figure of the public signifying the people "out there" who – contra to the open-minded talk-show host himself – might consider age-play sexual, deviant or just plain perverted. It is with the aim of educating this audience in mind that the show argues to probe the theme. This thin veneer of understanding, leaning on heterosexual matrimony as the normative frame for sexual contact, and steeped in the therapeutic discourse of self-help, nevertheless continuously slips and slides towards shades of the freaky. Meanwhile, the middle-aged couple awkwardly seated on stage become the freaky incarnate, despite their concluding remarks detaching baby play from perversion and paedophilia: "We're normal, working people, who just happen to like to dress in a certain way. We're not harming anybody ... Each to his own!"

The element of sensationalism seems hard indeed to dislodge from popular media coverage of sexual play off the mainstream, even when such play is safely placed within the socially sanctioned confines of heterosexual monogamy. Accompanied by affective audience responses assumed to express and echo those within the living room, the talk show resorts to the terminology of normality even when the preferences disclosed are stretching the boundaries of the very concept to the point of de-investing it of any analytical or descriptive force. Had the adult baby aficionados confessed to sexual motivations for play, their claims to normality would have simply fallen flat: a preference for dress is, after all, distinguishable from the libidinal turn-ons that Kyle, with perfectly puritan sensibility, couches in sexual sordidness.

Adult Baby Micro-Celebrities

In addition to talk shows, age-play, and diaper play in particular, is a natural fit for the televisual flow of sensationalist documentaries promising titillating glimpses of extraordinary sexual lives in a framework that is either humorous or moralising, or any combination thereof, laced with sexual norms and regulatory intent (see Arthurs 2004; Lunt and Stenner 2005). Adult babies have featured in various TV "shockumentaries", such as TLC's *My Strange Attraction* episode "An Adult Baby" (2011) featuring Riley, a 25-year-old age-playing transwoman, TLC's *My Crazy Obsession* episode "A Real Life Adult Baby" (2012) starring the 31-year-old adult baby Stanley who has also appeared in the National Geographic series *Taboo*, as well as Bankroft TV's *Extreme Love* episode, "Living as an Adult Baby" (2016), focusing on 21-year-old Jess who enjoys regression to infancy.

Different yet also notably similar in their execution, their uses of voice-over narration and humorous music, the shows introduce the littles, their play routines and some of their motivations which are invariably depicted as non-sexual – as distinct from BDSM even if connected to the dynamics of submission and domination. While CSI's "King Baby" episode, with its disclosures of rectal penetration, maps out baby play firmly in the hues of sexual kink, these episodes – much like the *Jeremy Kyle Show* – systematically frame out the sexual in their emphasis on sensations of comfort and safety that help the play participants to deal with the anxieties, pressures and responsibilities of adult life, provide fulfilment and compensate for actual childhoods rife with abuse.

In *My Strange Attraction*, Riley describes her preference as the means to "wash away all the stress of the big, tough world" while also disclosing her earlier experiences of being violently bullied. For Stanley, in *My Crazy Obsession*, play is not "sexual at all. And it's a feeling of being safe, something I didn't have when I was growing up. There was child abuse going on at the time, and being an adult baby became my way of coping with the world and my own problem." Addressing her entry into "little space" in *Extreme Love*, Jess identifies diapers as comforting and similarly connects her preference with experiences of childhood abuse. For Jess, age-play allows for reliving infancy in a "more innocent and pure way": "For me there's nothing sexual about my age-play or anything like that but for a lot of people it is a fetish or a kink." Jess' partner David is equally explicit about his disinterest: "age-play is not sexually stimulating to me in any way, shape or form. It is to other people but it's not for me."

Both Riley and Jess have an active social media presence – even something of a micro-celebrity status – through their YouTube channels and Riley's blog, first set up in 2006. Both also released videos addressing their participation in the TV shows. Riley's 2015 "My Strange Addiction Retrospective" looked at the experience of being on the show four years earlier. Riley explains her motivations for participating as a desire to be heard. She had a script to present even when knowing that the end result would inevitably be something different: "I knew that they were going to take what I said and chop it up in such a way that was not going to be ultimately flattering because reality TV is, sort of has a swing to it where ... a lot of it is focused on sort of punching down a little bit." For both Riley and Jess, television appearances were a means of expanding their social media presence while also being lucrative experiences in themselves, independent of any later feedback. The domestication of adult baby play in non-sexual terms within the shows nevertheless amputates the affective range and charge of their respective likes and activities.

Contra the neat compartmentalisation of sex and play in *My Strange Addiction*, Riley examined their more complex intermeshing in her blog very early on: "It's not sexual ... I like sex ... a lot, I like really kinky sex ... a lot, and I like incorporating diapers into bondage scenes, but diapers have always been about way more than sex, it's about happiness and protection and a lot of stuff I'm going to spend the rest of my life on a therapists couch for." Age-play, then, comes in a range of hues and thrills while the roles and positions occupied – and the dynamics connected to them – similarly alter. Like bondage and domination, it involves the pursuit of pleasure but equally it is about identities, attachments, "the discovery of new intensities, the diverse dimensions and potentials of 'lived bodies', as well as the development of contextual ethics" (Beckmann 2001).

In her video "Dear Ignorant People: Clearing Up Assumptions" (2016), Jess responded at length to the hateful comments she had received after her television appearance while also addressing the problems in how the *Extreme Love* episode had been put together. Her main complaint concerned the perception that the show gave of her early experiences of abuse in connection with her play preference:

If it makes you feel better to think that I'm dealing with abuse and it makes you accept this more then fine but the thing is, I'm not doing this because of abuse ...

My reasons for doing this are: it is a BDSM community and a lot of you think, "oh you say that you don't sexualise it or that's not sexual for you". In my relationship with my boyfriend and our DDLG relationship we do not practise it sexually – I do not have sex with him when I'm in little space ... Just because I don't sexualise it in my relationship doesn't mean that it's not sexualised, period, for me ...

What people in this kink or fetish get off on when their partner is acting as a child is the power and the control and the helplessness that the adult is embodying. It is a fetish and it's very common in the BDSM community to like to be humiliated or cut down to size and be controlled and when you're a child, or when you're a baby, you are very helpless and dependent on someone else –where you're basically forced to give them the power ... Everyone has different reasons for their kinks. For me, it makes me feel comfortable and happy and carefree and it releases my anxiety of the day – I like just to escape and go to another mind set and just kind of become something else.

Debunking the unequivocal separation of sex and play in the TV documentary, Jess' video presents a much more complex tapestry of preferences, intensities and pleasures where the sexual cuts into age-play without fully consuming or defining it, and where sensations of safety and comfort do not foreclose the pleasures of power play. Meanwhile, trauma caused by abuse is cut off from this tapestry as something that has been, that has since been managed and that is no longer re-enacted or worked through in scenes of play. Play, in short, is reframed and defined in terms of the diverse pleasures it affords without any need to isolate or exclude the sexual.

Independent of how specific media products – be these commercial TV shows, YouTube videos or something else – have been put together, the point is to not perceive of sexual desires and palates in a binary manner as being either present or absent in play practices. Following Tomkins, the question is one of qualities and registers of affect connected to bodily pleasure. For Tomkins (2008, 226), the affect of interest–excitement central to sexual pleasure involves optimal stimulation whereas that of enjoyment–joy generates release and relief, facilitates intimacy and social bonding.

Excitement necessitates the reduction of enjoyment, and vice versa (also Allen 2015, 60–64). At the same time, enjoyment is central to sexual plea-sure, as long as these joys are mutual – when, for example, all the partners involved enjoy bodily contact of the same sort or like similar things being done to their bodies. Enjoyment can also be complementary:

If you like to be supported and I like to hold you in my arms, we can enjoy such an embrace. If you like to be kissed and I like to kiss you, we may enjoy each other. If you like to be sucked or bitten and I like to suck and bite you, we may enjoy each other. If you like to have your skin rubbed and I like to do this to you, we can enjoy each other. If you enjoy sexual pleasure and I enjoy giving you sexual pleasure, we can enjoy each other. If you enjoy being hugged and I enjoy hugging you, it can be mutually enjoyable. If you enjoy being dominated and I enjoy controlling you, we may enjoy each other. (Tomkins 2008, 227)

Enjoyment taken in bodily proximity and interaction of all kinds is cen-tral to sexual experimentation and play. As Allen (2015, 65) points out, Tomkins' affect theory allows for considering sexuality "as a set of *affective curves* that are always characterized by the affects of excitement and/or enjoyment". The affective curve of enjoyment–joy may give way to interest-excitement as shifts in intensities and qualities of experience occur without being consciously registered. Furthermore, there are endless variations in the degrees of experience with any affect, which can be "enjoyed in innumerable ways" (Tomkins 2008, 78). An embrace may spark desires and inclinations of a sexual kind, or remain pleasurable as such. Play participants may experience different bodily intensities without this incompatibility being an obstacle to mutual pleasure. In other instances, incompatibilities in the "coarseness or gradation of intensity of interper-sonal affect" may render mutual enjoyment impossible (Tomkins 2008, 229). Rather than being an issue of the presence or absence of sexuality as such, play then involves negotiation over the compatibility of desires, needs, forms of sensation and interaction.

Adult Babies with Butt Plugs

Jan Soldat's 2016 documentary film *Coming of Age* provides a 14-minute vignette of adult baby play that is notably different from those addressed above. In one scene, the German 60-something male couple on whom the film focuses first recount the beginning of their relationship as a fisting date. Horst reclines on a sofa topless while Kalle, dressed in a plastic bib and diaper, sits in a playpen hugging a teddy bear with a markedly pensive expression, both of them facing a television screen showing gay porn. Answering Soldat's question of how the couple ended up doing diaper play, Kalle defines it as spontaneous improvisation contra Horst's suggestion that this was his longer-term fetish and a crucial interest in terms of his sexual identity:

> **Horst:** He had always been into diapers, right, Kalle?
> **Kalle:** Me? Well… As I've told you before, it's connected to my whole incontinence thing. I do it out of need to make something good of the situation. Just to look at it differently.

This exchange suggest that, rather than being driven to adult diaper baby play by an innate urge, long-term fascination or identification, Kalle – like the incontinent subjects of the television shows discussed elsewhere in this chapter – developed these routines as a means of coping with an uncomfortable physical condition by reframing it and turning it into something pleasurable within the circuits of play. The couple continue to discuss how their play has emerged and evolved and, in doing so, describe something of the broader dynamics of sexual play: of how people play along with scenarios coined, set and desired by others, rehearse and test out their rules until they seem to somehow fit. Play then comes across as exploration practised for the sake of pleasure, and as involving its own learning curves, tensions and releases:

> **Horst:** The first time is always forced anyway. You need to work it out to see what works, what doesn't work. The second time is always more relaxed and it gets better and better.
> **Kalle:** Just like any kind of a game. Some people like it, some don't. You can't force it. It either works or doesn't. It's that simple.

The scene unpacks diaper play as a realm of improvisation, repetition and learning. Unlike the television documentaries addressed above, it involves no attempt to uncover or position the roots of the preference in childhood events, traumas or family histories in ways that would fix or explain it in relation to the notion of identity. Rather, age-play is seen as unfolding as a response to later life events that has since grown into routines, habits and tastes. As such, play has gradually and by degrees come to define the couple's sexual life. There is no separation of play from sex, or from Horst and Kalle's habits of cohabitation more generally. Soldat shows Horst preparing Kalle's baby bottle, changing his diapers and eating his ass while masturbating without much change to their overall mode of interaction. Diaper play similarly smoothly leads to bondage with sleep constraints as Kalle decides to take a nap with his teddy bear. The playroom comes with baby gear, butt plugs and lube. Perhaps most notably, Kalle's age-play – unlike that of the subjects depicted in the television shows – involves no mimicry of an infant's voice or motions: his is a queer kind of senior baby with a penchant for hardcore porn.

As the couple continue to discuss their former relationships, marriages, children and families, Kalle, still in plastic baby wear, moves

Fig. 4.1
Kalle in his playroom. Photo by Jan Soldat.

from the playpen to a leather armchair, smoking a cigarette. Moving back to a more playful mood, he then starts to explicitly perform for Soldat's camera: "We could show a bit of this as well. Look, my diaper ass! Jan, look! ... It's a must!" Such performative inclusion of the filmmaker within the scene grows even more manifest in Soldat's other 2016 documentary film, *Happy Happy Baby*, featuring a group of men getting together for age-play. The three men on whom the film focuses all play toddlers, yet, despite their shared play scenarios of eating baby food, napping, watching children's films and playing with building blocks, their styles of age-play remain divergent. One of the men identifies as asexual and the two others as gay, yet without disclosing much of the sexual undertones involved in their respective play routines.

Sitting on his bed in a pile of soft toys, Mike describes discovering his penchant for age-play at the age of fourteen: "somehow I figured it out, through the internet. Of course it was a weird feeling for me in the beginning. You put a diaper on and this and that... Since then it became clear to me, not that I need the diapers, but that I had an inner feeling where my body says 'I am feeling good like this.'" Formerly married to a woman, Mike prefers men but also chooses to live without a partner. Tommi, whose younger male partner lives in a different city, explains his self-image as a three- or four-year-old while sitting on the floor of his playroom littered with toys, dressed in a bright green overall. For him, age-play is essentially about feeling "the affection, love and warmth of others ... for us, adult babies, or for me, it's the physical contact that I like. Cuddling for hours, playing with each other, hopping or running around ... There are adult men who like fixing their cars. That is a way of life and a fetish too."

Seated on his bed against a background of blue wallpaper decorated with little stars, surrounded by stuffed animals and with two teddy bears on his lap, Sveni similarly explains that "adult baby means to look for comfort, warmth and love. When I am AB, I am – and I think most of the others are too – asexual. This means that sex is of no importance to me." The lack of sexual interest would nevertheless not extend to all play participants. Speaking of his former daddy who would get aroused when changing his diapers and then proceed to have sex, Sveni notes: "As a baby I have a subordinate role. I personally don't have much to say, or anything to report." Despite the surroundings, his diapers and bib, Sveni – like the other two

Fig. 4.2
The play group in *Happy Happy Baby*. Photo by Jan Soldat.

men in the film – is out of his role as little during the interview, wearing glasses and speaking as an adult rather than a toddler, analytical even if somewhat guarded in his approach.

Similarly to the TV show adult babies addressed above, all three men emphasise the bodily sense of comfort and pleasure derived from age-play – from extended physical proximity to the sense of security afforded by diapers. These pleasures point to continuities in the enjoyment taken in physical sensation from infancy to adulthood. As Tomkins (2008, 232) notes, warmth, skin stimulation and body support experienced in early social communion commonly find their adult variations in activities such as "sun bathing, ocean and lake bathing and skin diving, and warm baths". In the case of these three German adult babies, such sensations are not sought or lived through adult derivatives so much as by returning to their manifestations in childcare. In this sense, the enjoyments of early care and adult bathing involve differences in degree – rather than those in kind – whereas age-play aims at doing away with even such distinction between the two by returning to the routines of the former. Such enjoyment can remain an end in itself, be part of sexual scenes amplified by excitement and driven by the dynamics of submission, domination, control and humiliation connected to the assigned roles and pre-agreed scripts of play. Again, the issue is one of gradations and degrees of experience.

All three men interviewed in *Happy Happy Baby* foreground the pleasures of ABDL role-play and Soldat's camera joins in to witness their play routines. Like several of Soldat's other films, this one witnesses people moving in and out of play roles, agreeing to the scenarios beforehand and reflecting on them afterwards. Andy, who plays daddy in their collective kindergarten space, instructs Sveni, Tommi and Mike on their forthcoming lunch scene: "You'll all get food, I will feed you and you can play around with it. I will bring each one of you over here ... One of you will say 'hungry'. Then another one 'me too!' and then like babies, everyone will say 'hungry'." As in Horst and Kalle's description of how their diaper play first came about, the scene highlights the centrality of feeling out the scenario and testing out one's role for the fit before engaging in play.

Mike appears to take particular joy in acting out baby on camera in ways that give rise to something of a performance. With Mike, the camera becomes a central component in or amplifier for the pleasures that he manifestly takes in toddler role-play: while documenting play habits, the camera also transforms their intensities by inviting contact with a virtual audience that its lens affords. This performative style of being differs from the displays of kink practice in Soldat's other films, which show what unfolds, for the most part, without the men – for these are all films focusing on the play routines of men –acknowledging his presence during the scenes. In the following Chapter 5, I move to thinking about the ethics and aesthetics of Soldat's documentary work on kink cultures in connection with the dynamics of BDSM play and the broader media presence of minoritarian sexual cultures.

5

Slaves, Prisoners and the Edge of Play

Jan Soldat's documentary film *The Incomplete* (2013) is a portrait of Klaus Johannes Wolf, a gay male slave. A small, stooped man in his sixties, Wolf is shown sitting on his bed, naked except for a leather collar, wrist and ankle cuffs, as well as a metal codpiece. He is placed firmly in the centre of the frame, with a chain attaching him by the neck to the bedframe. Describing his slave-play, Wolf argues for its exceptionality in contemporary culture that has eroded people's ability to play: "We, in our rational world that is getting more rational because everything gets more mechanical, like doing an endurance run that never ends, we are blocking the whole thing out. The whole ... game. The act of playing. We can't play any more. Our society cannot play any more."

Sketching out play as an alternative to the mechanical, repetitive and compulsive rhythms of contemporary society, Wolf, by implication, maps out his slave practice as organic, versatile and improvisational. The film displays slave-play as being at the core of his life as that which affords it intensity, focus and a sense of purpose while remaining bound to specific principles and limits. As a technique of the self, Wolf's slave-play is reminiscent of Caillois' (2001, 29) rule-bound and structured play category of ludus that "disciplines and enriches" spontaneous play, "provides an occasion for training and ... leads to the acquisition of a special skill, a particular mastery". In *The Incomplete*, BDSM scenes and the routines of everyday life are inextricably intermeshed. The role of a slave is depicted not as something that Wolf puts on and takes off, or moves in and out of, but rather as his overall mode of being in the world, relating to it and the people populating it. No effort therefore seems required for Wolf to enter a submissive headspace: fetish gear is his preferred form of

Fig. 5.1
Klaus Johannes Wolf in *The Incomplete*. Photo by Jan Soldat.

habit independent of whether his activities involve cooking, cleaning or browsing through family photo albums.

There is little playfulness to the scene described above, or to the film more generally. Rather, it pushes definitions of play as something occurring within magic circles bracketed off from other realms of life and operating with alternative sets of rules. In Wolf's case, such boundary maintenance simply does not apply. The scene equally pushes the notion of play as something light, fun and entertaining by default. Rather, slave-play emerges as that which brings purpose to Wolf's life and even makes it liveable in ways echoing Foucault's (1997, 163) discussion of sexuality as "our own creation, and much more than the discovery of a secret side of our desire", namely "a possibility for creative life". Wolf's domestic labour slave-play comes across as quotidian creativity where the sexual is quintessential to the fabric of everyday life, its texture, grain, modality and intensity. These dynamics can be understood through the notion of play – that which Wolf discusses as the opposite of the mechanical: "The whole ... game. The act of playing." Understood in this vein, role-play is seriously ludic, detached from the mandates of rationality and driven by the quest for bodily intensity – be this charge sexual or something else. The world at large presents itself as a potential play space, even if this world is, for Wolf, generally bereft of playfulness.

Starting with *The Incomplete* and moving into a discussion of Soldat's other documentary films on kink play – *Prison System 4614* (2015), *The Sixth Season* (2015), *Hotel Straussberg* (2014), *The Visit* (2015), *Law and Order* (2012), *A Weekend in Germany* (2013) and *Protocols* (2017) – this chapter explores their depiction of everyday lives rooted in sexual power play. Bringing together BDSM scholarship with film analysis, it inquires after the presence or absence of trauma in how the people in Soldat's films account for their play preferences, the ethical issues involved in presenting fringe fetish cultures on film, as well as the specifics of the film style deployed in all this. Spanning a wide range of BDSM preferences in the uses of physical restraints, forms of punishment, humiliation and control, Soldat's films depict play as elementary to how everyday lives are organised and lived – in fact as the dynamic that drives these lives. At the same time, they also evoke questions concerning the boundaries, or edges, of play.

Trauma and Play

The Incomplete witnesses the stories that Wolf tells about his life and follows him around in daily routines: arriving home, showering and changing to his preferred form of dress (as already described above), cooking and eating, cleaning at a friend's place and giving him oral sex, being urinated on and spanked at a slave training camp. There is no cathexis to Wolf's desire on a specific object, such as a permanent partner. Without a regular master, he moves in and out of locations, scenes and arrangements with other men, including the top friend he services and the masters operating the slave camp.

Occasionally pausing mid-sentence and speaking with a mild stammer, Wolf talks to the camera of his childhood and family, his work as a tax advisor and his former life in a religious confraternity. He shows personal photographs and shares autobiographical details, from when the brothers of the confraternity discovered his stash of condoms – and consequently his sexual identity – to his mother's dying moments, his grandfather's sadistic streak, and the social spectacle that was his father's funeral. Wolf recounts hurtful and meaningful life events and, in a round-about way, associates his slave-play with trauma: "A role-play, really this role-play where I can say, here I can bring my soul which has been quite a bit injured, and heal it again. It is, so to speak, a kind of psychotherapy. Without a psychiatrist." While the film does not dwell on precisely how Wolf's soul has been injured, how it becomes healed or what the specifics of his therapy routines might be, this discussion of role-play as personal psychotherapy resonates with accounts of BDSM play as somatic intervention, bodily reconnection and affective reworking of hurtful or traumatic experiences.

BDSM play derives some of its intensity from the incorporation of personal life experiences, attitudes and social power dynamics into sexual scenes in ways that also afford therapeutic possibilities of processing, self-discovery and resolution (Weiss 2006, 236–240; Weiss 2011, 16). Margot Weiss (2006, 240) points out that the pleasure of BDSM "lies in its depth, in the creation and subsequent transgression of boundaries around what one is and can be, what is safe and what is dangerous and what is set aside and what is reconnected". BDSM entails theatrical enactments of domination, submission, pain and pleasure that can provide arenas for examining and working through life experiences in a different shape, form and context. As a form of trauma play, BDSM has been examined as a means to increase, or restore, the liveability of bodies that have undergone harm (see Barker 2005; Barker et al. 2007; Weiss 2011; Hammers 2014).

In her discussion of BDSM as somatic intervention for sexual trauma among female rape survivors, Corie Hammers (2014, 69) sees it as affording a re-working of affect "into bodily and psychic (re)orientations to/with the world". Hammers notes that women engage in BDSM for the sake of physical pleasure, yet this can entail experiences extending beyond sexual satiation alone. Rape play, for example, allows for scripted and hence controlled re-enactments of trauma both past and present in order to reorient bodies that have been truncated or cut in their affective capacities (see also Weiss 2011, 147–150). As public witnessing, play scenes where "the trauma is spoken in both verbal and extra-verbal ways" make it possible to share the unbearable so that the body is no longer held hostage by previous experiences and "the somatic pain loosens its grip on the victim, unleashing in turn the becoming process" (Hammers 2014, 73). Rather than addressing affect as instantaneous, momentary and fleeting encounters and intensities, Hammers (2014, 70) conceptualises it as residues and traces that linger on in the body without fully leaving it, and that are therefore available for re-attunement and revitalisation. Operating through bodily disassociation where desire becomes cut off from one's body, trauma exposes "in stark terms a non-randomness of affect, contravening the notion that affect is a free radical beyond reach – beyond the social – beyond much of our conscious" (Hammers 2014, 84).

Trauma play, as addressed by Hammers, works through the capacities of what a specific body can or cannot do, and modulates how these capacities may wither or grow. In addition to associating his slave-play with healing from trauma, Wolf equally describes the heightened corporeal sense of focus, performance and intensity that play generates:

Wolf: I need no cardiovascular agents, no coffee, nothing. My blood flow is great. It's like when Usain Bolt, the sprinter, runs 100 meters in nine seconds. He's also in top shape. It's the adrenaline. Then everything feels right. My head is quite clear then. After that I can do my most complicated taxes. Because then your body's blood flow is at its best, it's well trained.

Soldat: So, like a jump-start?

Wolf: Yes! It's training. Really, it's like training. It's like training, just in a weird way.

Wolf's slave-play is not genital so much as connected to discovering the possibilities of pleasure through an eroticisation and affective intensification of the whole body (see Foucault 1997, 165) – by making use of the body, its "every nerve fiber, and every wayward thought" (Califia 1999, 176). Understood in this vein, power play results in an amplified sense of corporeal aliveness and capacity to act, whether this occurs in connection with trauma or not.

Associations between BDSM and trauma, when reiterated, also involve the risk of framing sexual play as a functional solution to a problem – and hence instrumental in its purposes – in ways that downplay the centrality of sheer bodily pleasure as its key motivation. Meg Barker and Darren Langdridge (2010, 69–70) note that the story "of SM as a 'healing' or 'therapeutic' practice which might take a person from a position of mental illness to psychological health ... from powerlessness to control over their own bodies ... or from fear and victimization to excitement and a movement away from past trauma" has been rearticulated and circulated widely enough to be instantly recognisable, even if this connection is not something assumed by default. The problem here, for Barker and Langdridge, lies in how this story both builds on and further amplifies the shame, pathologisation and marginalisation connected to SM and other minoritarian sexual likes. Furthermore, this narrative implies that as people overcome trauma through play, any desire or necessity for kink evaporates as one's non-normative sexual tastes become similarly cured (Barker and Langdridge 2010, 72).

While broadly re-circulated in all kinds of variations, accounts of trauma and healing are, however, only one sexual story connected to BDSM play among others, many of which emphasise its pleasures rather than instrumental functions or applications. Furthermore, stories of trauma are themselves multiple (Barker and Langdridge 2010, 73, 76). The appeal of trauma narratives is connected to their causal clarity as well as their emphasis on individual effort and self-discovery. This narrative certainly remains pervasive: the story of Christian Grey's healing from childhood trauma, his initiation into vanilla sex and physical intimacy in the *Fifty Shades of Grey* trilogy, as discussed in Chapter 3, remains one of the more visible recent examples of framing BDSM as trauma play and healing while also ramping up its cultural visibility, or ubiquity. As Ofer Parchev and Darren Langdridge point out, popular representations of BDSM "are often gross *mis*representations. People who engage in BDSM continue to be subject to considerable opprobrium, in large part as a result of the pathologizing discourses of the medical and legal professions ... Indeed, most of the traditional academic literature on BDSM has focused on aetiology, understanding these sexual practices as a form of pathology in need of treatment and cure" (Parchev and Langdridge 2017, 3, emphasis in the original).

In *The Incomplete*, Wolf recounts at length the legacy of the Third Reich in his family who were once heavily invested in its ideological machinery and describes slave-play as therapeutic and central to his wellbeing. The documentary portrait nevertheless remains void of therapeutic resolution as such: there is no talking cure at play. Soldat's refusal to frame *The Incomplete* in terms of trauma or to unravel the specifics of how Wolf has been damaged involves an ethical edge in its detachment from the dynamics of cause and effect, harm and remedy connected to BDSM play. While exploring Wolf's personal history, the film does little to contextualise or narrate, let alone "solve" the question of his specific desire, sexual bent or way of being in the world. Rather, the film operates with the register of recognition, that which Wolf addresses in terms of understanding: "What I'm looking for is understanding. The understanding to say: 'Uh-huh, he is like that.'" *The Incomplete* observes, witnesses, records and reorganises Wolf's autobiographical narrative, everyday routines and incidents into a cinematic whole that offers statements, impressions and perceptions. Edited down to 48 minutes from 14 hours of interviews, of criss-crossing stories and many things left undisclosed (Soldat 2014, 51), the film, in Ken Plummer's (1995, 21) terms, assembles a life story action around its

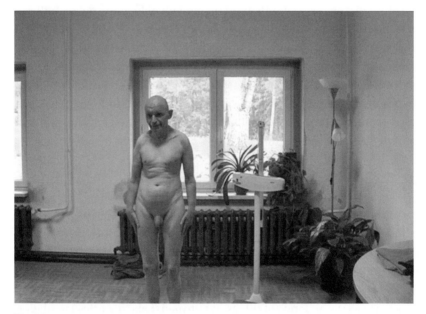

Fig. 5.2
Wolf at the slave training camp. Photo by Jan Soldat.

events and happenings without providing the viewer with the possibility to grasp Wolf's life or experience as such. As Soldat (2014, 57) himself notes, the film is characterised by emotional distance. For Soldat (2014, 59), it would be a compliment if the viewer fails to grasp the origins of Wolf's fetish after seeing *The Incomplete*.

Soldat's films are also void of psychological investigation more generally. The interview segments where men face the stationary camera seem to set the stage for a confession of sexual identities, tastes and acts, yet such a thing never quite unfolds in accounts of how the men's play preferences have come about, how they have evolved and what role they occupy in everyday arrangements. All in all, the films remain detached from the framework of therapy culture, which, through a pervasive language of emotionalism, depicts individuals as differently traumatised, damaged and scarred in ways that harbour a sense of powerlessness and possibly result in diminished capacities to act (Furedi 2003, 11, 135). Frank Furedi associates therapy culture with the accumulations of personal disclosure in the public sphere, as well as with the cultural penetration and extensive commodification of Freudian – and, more broadly, psychotherapeutic – discourses that, premised on individual fragility, define individuals through their emotional vulnerability (Furedi 2003; also Illouz 2007). In this framework, disclosures of sexual selves, preferences, memories, tensions or traumas come across as a therapeutic opening up that allows for causal explanations and possible resolutions. While Soldat's films do not disclose or avoid accounts of vulnerability and trauma, these are not foregrounded or dug into either. Rather, they emerge as threads and patterns among others within the horizontal film fabric.

"256,000 Shades of Gray"

Trauma literally means a distressing, painful and harmful experience, be it in the form of an emotional or psychological shock or a physical injury. As such, the notion of trauma can be – and has been – malleable in discussing a range of experiences, from virtually anything negative and hurtful to that which leaves permanent marks and reduces one's aliveness and capacity to act, as well as all kinds of things in between. Sexual stories circulating through the media operate with degrees of opaqueness that the notion of trauma entails while eagerly grabbing it in order to pin down and resolve unusual orientations – remembering, for example, the role given to Jess' childhood experiences in *Extreme Love*, as discussed in the previous chapter.

Trauma plays a central role in feminist and queer theorisations of sexual fantasy and desire, especially in the framework of psychoanalysis and in connection with violently marginalised communities (e.g. Cvetkovich 2003; Berlant 2012, 74–75). In psychoanalytical accounts, trauma haunts sexual lives from the discovery of the mother's lack of penis to male castration anxiety and the state of female castration to later stages of development and life events within and outside the family. This frame for understanding sexuality revolves around, and draws its force from, the tropes of lack and loss. The role of trauma in sexual stories is further supported by therapy culture and the pervasiveness of Freudian (and post-Freudian) discourses within that which Eva Illouz (2007) identifies as emotional capitalism.

In their introduction to the work of Silvan Tomkins in the 1995 *Shame and Its Sisters*, Eve Kosofsky Sedgwick and Adam Frank contextualise its importance against the dominance of social constructivist and discursive approaches which, under the banner of anti-essentialism, have worked to downplay the role of the embodied, the affective and the material. While this complaint is by now familiar within the so-called affective turn in cultural theory (e.g. Koivunen 2010; Liljeström and Paasonen 2010; Seigworth and Gregg 2010), it was less so at their time of writing. More specifically, critiquing the centrality of figures such as Jacques Lacan, Sedgwick and Frank (1995, 20) point out that, despite the subtlety that psychoanalytical work entails, it remains predictable in its patterns, as well as unable to accommodate differences in qualities of experience: "it's still like a scanner or copier that can reproduce any work of art in 256,000 shades of gray. However infinitesimally subtle its discrimination may be, there are crucial knowledges it simply cannot transmit unless it's equipped to deal with the coarsely reductive possibility that red is different from yellow is different again from blue."

The appeal of Tomkins' work is then largely due to the fuller colour spectrum that it opens up and operates with. For Sedgwick and Frank (1995, 2–7), this appeal is manifold, ranging from the specific grain of his textual voice to the novel avenues that his affect theory offers in its empirical focus and resistance to heterosexist teleologies such as those that can be found in much psychology and psychoanalytical writing. Tomkins' affect theory allows for other points of departure for thinking about experience in terms of the materiality of bodies and their complex capacities. Queer scholars have especially returned to his discussion of shame ever since Sedgwick and Frank foregrounded its centrality in the framework of queer theory. Tomkins' eight other registers of primary affect have been much less enthusiastically probed, despite the centrality of excitement and enjoyment that he associated with sexuality in particular.

Taking up Tomkins' argument of sexuality as rooted in excitement, Allen (2015, 4–5) argues for turning away from the register of shame–humiliation towards the more positive range of affect in feminist and queer theorisations of sexuality. Tomkins' conceptualisation of affective amplification provides possibilities for telling stories about sexuality rooted in the affective registers of surprise, interest, excitement, enjoyment and joy, rather than in the heavy circuits in lack and trauma. Furthermore, as Allen (2015, 42) points out, Tomkins' affect theory is unconcerned with the origins of diverse sexual preferences and, given its insistence on the autonomy of affect – on any affect having any object – it also veers away from normativity in ways that necessitate no categorisation or policing of sexual normality. This anti-normative streak finds reverberations in Soldat's documentary films and the additional hues and tones that they offer for thinking and telling stories about sexuality – in addition to all the available shades of grey.

Different theoretical frameworks afford different registers for thinking about sexuality. The same applies to film and media work exploring or otherwise addressing diverse sexualities. Tomkins' emphasis on enjoyment and excitement in and for sex resonates with the possibilities that conceptualisations of play afford in thinking about pleasure. In their markedly serious approach to sexual play, Soldat's films examine the enjoyment and excitement involved in scenes of humiliation, pain and torture in ways reminiscent of Tomkins' discussion of the autonomy of affect. These negative affective intensities hardly cancel out or reduce the positive ones but rather support them and amplify the overall intensity, arousal and appeal that play routines and scenes hold. Soldat's films propose that trauma can motivate sexual power play or play no apparent role within it. Applications of play in studies of sexuality similarly do not foreclose the presence of trauma, or downplay any of its visceral force: they just do not start from the premise of trauma always already being present, lodged in the centre of sexual lives or driving particular sexual desires and habits of play.

Ethics of Film Style

Soldat's films *Law and Order* and *A Weekend in Germany* both focus on the mundane preoccupations of a retired senior male couple, Manfred and Jürgen, as they sunbathe in the nude, do gardening, have lunch, chat, joke, tease one another, cruise for sexual partners online, encounter Jehovah's witnesses doing their rounds handing out *Watchtower* magazines, set up and film their BDSM sessions and discuss their lives. The camera documents the details of their interior décor with the same care, or detachment, as that involved in the depiction of the couple's sexual play sessions. In *A Weekend in Germany*, their friend Rosi, a man of the same generation, joins in for some play, yet the camera is as interested in their conversation on a relative winning a giant chocolate egg in a lottery as it is in their performance of synchronised caning.

This is in line with how moments of fleshy intensity unfold in Soldat's films more generally without any of the overall rhythm, tempo, camera angle or image size changing. In most instances, only fragments of sexual acts are shown. Some scenes of play, such as those set up by Manfred and Jürgen, are positioned in the middle of the frame while others, such as those in *Hotel Straussberg*, take place at its edges or are shown only in part. The general lack of close-ups or zooms further distinguishes Soldat's film style from that of pornography that largely aims at an optimised exposure and visibility of body parts, orifices and acts. In *The Incomplete*, a static camera witnesses Wolf's experiences at a slave training camp, yet the mode of cinematography remains non-intimate: images of his bruised buttocks are only made visible on a screen that Wolf is himself later watching.

Regularly sexually explicit in their subject matter, Soldat's films are markedly laconic in their execution and delivery. Their unhurried tempo builds on long and medium shots extended enough to allow for observation. There is no camera movement within the shots: no pans, tilts or zooms. With the sole exception of a scene in *The Visit*, the camera does not move or follow its subjects. Moving out of the frame, people then also move beyond the film's visual reach. Refusing to explain much of the sexual palates, orientations and preferences they address, the films – *The Incomplete* included – witness sexual lives by reorganising that which has taken place in front of camera and what people have decided to show and tell without explaining much of it. Soldat's camera does not aim at inconspicuousness as much as heightened awareness of its presence. People face the camera, look directly at it, talk to the director behind it and occasionally walk off.

Soldat's film style can be characterised in terms of its particular ethics and "aesthetics of the frame; that is, as an aesthetics that foregrounds documentary participation in the real" (Hongisto 2015, 4). There is no aim towards the transparency or immediacy of the medium. Films begin and end abruptly without an added layer of music or voice-over, editing is direct to the point of being blunt and cuts are marked with flashes of black. The camera's immobility makes its presence impossible to miss for either those within the frame or those watching the films and allows for no voyeurism or apparent intimacy towards the people appearing on screen. The awareness of seeing and being seen unavoidably also evokes the question of what the audience cannot see. This particular style of execution, combined with the apparent ease with which the people relate to the presence of Soldat and his camera in their domestic spaces of play, is one of the central reasons why I have been so drawn to his work when thinking about sexuality and play. While laconic and mundane, the films are also extraordinary.

Soldat's films explore niche fetish cultures that the director himself is not part of and display everyday lives grounded in intense sexual play. Doubling as director and cameraman, Soldat is present in, but does not participate in, the scenes. The films do not position the people appearing in them as objects of knowledge or set out to solve the puzzles offered by their kink preference. Their dynamic is one of mundane outness, of living out a sexual life where the sexual play and other routines of life are not marked apart from one another (cf. Barker 2005; Weiss 2006, 2011). As such, they bring onscreen practices routinely deemed obscene – literally ones to be put "out of sight" (Williams 2004, 4; Attwood 2009, xiv) – by detaching them from the frameworks of both secrecy and sensationalism. In different ways, the films – and, centrally, their subjects – do not so much challenge as disregard assumptions of sex being simply a private affair or non-normative sexual tastes being ones best kept hidden. In contrast, theirs is a world of mundane, unspectacular outness, "public in the sense of accessible" (Berlant and Warner 2000, 326). Since sexuality poses no secrets to out, being already in the open, there is no particular underlying mystery or dilemma offered for uncovering, analysis or resolution. Consequently, the persistent links between sex, privacy, intimacy and secrecy are redrawn, if not simply ignored.

The physical spaces or sexual routines displayed in Soldat's films are not openly accessible as such, yet they gain certain publicness through their cinematic depiction. Soldat meets and contacts the people online on the basis of their active engagement in kink cultures. In this sense, outness is the very premise of film practice, and one visually echoed in the cinematic uses of natural light. The films are predominantly shot during daytime with no additional lighting. In one scene after another, rooms are bathed in daylight and people are shot against windows. With the understandable exception of playrooms, such as the windowless cells of a private prison, the locations are primarily domestic, filled with personal belongings, keepsakes and utilitarian objects. The prison in question, providing its inmates with their forms of confinement, punishment and isolation of choice, is upstairs from the home of Arwed and Dennis, the couple running it, whose relationship plays a key role in *Prison System 4614*, *The Sixth Season* and *The Visit*.

In Soldat's films, sexual play is not cornered off, or easily confined in specific spaces, just as there is no variation in the narrative rhythm or tempo of scenes focusing on a scrotum being stroked with nettles or those documenting domestic squabbles over which frozen meals to microwave for dinner (*A Weekend in Germany*). Accounts of first meeting one's partner intersect with shots of eating their ass freshly out of diapers (*Coming of Age*), and a chat with the director on which rubber shorts to display is disrupted when a partner wants to get on with the ass spanking (*Law and Order*). This horizontality of narration, combined with the default outness of the sexual lives and the events unfolding in front of the camera, provides ample possibilities for thinking through the interconnections of sex and play in ways that necessitate no dichotomous separation between the concepts, or the fencing off of sexual play into specific magic circles allowing for exceptional bodily engagements.

Many of Soldat's films focus on ageing men and all of them can only be seen in cinemas during film festivals. Visual materials of elderly gay men's sexual practices have been circulated on the Web since its early days for the purposes of humour and shock, as in the well-known instance of "Lemon Party", a still image of senior men engaging in an oral sex threesome, the effect of which depends on "the (homo)sexualized, elderly, or overweight body" being perceived "in terms of disgust and amusement" (Jones 2010, 128; also Paasonen 2011, 223). Media culture is increasingly focused on the speedy circulation, spreadability and mashability of digital content as it becomes endlessly linked, copied, edited, remixed and grabbed for novel purposes. These circulations are fast and their routes impossible for the ones generating the content to control. The visibility of sexual cultures online allows for self-organisation as well as greater degrees of self-control in comparison with how these cultures are presented, framed and shown in other forms of media – including the television documentaries addressed in Chapter 4. At the same time, online visibility results in potential vulnerability, given the impossibility of controlling the context in which it unfolds, how, where, with or for whom.

Soldat's films are not available on either television or open online platforms. As such, the work remains inaccessible to those wanting to freely remix it, grab clips or craft animated GIFs from it. Soldat's work operates within a film culture of limited yet manifest public accessibility (cf. Ryberg 2012, 33–34). As old school as this solution of screening films in cinemas during festivals may seem for a director born in the 1980s, the lack of online and televisual exposure allows for both authorial control and degrees of privacy for those appearing in Soldat's films. The few trailers available online are laconic – hardly teasers – and they generally show little of their subjects that would be identifiable. The same goes for still images of the films in circulation with approval, such as those included as illustrations for this book. In sum, the context of film culture can be seen as providing an intimate and limited public for minoritarian sexual cultures and tastes of the kind that remains unavailable on open online platforms and their circuits of constant, uncontrollable redistribution and repurposing.

Willing Prisoners

Shot in the private prison that also features in three other Soldat films, *Hotel Straussberg* documents an army prison play event. The flow of events is quotidian, with scenes of guards preparing dinner and going through army drills, prisoners spending their time in cells, participating in organised outings, being placed in confinement, kissing and having oral sex with one another. In one notable scene, three prisoners, two of them cuffed to the wall and the third chained to the ceiling, improvise a football game by kicking a wooden doorstop from one to another until it lands between the legs of a man who – chained as he is to the wall – is unable to move enough to set the wood block back in motion. The shot cuts to

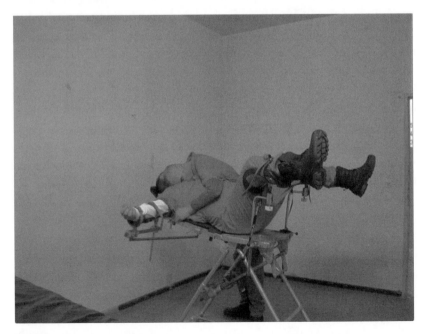

Fig. 5.3
Prisoners in *Hotel Straussberg*. Photo by Jan Soldat.

an image of the man's legs and his hapless motions as he tries to reach the doorstop, to little avail and to some shared amusement. The scene is one of play within a scene of play. While the prison event is pre-scripted and pre-agreed, and driven by the men's specifically articulated individual play preferences, the scene is one of spontaneous, impromptu fun. Similar lightheartedness reoccurs in Soldat's other films on kink play that pause to observe minor mundane incidents, details and occasional absurdities.

As in *Law and Order* and *The Weekend in Germany*, scenes of play are porous and feed into chitchat and the management of domestic chores. Even as the prison event participants in *Hotel Straussberg* are in role costume, they do not systematically stick to the assigned roles of guards and prisoners but fall into small talk over health, football, hairstyle, places of birth and residence. When prison play is led by Arwed in *Prison System 4614*, participants remain more firmly in their roles. As warden, Arwed communicates, corrects and punishes his prisoners in a raised voice without generally slipping into niceties.

The five-minute impromptu film *The Visit* shows Arwed giving a tour of the prison to his mother and grandmother, exhibiting the cells and props to his curious and somewhat baffled visitors without fully breaking his performance as warden. As Arwed explains the function of chains and constraints with a prisoner readily at hand, another inmate meanders in, laughs at the grandmother's comment and clowns for the camera. As Arwed continues with his demonstration, barking at a prisoner, his grandmother notes on his altered demeanour: "His voice is louder than it used to be. His voice has never been loud." The film is lighthearted, the prison players move in and out of roles, or balance somewhere in between them, break into smiles and casual conversations in the midst of the event.

The prison operates with multiple sets of rules, both those agreed with the individual prisoners desiring specific forms and styles of isolation, interrogation and torture and those cutting through play more broadly as the limits that wardens hold in their uses of punishment and in the overall structure of drama that the event entails. Since the framework is one of a military-style prison, scenes of hooded water torture and humiliation play, framed as ones of forced interrogation, readily evoke associations with the infamous 2004 incident of US military torture at Abu Ghraib. Addressing the "disturbing parallel" between Abu Ghraib and scripted

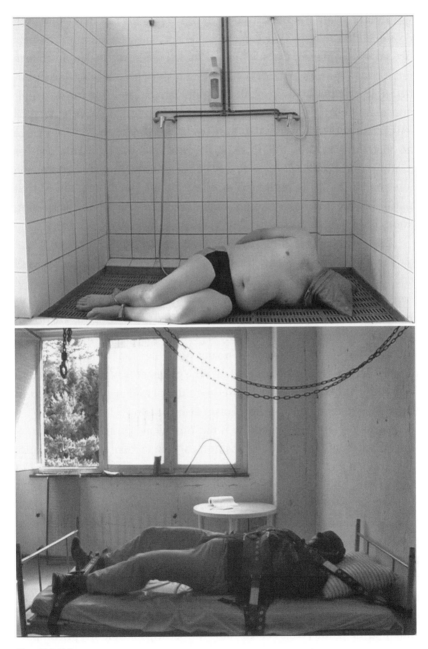

Figs. 5.4–5.5
Inmates in *Prison System 4614*. Photo by Jan Soldat.

BDSM interrogation scenes, Weiss (2009, 181) points out that while both rely on feedback loops between the social and the scene of performance, they do so in different ways: while an "effective SM sutures performance to the social in ways that feel deeply real for the practitioners", the photographic documentation of Abu Ghraib "effectively transforms a political real – torture – into a … sexual fantasy". Although the photographs depicted torture techniques that have been deployed by the US army since the Vietnam war – including sleep deprivation, water boarding, stress positions and humiliation – they were framed in the media as borrowing from the aesthetics of online porn in ways that tapped into, and further supported, the pathologisation of sadomasochism as a sexual perversion (Weiss 2009, 189).

This allowed for shifting attention away from the structures giving rise to torture in scenes of war to the potential pathologies and proclivities of individual military personnel and, in doing so, allowed depoliticisation of the photographs. I would further suggest that this detachment was bolstered by the overall framing of play that helped to reconfigure the prison space into a magic circle assumedly separate from other realms of life, as well as detached from the codes, norms and rules that otherwise govern military conduct (e.g. Caillois 2001, 6). The frame of play further helped to reconfigure the scene as a dramatised enactment and display distinct from the routine manoeuvres and roles of an army prison.

These globally circulated, by now somewhat iconic, images of torture and humiliation involving positions of spectacular power inequality may provide fuel for sexual fantasies and desires among those drawn to submission, domination, humiliation and pain play. However, as Weiss argues, the issue would not be one of copies and originals, of a BDSM scene copying or emulating a scene of torture, or vice versa. Scenes of power exchange in BDSM "derive their intensity and erotic charge from replaying real, sociohistorical structures of exploitation and power inequity" in ways that performatively alter them (Weiss 2009, 183). Actual contexts, histories and relationships provide the play scenes with a sense of realism and credibility that then frames the scene of desire for the individual participants (Weiss 2009, 186). The setting for Soldat's prison play films is a former military barrack. While making use of army equipment such as gas masks, it also features props such as helmets befitting knights and iron suspension cages too antique and elaborate to fit into any military technique manuals. Although rooted in a sense of realness, the prison is markedly fantastic, its rules unpredictable and unstable beyond the overall dynamic of submission and domination, as encapsulated in the roles and uniforms of inmates and wardens. As John Mercer (2004) has shown, prison fantasies have, along with army barracks and other all-male environments, long been key elements in mainstream US gay video porn. In such self-contained environments, "the social conventions of the outside world ... do not apply" and "hierarchical power relations can be played out" through the roles of passive, submissive prisoners and dominant wardens (Mercer 2004, 162). The private prison allows for exploring such scenes as BDSM practice.

Sitting on a sofa with a beer, describing his initiation to prison play after meeting Arwed in *Prison System 4614*, Dennis notes on its exceptionality: "I thought to myself: He built a prison? Why would anyone build a prison? ... Maybe because he wants to be locked in there, okay. How many of those exist in Germany? Not so many. But it's nice that he built his own prison. It's like having a hobby knitting for the World Hunger Aid. A hobby that you never had before. Prison is quite unusual. I hadn't heard about it as an S&M fantasy. Prison? Alright. Sounds nice." Chuckling at Dennis' side, Arwed spreads his hands far apart to explain the position of prison play within the overall BDSM scene. "Let's say, if the whole fetish scene is as big as this room, then prison play is this big. It's quite small." Here, Arwed indicates the space of an inch between his fingers. Like diaper and adult baby play, prison play lies at the fringes of the BDSM scene as a fetish that may be rare but is also shared and cherished.

Arwed and Dennis explain in tandem that they do not want the event to be about, or to involve, sex: "It doesn't work like that. Most of the guys, or at least 99.99% of them want to play prison. To them detention and lack of iron are the worst things they can imagine. Impossible not being able to wear hand and leg cuffs! And maybe also being kept horny for five days. Simply that. What happens a lot is, if they happen to come, then they usually go. Because they're not horny anymore." The intensities of the prison events oscillate within the affective registers of enjoyment–joy, surprise–startle and interest–excitement, despite the play being premised on, and acted out as, a series of discomforts disallowing sexual release and extensively constraining the inmates' uses of their own bodies. Within the event, routines of humiliation feed pleasure, yet care has to be put into modulating them and preserving their preferred intensity, rhythm and tempo.

The structure of Arwed and Dennis' events is designed to keep the prisoners sexually frustrated and deprived just enough to maintain the overall play dynamic but also to control the movement of players in and out of headspace. While many move out of confinement smoothly and joyfully once the cell doors are opened, one inmate – a serious head player who cannot shift between roles and ways of being with any ease – is described as having required twelve hours to "snap out of the situation". Another inmate describes his annual visit as allowing him to "completely shut down" and to let go of himself. Following this principle, *The Sixth Season* shows Dennis providing Arwed with a week-long forced break from running the place, as well as his farm, by becoming an inmate and being forced to let things go instead. Arwed is taken by surprise by a visiting master, imprisoned, put in a cell and explained the rules and daily routines that include punishments occurring in response to violating the rules, groundlessly, as well as for the warden's – that is, Dennis' – pleasure. As prisoner, Arwed is appropriately impassive, grumpy and resistant even though conforming to the overall rules of the game. He does not communicate with Soldat's camera when his routines are shot, and does not answer Dennis' queries of concern, yet moments and gestures of tenderness pattern the play, and no safe words are required.

From the perspective of BDSM practitioners, any default separation of sex and play would come across as meaningless, or even absurd. Involving improvisation within the bounds of pre-established agreements between partners, articulated guidelines, soft and hard boundaries and possible safe words, BDSM play stages the scene of excitement in notably theatrical terms (e.g. Lewis 2011, 5–6; also Hammers 2014). Weiss (2011, 17) identifies this as "paradigmatic theatricality" manifest in how sexual encounters are called scenes, how engagements with partners are called play and how central a position roles, props and costumes of different kinds occupy in the practice. As such, BDSM is undoubtedly an exceptionally fitting context for any examination of sex as play geared towards pleasure. As Weiss stresses throughout her *Techniques of Pleasure*, the role of the broader

Fig. 5.6
Arwed imprisoned in *The Sixth Season.* Photo by Jan Soldat.

scene of BDSM lifestyle and culture nevertheless remains crucial to understanding the context in which play unfolds. A shift from being kinky to being a BDSM practitioner therefore necessitates "participation in a social, sexual, and educational community that teaches techniques of the self alongside rope bondage and flogging skills" (Weiss 2011, 12). Wolf's slave training camp and Arwed and Dennis' prison events are manifestations of such community.

The Edges of Play

The code of the "safe, sane and consensual" formulated within BDSM culture has become a normative code crucial to its social organisation as "the primary way practitioners distinguish between good, safe, acceptable SM and bad, unsafe, unacceptable practice" (Weiss 2011, 80). In other words, these rules are a means of drawing boundaries between what qualifies as BDSM, or what is recognised as such, and that which falls outside its boundaries. In this sense, the rules are normative and rely on hierarchies of value. In their discussion of the code, Parchev and Langdridge (2017, 12) identify a gap between this infrastructure and explorations of fantasy that break against, or exceed, its principles. This involves somewhat complex dynamics where the code marks play practice apart from things deemed unsafe, insane, non-consensual or abusive, and therefore unacceptable. The code nevertheless emphasises consent over safety so that certain knowing risks are accepted, in a similar way to in extreme sports:

> BDSM practices that involve high levels of risk (as is seen in so-called "edge play"), with this on occasion even constituting their ultimate purpose, violate the social codes that resist the link between sexuality and death, however. Prioritizing consensuality over the universal prohibition of risk in sexual practice leads to the violation of these essential codes, enabling the community to forge a new mode of subjectivity that gives room to fantasies and urges that would otherwise be delegitimized within the dominant hegemonic discourse of reproductive (genitally driven) sexuality. (Parchev and Langdridge 2017, 12)

Among BDSM practitioners, and within society at large, the desire to seek death or to be eaten as a form of sexual enjoyment remains irrational and abject. As such, it points to the disciplining of individuals choosing to put their bodies at risk, as well as to the mandates of life and health within the BDSM subculture (Parchev and Langridge 2017, 13). Although the edge of edge play may not be a fixed limit so much as something that changes according to the practitioner's "ability, knowledge, experience, and confidence level" (Weiss 2011, 87), there would be little doubt as to permanent bodily harm, or death, being a very fixed edge and boundary indeed. The edge of play involved in cannibalism fantasies also marks the edges of what is recognised as BDSM practice or power play.

Harviainen (2011, 67) sees BDSM as live-action role-play that allows for immersion through continual characters and play spaces offering impressions, or illusions, of novel realities. The pleasures it provides can linger on in the register of enjoyment–joy or interest–excitement, bodies can be sexually attuned to one another or focused on their solitary sensations that emerge as people "consensually take on dominant and submissive roles, for the purpose of inflicting things such as pain and humiliation, in order to create pleasure for all participants" (Harviainen 2011, 59). Death and permanent bodily harm fall firmly in the category of irreversible scenes that remove the space separating the player from the role and a play scene from a life. As the very endpoint and polar opposite of aliveness, death hollows out the space of play as exploration of bodily potentialities by cancelling out any new lines of improvisation and carnal thrills of sensation.

Soldat's 2017 film, *Protocols*, explores fantasies of being inspected, humiliated, tortured, butchered and eaten. The style of delivery is familiar from his other work, from the unmoving camera to the people talking to it while seated against windows. *Protocols* nevertheless stands out amidst Soldat's other films on kink play in featuring three actors shot in backlight so that their facial features remain hidden, delivering the narratives of the men that he has had conversations with: in fact the film's stripped-down aesthetic consists of three scenes with talking heads whose facial gestures and expressions cannot be seen. The double layer of anonymity alone – the interview stories being detached from any specific people and the actors being rendered difficult to recognise – speaks of the far-out character of cannibalism fantasies within fetish cultures and of the ethical challenge of cinematically depicting them. The sense of distance and darkness is amplified by the lack of light: the skies seen from windows are of heavy, wet, wintry grey and there are no additional sources of lighting. If *The Incomplete* is characterised by emotional distance, *Protocols* involves an emotional detachment, or amputation, that puts its subjects out of reach.

The first of the men describes his play-dates: "the Dom, the butcher, trains me as if I were a pig, then tortures me and fake-slaughters me". At Soldat's suggestion, he provides further detail on the role-play scenario: "I've done slaughter-play where I was lying on my back on a table or hanging upside down from the ceiling ... For me it's a very exciting feeling, as the cold steel slides on my belly, and the tip of the knife pokes inside it. That's the slaughtering moment that usually leads to ejaculation. Or ... once I was locked in a cage and was fattened up. Or I get tied like a rolled roast with thick rope, so that the fat pops out." Despite the bodily harm that these play-dates result in, the arousal they evoke inspires further variation. Although aroused by the possibility of transgressing his current limits in scenes where his flesh would be carved out and eaten so that he would physically become a roast, the man nevertheless draws the line at permanent bodily damage. For the other two men interviewed in the film, the very fantasy, and aim, is to be killed and eaten: there is no realm left for role-play.

Cannibalism, along with incest, represents one of the most funda-mental social taboos. Like any taboo, it comes with the possibility of being breached: in fact the option of transgression shapes the taboo's contours and boundaries, provides these with a magnetic charge and helps to uphold them (Bataille 1986, 63–64). There are highly concrete limits – legal, emotional and social alike – to living out fantasies of being fattened, cut up and slaughtered unless one is able to commit to ending a life. Such scenes can be explored, and to a degree enacted, through role-play even if the tra-jectory of the fantasy itself, should it run its full course, would exhaust the possibilities of exploration and any shape of bodily affectation for at least one of the participants involved.

For the prison event participants in Soldat's films, the pleasures of play involve submission and lack of control in the role of inmate. For the adult babies and diaper players addressed in the previous chapter, these pleasures are connected to sensations of physical comfort and sexual excitement. For Manfred and Jürgen, BDSM play connects to bodily inten-sities and forms of social leisure. And, for his part, Wolf describes slave role-play as affording the exploration and expansion of what a body can do while also transforming him into an object: "A slave is also a thing. He has no personality: he is a thing, a product. Not only is he emasculated, but you can also see the entire person, completely naked." In the fantasies of being eaten, such transformation to a thing or product is taken to its extreme. If carried out, the fantasy would turn the naked body into dead, consum-able meat and, eventually, into nothing at all. The third man interviewed in *Protocols* frames his particular fantasy as a matter of his particular, long-standing body image:

Every person has a perception of their own body. For every body part or for the body as a whole. I feel, I am made of many parts that do not make a whole. This is a thought I've had since I was a child. That I am made of this piece, that piece and another … And that they are sewn together with a needle and a thread. Oh! I also remember when I was eight, I was at a butcher shop and saw a piece of pork on a plate. Next to it another piece and another. I always wondered, why can't I be that pig?

Similarly to a meat chart displayed at a butcher's shop that shows the body of a pig divided into distinct sections – from the loin to ham, spareribs, jowl and side, all resulting in specific cuts of steaks, roast, chops, ribs, bacon, ham slices, sirloin and tenderloin – the man describes his bodily perception as one of a patchwork of meat. This does not mean that his body would not be able to operate, sense or perceive, but neither does it mean that the man in question would be interested in, or aim at, fusing it all more firmly together. The fantasy of becoming pig, or meat, means resolving the issue by cutting the thread that holds the diverse pieces of meat in connection with one another. Becoming-pig is, by definition, a radical unbecoming of the self as annulment of all bodily capacities, be these affective, sensory or cognitive.

Play for the Sake of Pleasure

Soldat's documentary films are quickly recognisable in their camera styles, forms of display, editing, tempo and sense of horizontality where mundane material objects are depicted with the same degree of attention as the mostly stationary people appearing in them. The films discussed above map a variety of fetish play revolving in their registers of submission and domination as well as in their hues of pleasure that can, as in the case of *Protocols*, be dark and grim to the point of questioning the very applicability of the notion of play.

There is little investment in these films on the question of "why" people's sexual preferences and practices are what they are. Instead, the films knowingly focus on the question of "how" people are, how they play and how they experience their particular routines. The question of "how" may involve describing the context of a specific fantasy or fetish by, for example, relating early experiences of enjoying a particular feel of texture, confinement or accessory. There is nevertheless no investment in closure or resolution in what footage gets edited in, no matter what that specific kink preference addressed might be. All this necessitates taking the pleasures and carnal intensities that the men in front of the camera describe seriously and at face value, as well as respecting the accounts that they are willing to make. When a man dreaming of being eaten describes how his sensations of fear would not make him back out from the final plan states, "I don't want to change my fantasies", that is all that remains to be said on the topic.

Soldat's films are strikingly different from media narratives conveying BDSM as pathological behaviour that is risky, bizarre, baffling, amusing in its manifestations and possibly something much better cured and straightened out. It is certainly not surprising for independent documentary films to differ from commercial media products such as television shockumentaries in their framing, aesthetics, politics, editorial style or subject choice. Such differences are nevertheless central for understanding how documentary footage on minoritarian sexual cultures is assembled and offered for public consumption. Soldat's films are unconcerned with sexual hierarchies governed by the notions of normality categorising preferences and kinks according to their healthiness, appropriateness, perversion, deviancy or risk. This is the case even with films where preferences go well beyond that which most would understand as play – as in the case of sexual cannibalism, also known as "vorarephilia". The laconic film style echoes the general aim of showing but not accentuating that which may titillate, shock, fascinate or amuse viewers. This results in a striking lack of zooms and close-ups in scenes of sex, as well as in a style of editing that refuses to highlight the role and centrality of such scenes within the cinematic whole. As argued above, this stylistic resolution comes with ethical gravity that, combined with the films' limited public circulation and visibility, offers a very distinct solution to the dilemma of audiovisually depicting minoritarian fetishes in a media culture saturated with images probing all spectrums of sexual likes with something of a bottomless greed.

Much like commercial online pornography that has, throughout the 2000s, amply harvested the aesthetics of alternative, independent and kink pornographies in the search for novelties to grab the attention of potential consumers, popular media culture feasts on sexual routines and attachments that are novel, atypical or otherwise striking. Documentaries circulating in Finnish TV programming alone at the time of writing this book have ranged from men loving sex dolls and fantasising about their advanced robotic functions to men dressing up as female latex dolls and women being in romantic relations with inanimate objects, such as fences, bows, landmark walls and towers. While diverse in their execution, the programmes are structured by a similar sense of titillation and salacious uncovering of sexual likes to the ones examining adult babies discussed in the previous chapter. The lifestyle slaves, prisoners, subjects of military torture and willing objects of culinary consumption contributing to

Soldat's films would be similarly guaranteed to grab audience attention, should they enter this televisual flow.

The increasing media attention and visibility of fringe sexual cultures goes hand in hand with their commercialisation – as in the case of *Fifty Shades*-inspired BDSM kits or the broader popular markets of kink play, or the much more modest range of commodities connected to ABDL. Several cultural critics have identified BDSM as "a paradigmatic consumer sexuality because of its tremendous market appeal, its ever-expanding paraphernalia, its non-reproductive nature, and its affinity with the leisure demands of late capitalism" (Weiss 2011, 104). Combined with the emergence of online forums and information resources connected to all kinds of sexual preferences, identifications and likes, this ongoing commercialisation of kink has had tangible effects on how the sexual cultures themselves operate, how they can be participated in and at what cost. A scene in *Prison System 4614* comments on these transformations as Soldat asks an inmate where he used to shop for his kink gear decades ago when first setting out to play, given the lack of specialised shops or online commerce. "Back then there was nothing at all," the man cuffed to the metal bars of his cell sternly notes, and he explains purchasing his first set of handcuffs from a gun shop. Prison events particularly catering to his kink would have, at that point in time, seemed like an improbable fancy.

More generally, BDSM complicates and challenges understandings of sexuality as based on notions of stability: "The pleasure of this play lies in its depth, in the creation and subsequent transgression of boundaries around what one is and can be, what is safe and what is dangerous and what is set aside, and what is reconnected" (Weisss 2006, 240). As scholars of BDSM have repeatedly pointed out, it involves and operates through the mutability of bodily capacities. Drawing on Andrea Beckmann's (2001) study of London-based BDSM cultures, Smith (2009, 23) further argues that "for practitioners, masochism is a form of human expression drawing on sexual dissidence, pleasure, escapism, transcendence and the refusal of normal genital sexuality, allowing for safer sex explorations of the lived body and its transformative potentials". While the following, final Chapter 6 explores the relations between sexual identity taxonomies and the notion of play in more detail, the point here is that the resistance to stories of origin or essence in Soldat's films echoes conceptualisations within BDSM culture where the notion of play is a means of identifying forms of doing over those of being.

In their matter-of-fact foregrounding of sexual play over the formation of identities or their location in taxonomies of normality, Soldat's films allow for alternative ways of witnessing and recognising sexual preferences and likes, as well as for telling different kinds of stories – often fragmented and open – about sexual lives. These are not accounts of sexual identities so much as ones of pleasures and practices. Weiss points out that many practitioners "see BDSM as that which they do (not something that they are), a sexuality organized around practices. As an obvious example, people who do BDSM are generally called 'practitioners' or 'players,' not something like 'BDSMuals'" (Weiss 2011, 11). This separation between doing and being, between proclivity and essence, echoes Foucault's examination of the late-nineteenth-century category of the homosexual. The newly invented label of homosexual fixed individuals as representatives of a broader type characterised by its inner qualities, in contrast to the earlier notion of "the sodomite", defined through the acts that men performed and the practices that they engaged in. While the sodomite described a "temporary aberration" from the sexual norm, "the homosexual was now a species" (Foucault 1990, 43). In other words, a shift from "doing" to "being", connected to the assumed inner essence of a person rooted in sexuality, was central to the articulation of identities deviating from normality. For its part, the rationale of the term "men who have sex with men", used since the 1990s, builds precisely on the separation of sexual identity from the sexual activities that people may engage in.

For Foucault (1997, 152, 165–166), the specific mixture of rules and openness in SM affords novel possibilities for pleasure and the intensification of sexual encounters. Contra the relations and operations of social power where mobility between different roles and positions is constrained, the relations within SM are fluid and strategic: "even when the roles are stabilized you know very well that it is always a game. Either the rules are transgressed, or there is an agreement, either explicit or tacit, that makes them aware of certain boundaries. ... It is an acting-out of power structures by a strategic game that is able to give sexual pleasure or bodily pleasure" (Foucault 1997, 169). Califia (1999, 173) makes a similar point, noting that while BDSM scenes are cut through by social relations of power and oppression to the same degree as any other part of culture, the roles of bottoms and tops adopted in play are assigned according to sexual likes and needs, as well as according to how the participants "feel about their particular partners, or which outfits are clean and ready to wear". Understood in this vein, fantasy contributes to the specific affective charge of individual (and social) lives and fuels acts of sexual play.

To state the obvious, sexual play is not a realm of freedom external to culture, society, economy or politics. As Weiss (2011, 6) points out, rather than existing "in a bracketed space of play", SM performances are deeply embedded in capitalist cultural formations, social histories of privilege and oppression, as well as in the complex, interlacing categories of identity. The pleasures involved in testing out, or stepping in and out of, different positions in role-play can be intense precisely because the scripts and norms they entail are so viscerally lived and felt (see Brown 2015, 5–6; Harviainen 2011; Weiss 2011, 17–19; also Harrison and Holm 2013). However, if such play is interpreted as literally indicative of normative power, there is a risk of seeing power play as either an extension or a subversion of social hierarchies in ways that do away with the complexities of sexual desire, investment and attachment – and, therefore, ultimately with the force of sexuality itself (see also Smith 2009; Weiss 2011, 230). An alternative avenue of interpretation involves seeing sexual play as integrated in, drawing on and cutting through the fabric of everyday life and its temporalities, and as providing it with a specific affective intensity and flavour.

6

Ripples Across Identities

While knowing decisions are involved in setting up scenes of sexual play – that which one is setting out to do, with whom and how – the fantasies and desires connected to them are hardly mere rational affairs. There is rawness, immediacy and fickleness to sexual desire, to what one yearns for and what quickly puts one off. Similar contingency applies to how these registers of likes, dislikes and potentialities are gradually transformed through and across bodily encounters and experimentations, and to how the affective registers of enjoyment and excitement oscillate in physical intimacies of different kinds.

For Tomkins (2008, 191), the affect of excitement is that which defines the self: "I am, above all, what excites me." The appeal and excitement of things nevertheless depends on their novelty and complexity, for intensities fade in the course of repetition and familiarity as attention and interest continue to gravitate towards different objects, choreographies and possibilities. Surprises always remain possible in the realm of sexuality as sensations that can fuel interest and excitement, or become enmeshed with shame and disgust in ways that curb, rather than amplify, sexual desire. Desire, again, resists its congealment in clear-cut categories of sexual identity for the very reason that its objects, trajectories and shapes are not constant, predictable or knowable as such. For as Califia (1999, 272) notes, "desire is notorious for leaping fences. If we will let it, it will connect us despite obstacles of class, race, age ... or gender." At the same time, identity categories remain crucial to how sexual desires circulate and how people make sense of them, themselves, the surrounding world and their multiple entanglements with one another. The oscillating affective registers of interest and joy, disgust and shame rooted in both personal histories and social norms are entangled in sexual lives and acts of play in a complex fashion. These acts, or scenes, are propelled by the restlessness of desire, supported by fantasy and playful mood, and geared towards bodily discovery, novelty and variations of pleasure.

In the paradoxes and variations that it involves, sexuality may remain "unruly, ecstatic, routine, mysterious, transgressive, confusing, unpredictable, and changeable over the lifespan" (Iasenza 2010, 291). Extending beyond moments of satiation, sexual desire moves towards and becomes attached to different scenes and objects, and as its forms are reorganised, so is one's sense of self (Berlant 2012, 65; also Grosz 1995a, 293). Sexual tastes, preferences and orientations evolve and vary. People of all kinds of orientations and identifications "may experience variations in their erotic and affectionate feelings as they encounter different situations, relationships, and life stages" (Diamond 2009, 3). What one desires at twenty is – most likely, or with any luck – a different configuration from that which the same person prefers, or craves, at the age of fifty, be this in terms of sexual acts, the partners' bodily aesthetics, relationship arrangements, emotional proximities or distances. In their discussion of affect and sexual experimentation, Jonathan Bollen and David McInnes identify this as the "erotics of unpredictability":

It is an erotics of not knowing in advance what is going to happen and of finding this out through the interactive experience of doing sex together. When bodies enter into sex with an open and exploratory attitude to what will transpire, they enter an intercorporeal assemblage where bodily capacities to affect others and be affected interact and intermingle. Where the possibilities of sex are not foreclosed in advance and where pride in the performance of sexual competence is no longer guaranteed, the affective dimension of power and the transformative potential of interaction will be enhanced. (Bollen and McInnes 2006, 112)

In broad agreement with Bollen and McInnes' discussion of the transformative capacities of sexual experimentality, my key argument in this book is that sex, understood through the framework of play as pleasure-seeking activity that is an end in itself, opens up the bodily horizons of possibility and, by doing so, pushes the boundaries of previously defined or recognised sexual tastes and preferences. In this concluding chapter, I explore in more detail what this argument implies in terms of sexual identities and what it may contribute to feminist and queer theorisations of sexuality more generally.

Bodies Re-attuned

All kinds of play – from experimentations with toys and paraphernalia to scripted role-playing or meandering, tactile exploration of bodily textures – entail an openness of becoming where the sense of one's sexual self may be pushed towards novel opportunities. As discussed in the context of age-play in Chapter 4, the pleasures of play can revolve around comfort and safety or move in the sharp registers of sexual excitements and thrills: in all instances, bodies move from one state to another. This movement, in the circuits of play, remains pleasurable in itself.

In furry fandom, people adopt the personae (or fursonae) of anthropomorphised non-human animals. Although the majority of furries prefer wearing only tails or ears as markers of their fursona, cartoon-like cat, dog, fox, rabbit, unicorn or wolf fursuits encase the players more fully in their embrace and set novel styles for their movement and perception by, for example, reframing their line of sight or by limiting their capacity of hearing (Satinsky and Green 2016, 108–110). The pleasures of fursuits vary from sensations of comfort to sexual frissons afforded by the transforma-tion into a hybrid human–animal–costume assemblage. Furry fandom is regularly depicted in the media as a kink activity, whereas furries them-selves do not necessarily identify sex as a key motivation for their role-play (Gerbasi et al. 2008; Satinsky and Green 2016, 109–110). Fursonas, and their respective costumes, enable different ways of being and relating to others while the diversity of sexual preferences, fetishes and identifications within the fandom – identified in one study as ranging from gay, straight and bisexual to pansexual, heteroflexible, homoflexible, asexual, unsure, grey-a, demisexual, 90% straight, floater, lesbian, trysexual, bicurious or zoosexual – affords an openness of opportunities in terms of what and how one might want to be (see Satinsky and Green 2016, 113–116). Within furry fandom, the categories of humans, animals and hybrid creatures of various kinds, as well as those connected to the trajectories of sexual desire, can all be played, and played with, if they seem to fit or titillate. Playfulness then cuts through this scene as experimentation and openness

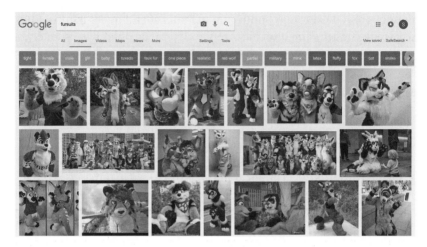

Fig. 6.1
Google Image search for "fursuits".

that fuel interactions from conventions to online exchanges and personal explorations.

Also when considered beyond specific niches or subcultures, sexual play opens up one's sense of bodily horizons of possibility and, in doing so, pushes the boundaries of previously defined identifications. This is also a point made by Smith (2009, 23) who, in her discussion on erotica reading, detaches the transformative potentials of the lived body from any specific or fixed notion of sexual identity. The intensifications of the body afforded by masochist sexual fiction, for example, "need not be the exclusive property of one sexual identity and may well offer pleasures to those readers who would identify themselves as without masochistic tendencies" (Smith 2009, 23; also Pääkkölä 2016, 33). Smith rather sees such potential as matters of embodied capacity and affective intensity that may resonate across categories of identity. Such an emphasis on bodily potentialities, changing sexual palates and fickle desires sets in motion, and rubs against, the logic of categorisation central to the politics of identity (also Probyn 2000, 75). This is crucial in that the framing of sexuality as a matter of identity may, perhaps paradoxically, result in myopia towards "phenomena like fantasy, desire, repression, pleasure, fear, and the unconscious, however one ultimately wishes to explain them, that in many senses make up sexuality" (Kulick 2000, 271).

This is also decisive since the taxonomy of sexual identities, and the fixing of desires and orientations into distinct types that it connects to, may not correspond with how people make sense of themselves and their intimate connections – one needs to only consider the range of identity markers deployed by furries for the purpose, as referenced just above. Historically, the categories of sexual orientation have been defined through perceived deviations from the norm. While the nineteenth-century homosexual was defined through its queer orientations, "the heterosexual would be presumed to be neutral" (Ahmed 2006, 69; Foucault 1990). The power of the norm lies largely in it needing no specific definition: it is the taken-for-granted mode of being, the boundaries and edges of which become marked out through violations, deviations and transgressions. Within the framework of identity politics, identity categories allow for personal trajectories of desire and attachment to be "wedded to the public construction of a group identity and to a political strategy for social change" (Epstein 1994, 192). Writing on the politics of identity connected to men having public sex with men in the early 1980s, Califia argued that

Before "being gay" became a political identity as much as a sexual one, anyone arrested in a tearoom was considered just as queer as a drag queen or a hustler. Oddly enough, it is the burgeoning gay movement with its demand confrontation and the concomitant demand that everybody choose a side which has left these men without a gay *or* straight identity, vulnerable to the contempt of both cops and activists.

The gay community has less and less tolerance for folk whose sexuality cannot be clearly defined as heterosexual or homosexual or who have eroticized something other than gender. (Califia 1999, 25, emphasis in the original)

The dilemma or challenge that bisexuality, with its non-binary orientations of desire, has been seen to pose for feminist and lesbian politics speaks of similar attachment to clearly defined, binary categories of sexual identity drawn along the dividing axis of queer and straight (see Däumer 1992; Rust 1995; Diamond 2009, 61–62). The attachments that identity politics afford may be compelling on a number of levels, yet they can equally come across as limiting and exclusive in their resistance to transformations in scenes of desire (see Diamond 2009, 6). Furthermore, as Stephen Epstein (1994, 192) points out, "the organization of an oppositional politics around the given categories of identity" is a limited strategy for challenging the regimes of normalisation themselves.

The flexibility between ways of perceiving one's sexual self and the acts that one may enjoy engaging in, or witnessing, has been explored within sex research for some decades. More recently, it has become addressed as "flexisexuality" and "heteroflexibility" and as "mostly straight" practices and desires (Savin-Williams and Vrangalova 2012; McCormack 2018). In her extensive analysis of sexual fluidity among women, Lisa M. Diamond (2009) identifies it firmly with female sexuality, arguing that common understandings of sexual identity based on fixity are derived from studies focusing on men, and that these models therefore come with an abrupt male bias. While there are many valuable insights to Diamond's study, it operates within a conceptual gender binary that may speak less of what people identifying as men and women *do* or what trajectories their sexual desire and pleasures take than of how these people are willing to disclose and describe their desires, acts and engagements. Furthermore, there is by now ample evidence of flexible and contingent sexual practices among men challenging the notion of fixity and stability drawn along the axis of binary gender (e.g. Carrillo and Hoffman 2018; Robards 2018; Scoats et al. 2018; Silva 2018).

In her exploration of male sexual flexibility, Jane Ward (2015, 27) notes that white American men identifying as straight describe their sexual encounters with one another as "experimentation", "accident", "joke" and "game". In this context, the vocabulary of playfulness is – similarly to within discussions of childhood sexual exploration – deployed to frame sex among men as non-serious, light, random and accidental rather than an issue of orientation, attachment or identity. According to Ward (2015, 7), "white straight-identifying men manufacture opportunities for sexual contact with other men in a remarkably wide range of setting" while also wrapping such exchanges in the dynamics of fascination, repulsion and humour. There is little new to such flexibility of sexual practice, remembering how Califia's (1999, 26) interviewee summed up the education received from tearoom sex: "I've learnt that there's no such thing as heterosexual. They can all be had." There may nevertheless be newness to how people – and representatives of the younger generation in particular – approach and disclose such flexibility outside a framing of sexual shame and secrecy (Ward 2015, 10–12; McCormack 2018).

In her survey of Finnish adolescents' relations with pornography, Sanna Spišák (forthcoming) gave the study participants the task of defining their own sexual identifications without any fixed pointers. The open-ended answers, ninety-eight in total, resulted in nine different categorisations: heterosexual, homosexual, lesbian, bisexual, pansexual, demisexual, asexual, polysexual and non-defined. The respondents did not seem to express much affective attachment to these self-identified sexual markers: for some, it was too early to tell, while others were uncertain, yet to define themselves or wanted to keep their options open. Such "complex, diverse and multifaceted" (Spišák forthcoming) sexual identifications point to the possibility that non-binary categories may not hold much appeal to at least some members of a younger generation (also Marsh 2016).

In a 2015 survey conducted by US trend forecasting agency J. Walter Thompson Innovation Group, only 48 per cent of young peopled aged 14 to 20 (e.g. "Generation Z") identified as exclusively heterosexual, compared with 65 per cent of those aged 21 to 34 (e.g. "Millennials"). Summing up the survey results for *Vice*, Zing Tsjeng (2016) defines teenagers' "queer AF": "On a scale of zero to six, where zero signified 'completely straight' and six meant 'completely homosexual,' more than a third of the young demographic chose a number between one and five, indicating that they were bisexual to some degree. Only 24 percent of their older counterparts identified this way." These two surveys were conducted in two clearly different contexts and with relatively small samples. They are far from being representative of a generation, or generalisable in their findings within these specific countries, let alone beyond their borders. Their means of mapping out sexual variation were distinct: whereas Spišák left the questions of sexual orientation open to any definition, the trend survey built on the Kinsey scale by mapping out sexual variation from the fully straight to the "queer as fuck" along a binary continuum.

An understanding of the sexual self as a work in progress that may be fickle or even unpredictable in its desires in fact implies something of a profound shift in discourses of sexual identity. Rather than figuring sexual identity as a firm sense of who one is that one comes to understand and know, the two surveys point to identity categories as working definitions descriptive of the present moment, and possibly something of the recent past, yet without pinning or closing down the possibilities that tomorrow may bring. Such a malleable view of one's sexual self would be at odds with any default framing based on mutually exclusive categories, given the space that it leaves for figuring things out in another way. It would equally be at odds with the notion of sexual identity as a point of individual and collective identification paving the way for political action. Rather than an issue of categories, sexual orientation becomes understandable as gradations and spectrums (also Savin-Williams 2014). It is neverthe-less crucial to point out that the flexibility addressed in the two surveys seems to primarily revolve around heterosexuality as that which one may do exclusively, or not, move in and out from, or perform with diverse trimmings. Slipping out of the straight would not seem to be a huge deal for many. While it would hardly be apt to claim that heteronormativity has suddenly lost its firm grip as an organising principle of intimacies and social arrangements, it is fair to argue that the coercive power of het-erosexuality – and that of normative heterosexuality in particular (Rossi 2011) – is limited in how the young people responding to these surveys figure out their own ways of being and interacting with others. This may be seen as one more example of the privileges afforded by heteronormativity for subjects to negotiate its boundaries who nevertheless reap the benefits afforded by their location within the sexual hierarchy as "mostly straight". Those situated at its outer edges may find more purpose in sticking to and articulating their specific identifications for the purposes of political transformation.

Attwood (2011, 86–87) identifies the flexibility and playfulness of sexual identities with how sex is increasingly framed as a leisure activity and an arena of consumption rife with "hedonistic lads and ladettes, bi-curious girls and just-gay-enough boys, characterised by 'heteroflexibility' ... and 'metrosexuality', a term coined by Mark Simpson ... to describe the emergence of a figure for whom sexual identity is forged, not through sex acts or sexual orientation, but through mediation, consumerism and the development of lifestyle." These novel markets of sex figure it in terms of taste cultures, which, like lifestyle preferences more generally, develop and vary across people's lifespans (Attwood 2007; Probyn 2000,

27–32). Sexuality, then, is seen as an individual project: a form of pleasure and creativity but also one of duty, responsibility, skill, performance and play (Attwood and Smith 2013, 326). Figured in this vein as the constant accumulation of experiences, commodities and pleasures, sexuality, in a similar way to other tastes or consumer preferences, entails the perpetual promise of novelty and change. This means that one's horizons of possibility remain to a degree open: there is always the possibility to shop around for something else.

Fields of Variation

As discussed in Chapter 2, so-called classic conceptualisations of play have largely zoned off sex from their field of inquiry as activities that are not wholly autotelic in the sense of having a purpose in and not apart from itself. At the same time, both Huizinga (1949, 43) and Caillois (2001, 27, 34), in their respective discussions of play and playfulness connected to improvisation and joy, address what they identify as illicit, casual, abnormal and strange sexual practices falling outside the social norm. Following their line of reasoning, it might then seem that the vast and wondrous landscape of unruly, kinky, queer and subcultural sex is the prime location for theorising the visceral appeal of sexual play. I believe that a more productive path nevertheless involves reconsidering the very notion of the norm as the affective hub and centre of focus around which theorisations of sexuality revolve. This, again, necessitates tackling the illusory homogeneity, coherence and authority of the heterosexual norm (Beasley et al. 2015, 683) – or that which Califia (1999, 215) once addressed as "the mythology of sexual normalcy". Here, queer inquiry involves a refusal to work with, or to start from, oppositional binaries, such as those drawing boundaries between "us and them, in and out, gay and straight" (Hillis 2009, 21).

If the non-normative, unruly, deviant or queer is taken up as the figure of transgression, play and exploration within sexuality, then the straight is to forever remain its opposite as that which is contained, immutable, non-playful and non-curious. Weiss (2011, 159) addresses this line of reasoning as reaffirming "a static hierarchy of sex practices based on oppositionality" and as constructing a series of comparative oppositions, solidifying them and effacing their internal differentiations within queer analysis.

Unruliness in the realm of the sexual, as encapsulated in the term queer, both necessitates and postulates rigidity and fixity as its points of comparison. As Beasley, Holmes and Brook (2015, 681) note, this regularly involves an articulation of heterosexuality "as a static monolith, an unvarying, commanding mass, and queer theories, identities and practices as the only potential source for a less oppressive sexuality". Such binary figures push against queer theory's project of destabilising the notion of the normal, the enactments of which remain at the heart of the mechanisms of social power and engender binary hierarchical divides between heterosexuality and homosexuality, straightness and its others (e.g. Warner 2000; Eng et al. 2005; Love 2011).

If sexuality is conceptualised as spectrums of variation that unfold in experimental play geared towards bodily intensification and pleasure, as has been the central aim of this book, then the issue cannot be one of stability, fixity or normality inasmuch as contingency and volatility. Rather than fuelling or supporting an understanding of heterosexuality as uninteresting, "nasty, boring and normative" (Beasley et al. 2015, 682) in contrast to the vicariousness of the queer occupying the outer circles of the sexual hierarchy, examining all kinds of sexual routines in terms of their variations opens up much less compartmentalised and dualistic lines of inquiry.

In *Queer Phenomenology*, Sara Ahmed (2006, 66–67) argues that straightness derives its character from being "in line", when "the line taken by the body corresponds with other lines that are already given" contra to those bodies that, in failing to line up, come across as queer. Normativity, then, is a matter of exhausting regularity and repetition as straight bodies move with no deviation towards the bodies of an opposite gender (Ahmed 2006, 70, 78). Understood in this vein, what factually happens in sexual couplings between bodies seen as being "in line" is secondary to how the dividing lines of straight and queer orientation allow subjects different degrees of mobility, visibility and acceptability. People understood as straight may engage in kinky role-play, casual and public sex of the kind that fall outside the bounds of Rubin's "virtuous circle" without violating the boundaries of heteronormativity as such. In other words, non-normative heterosexual practices do not in any causal way challenge heteronormativity as a broader, hierarchical organising principle of orientations and ways of being (see also Rossi 2011, 10, 19).

Beasley, Holmes and Brook (2015, 685) pose the issue somewhat differently in their circular figure of heterosexuality that ranges from the normative to the heretical. In the heart of this model – as in the elusive core of Rubin's good sex – heterosexuality remains close enough to the norm to be conflated with heteronormativity, yet the further the ways of doing heterosexuality travel from this core as divergence, transgression, subversion, dissidence and heresy, the more disjointed their relations to the norm become. As deviation, these involve kinky and non-stereotypical gendered and sexual alignments where it is not necessarily the female partner who is penetrated, and as subversion they connect with practices of non-cohabitation in sexual partnership (Beasley et al. 2015, 688–690). I would nevertheless argue that, in the framework of straightness, the constant, inevitable violations of the norm of good sex can be ignored and the boundaries of acceptable normality bent comfortably enough to accommodate them so that transgression or subversion do not necessarily become registered as such. The same may well apply to non-straight orientations that approximate enough elements of good sex to not challenge the majority of the sexual hierarchy. This ultimately means that while a binary straight–queer divide explains positions of privilege and the lack thereof, it will fall short in explaining much of how sexual lives unfold as differences in tastes, orientations and desires.

Mapping out queer in relation to a solidified norm of the straight renders visible social relations of power and hierarchies that weigh and matter. At the same time, any theoretical approach foregrounding transgression, subversion and lack of fixity becomes defined in relation to that which remains immobile and normative: after all, a desire to go beyond fixity may itself serve to fix (Ahmed 2000, 84). According to a by now familiar line of critique targeted at queer theory, it is reactive and negative in mapping out norms – such as heteronormativity and normative categories of identity – in order to challenge, circumvent and subvert them (e.g. Grosz 1995b, 224). Since evoking the norm is also a means of performatively reiterating it, queer critique remains captured within the normative logic. In the course of such reiteration, norms may become articulated as more coherent and solid than they otherwise appear.

Addressing antinormativity in queer theory, Vicky Kirby (2015, 97) questions "why the center, the norm, the rule, is routinely accepted

as a fixed reference point *against which* deviation, change, and singu-
larity – the exception – must be measured". Kirby points out that a society
is not identified through its internal coherence, nor is an individual identifiable in terms of her internal unity or consistency. A norm would be
"similarly erratic: if it is accurate to describe a norm as a constant, then
what persists is something inherently mutable" (Kirby 2015, 99). Following
this line of reasoning, contingency is all that ultimately remains, whether
one is discussing sexual norms, categories of identity, shapes of fantasy or
experiences of lust – no matter how firm the hold of social norms and categories may feel.

Juxtapositions of the queer and the straight performatively produce,
or even postulate, differences in kind between sexual desires, practices
and appetites that become thus categorised for the simple reason that
binary forms "divide a field of objects, bodies, or ideas into two domains"
(Levine 2017, 84). This means reducing the notion of difference to opposition (to a norm) within a struggle of two terms forming a conceptual
pair (Grosz 2005, 5). For as Grosz (2005, 6) further explains, "Dualisms,
relations of binary opposition, in fact do not involve two terms at all, but
two tendencies or impulses, only one of which is the ground of the other,
the force which, in elaborating or differentiating itself, generates a term (or
many) that maps, solidifies and orders this ground according to its terms."
Here, Henri Bergson's distinction between differences in kind and those
in degree emerges once again. As Grosz (2005, 4) points out, Bergson, like
Deleuze after him, examined the interrelation of difference and specificity where "as each touches upon one it elides the other". Understood in
this vein, difference cannot be binary and the notion of difference cannot
be used for equalising or neutralising differences between things. Rather,
difference is that which generates ever more variation and differentiation
(Grosz 2005, 7).

When operating with differences in kind in the realm of sexuality,
the task becomes one of charting sexual taxonomies, be these binary
ones such as the queer and the straight; broad ones such as those separating the heterosexual from the homosexual, bisexual and asexual; or
much more nuanced ones, such as the categories of abrosexuality based
on fluidity, ceterosexuality involving attraction to non-binary people,
placiosexuality centred on performing rather than being the recipient of

sexual acts or quoisexuality, averse to any extant labels. As a strategy of classification, sexual taxonomy necessitates distinctions between its individual categories.

The sexual taxonomies that Kinsey so enthusiastically coined within his scale of sexual orientation helped to illustrate the range of sexual preferences and behaviours while also mapping out heterosexuality and homosexuality as a continuum rather than as discrete categories of identity (Epstein 1994, 191). In this sense, they brought the notions of diversity and variation to the core of sexual lives. These taxonomies nevertheless – and possibly paradoxically – gained a performative force of their own as forms of classification and knowledge feeding into the politics of identity. The logic of sexual taxonomy entails a certain drama in how the traffic across different positions and markers of identity becomes accounted for, from the social tensions involved in "coming out" to the trajectories of "turning" lesbian or gay, possibly going or turning back to straightness, or remaining within the no-man's land of bisexuality (Diamond 2009, 63–64, 137).

If one approaches the spectrum of sexual fantasy, desire and orientation in terms of differences in degree – as fields of variation and differentiation – the issue is one of intensities and gradations that necessitate no pigeonholes to separate them, to turn towards or away from. Contra the taxonomical principles of sexual normativity, desire, as fields of variation, is resistant to such forms of capture. Conceptualisations of play and playfulness are a means of working through differences in degree on levels both individual and collective, as already discussed above in the context of childhood, teenage and adult sexual play.

The Problem with Identity and Pornography

The notion of identity is an epistemological as well as methodological issue that orients analytical attention towards certain premises and trajectories in studies of sexuality and media. As such, it has methodological reverberations. According to a routine line of thinking, watching a porn video is indicative of that video somehow communicating to, or speaking of, that person's sexual preference, bent and identity: watching gay porn, for example, might not precisely make one gay but speak of inner, ontological gayness now manifesting itself. A preference for any other porn category, let alone a distinct niche, would, according to this logic, similarly communicate issues concerning sexual identity which, following Foucault, entails a more profound truth concerning one's inner self, or being. Meanwhile, according to available empirical studies, women identifying as straight and queer alike broadly consume gay porn, as do men self-identifying as "totally straight" (Neville 2015; Robards 2018). Consumers of different ages report watching pornography out of interest, sexual arousal, curiosity and fun. People describe watching things they like or would want to do, those that they do not want or cannot do, as well as coming across things without much planning or premeditation involved, possibly in search of serendipitous thrills (e.g. McKee et al. 2008; Smith et al. 2015; Paasonen et al. 2015). The motivations of amateur pornographers – at least those of people uploading their content without any financial reward – become similarly associated with personal sexual desires, fascinations and orientations in ways that frame the outcome as expressions of the sexual self. This premise, like the one concerning porn consumers, simplifies the issue by conflating the motivations of pleasure and playful exploration of sexual imagery with the notion of sexual identity as one tied to specific pornographic niches. In doing so, it locks down the potential ways of conceptualising both porn consumption and production.

Consider, for example, a singular image of amateur pornography that I first encountered in Sergio Messina's presentation on "realcore" Usenet alt.fetish porn during the first Netporn Conference in 2005. The image is shot in a bathroom with white tiling partly visible in the background, and displays the crotch area of a man standing with his legs apart, his left leg slightly elevated. In his left hand, the man holds a white leather Nike basketball sneaker with a blue Swoosh logo while taking the picture with his right hand. The man's reddish, tumescent penis has been neatly inserted under the white shoelaces – or, perhaps better, laced into the shoe in a scene of self-bondage. The sneaker in question is rather diminutive in size: something fitting a boy but also of the size to snugly fit the penis. Nothing much takes place in the photograph other than the simple display of the sneaker and penis placed squarely in the centre of the frame. Both laconic and peculiarly spectacular, this image remained with me from the first viewing, and later inspired a book chapter addressing its haptic qualities and the methodology of close looking (Paasonen 2010).

Interpreted in the conceptual framework of sexual identity, the image, coined by an anonymous amateur in and for newsgroup exchange, would most likely be seen as indicative of the man's personal sexual fantasies, desires and attachments as a sneaker fetishist particularly bent towards play with the basketball shoes of teenagers. Understood in this vein, the image would then make it possible to pin down its author within a sexual taxonomy as a fetishist with possible homosexual orientations and a preference for young people. However, if one sets out to explore the image from the perspective of play, the interpretative frame is transformed in substantial ways.

When discussing the image with Messina some years later, he noted that it was part of an exchange where Usenet newsgroup members inspired one another to envision and execute shots involving sneakers. In other words, the context and scene was one of mediated online play where scenarios and props were picked up, explored, developed, shared and discussed among participants with the aid of photos and text. Similarly to the online pervy role-play practices in Silja Nielsen's survey among Finnish teen girls, discussed in Chapter 4, the exchange evolved as improvisation within certain mutually agreed parameters motivated by interest, curiosity and pleasure afforded by the activity itself. This particular sneaker image then emerged from communal fantasies of "what if" – from explorations of what "sneaker fuck" scenarios might look like or include. Interpreting the outcome through the prism of identity therefore fails to grasp the essential of where, how and why the image originated in the first place. While singular, the example is useful in illustrating the centrality of playful openness and experimentation in sexual engagements of all kinds, as well as the default limitations that emerge if such engagements are primarily examined within or reduced to the framework of sexual identity as expressive of specific forms of desire.

Contingencies of Flesh

Experiences of bodies and selves are variable, sometimes to the point of disturbing. There may be little to being a body, or being in a body, that can, in the framework of contemporary media culture, be considered as straightforwardly effortless. Mundane routines involve the navigation of ever so slightly changing yet characteristically tenacious cultural templates concerning body shapes, sizes and tones, styles of movement and forms of display (Coleman 2009; Kyrölä 2014). How we perceive our bodies and the transformations they undergo with age, what we make of the bodies of others or of these bodies coming together, is all undercut by complex economies of worth and desirability connected to the categories of gender, ethnicity, age, sexuality, ability, size, class, race, profession and religion alike. Such categories function as moulds through which to perceive and be perceived, classified and assumed to be figured out, even while their complex intersectional entanglements translate as much more convoluted forms of experience and agency. There is heavy weight to categories of identity, whether these be something resisted, successfully mastered or ambivalently navigated.

Comfortably occupying one's own skin is a skill possibly strenuous to accomplish, given the degree to which it involves the negotiation and calibration of norms and expectations that both orient and fix ways of being in the world. This accomplishment is rendered even more difficult by the thick materiality of bodies that does not remain the same from one moment to another. Bodies grow and diminish, bloat, leak and bleed, reproduce, lose limbs and parts, grow muscle and fat, sprout and shed hair, scar and limp. It is obvious that bodies age, with the timer constantly ticking, and thereby move from one chronological category to another – from infancy to childhood, adolescence, youth, variations of adulthood and middle age, seniority and old age. Yet other ways and styles of occupying and negotiating identity categories remain equally, albeit not identically, on the move. Ways of improvising, occupying or resisting identity categories through which we are defined are never steady or constant. All kinds of traffic occur in vocational, educational and professional trajectories, political and religious underpinnings. In addition, sexuality remains forever a fickle thing, despite the taxonomies that are in place for classifying preferences, orientations and desires, for living them out, for promoting their cultural visibility or, in contrast, for truncating them.

Put in new materialist terms, the issue is one of duration as difference, "the inevitable force of differentiation and elaboration, which is also another name for becoming. Becoming is the operation of self-differentiation, the elaboration of a difference within a thing, a quality or a system that emerges or actualizes only in duration" (Grosz 2005, 4). Following Grosz, duration both undoes and makes as it fractures the past while holding the future open. Becoming is by necessity also an issue of unbecoming, for in encounters with the world, novel connections are constantly forged while others are shut down.

As people live out their lives, experiment with their bodies and those of others, sensory experiences layer and sexual palates evolve, possibly in surprising ways. Sedgwick (2003, 238) discusses something of this kind when writing on self-recognition as "identification with what is, at any given moment, understood to be the growing edge of a self", detached from "desire to fix, to render self-evident or self-identical or unchanging, the boundaries of personhood". In and across these encounters, appetites alter and bodily boundaries of comfort become redrawn (Grosz 1994, 165; Probyn 2000, 70, 147; Paasonen 2011, 202; Berlant 2012, 6). Such mutability of bodily horizons of possibility can be seen as central to the appeal and force of sexuality as that which supports and amplifies feelings of aliveness. Or, as Grosz (2005, 10) puts it, "Durational force, the force of temporality is the movement of complication, dispersion or difference that makes any becoming possible and the world a site of endless and unchartable becomings." Things, in sum, do not remain the same, or even all too stable, as experiences layer and fade.

There is nevertheless a tenacity to bodies and their archives of sensation that is crucial to one's very sense of self. The feel of a serendipitous touch – careless, hesitant, caressing, firm or anxious – may shoot violent shivers through the body that continue to resonate as embodied memories for years to come, even as the immediacy of sensation remains impossible to recapture, being permanently out of reach (Grosz 1994, 286). Sensations that one may desperately wish to forget – from the traumatic to the embarrassing or the unpleasant – linger on in somatic archives, generating unpredictable patterns of interference as flashbacks and reverberations while others are cherished as the stuff of sexual fantasy (Paasonen 2011, 202–205). Despite their occasional or persistent discomforts, such layered memories of bodies, places, motions, sensations and intensities give bodies a sense of depth as they accumulate "in habit, in reflex, in desire, in tendency" (Massumi 2015, 4). Sexual play both reverberates with these steadily accumulating and unstable somatic archives and contributes to them by expanding their previously registered shapes, depths and boundaries.

Bodies carry "tendencies reviving the past and already striving towards a future" (Massumi 2015, 54). Both memories and fantasies of bodily encounters, motions and sensations layer into somatic archives that feed acts of sexual play. Play then feeds back into both memories and fantasies. Sexual play – be it elaborate fetish role-play, a BDSM session, self-exploration with sex toys, a teasing game of tickles played with an intimate partner, or a flirtatious exchange of nude pictures with a virtual stranger – is imaginative and improvisatory activity connected to fantasy. Yet it is not literally about "acting out" sexual fantasies since what unfolds is in part improvisational variation on a theme. Sexual fantasies can themselves be understood as forms of thought play geared towards intensity of experience that can borrow from and reference a broad range of sources – from expert advice columns to fictions both highbrow and lowbrow, from memories to friends' accounts of their erotic adventures, from the curiosity felt towards the touch and feel of textures and bodies to interest felt towards taboos and things framed out from the "the virtuous circle" of good sex. Deeply social yet embedded in personal histories, fantasies are open to influences and stubborn in how they linger.

As such, fantasies can be both prospective and retrospective in their temporal orientation and move back and forth between that which has been, what could have been, what can be and what currently is. Looking both forward and back, inwards and out, fantasies provide affective fuel for sexual desire as that which orients people in their acts of play and in their relationships to others. Fantasies can equally emerge from the momentary dynamics of interaction without either tapping into embodied histories or orienting the shapes that future investigations take.

Pressing Circuits of Desire

Play in the realm of sexuality can be seen as both ludic and serious. As Huizinga (1949, 5) notes at the very outset of his book, "play can be very serious indeed". Play can proceed "with the utmost seriousness, with an absorption, a devotion that passes into rapture and, temporarily at least, completely abolishes that troublesome 'only' feeling": consequently, the "contrast between play and seriousness is always fluid" (Huizinga 1949, 8). It can be further asked whether such contrast is even to be presumed, given how central the intensities of absorption and purpose of play are to the pleasures it generates – and whether such a contrast is warranted in the first place.

Sexual desire can be highly inconvenient, "overwhelm thought, shatter intention, violate principles, and perturb identity" (Berlant 2012, 26; also Berlant and Edelman 2014, 117), or "[e]xcessive, redundant, and superfluous in its languid and fervent overachieving" (Grosz 1994, viii). Desire can generate pleasure despite the circumstances or the availability of preferred partners: its "fundamental ruthlessness is a source of creativity that produces new optimism, new narratives of possibility, even erotic experimentality" (Berlant 2012, 43). It then follows that sexual desire does not necessarily "restrict itself to the most suitable person, in the most suitable place" and can forsake us "when we do find that person, whatever the presence or absence of technical virtuosity on offer" (Segal 1994, 104). Its nervous urgency can push people beyond their zones of safety and comfort towards the risk of relationships severed, professional reputations compromised and personal health damaged. Such risks, with their edges of potential harm and loss, may also hold considerable affective appeal as figures of fantasy around which desires grow, stick, layer and flicker (also Attwood and Smith 2013, 333).

Animated by sexual desire, people can feel compelled towards their acts of play: the men that Jamie Hakim (2016) interviewed for his study of chemsex describe the intensity of desire as being such that only ripping off the other man's skin would have felt like getting close enough. Describing their desire for a lover, Califia (1999, 213) resorts to only a notch more moderate phrasing: "The pleasure, the excitement, the necessity of colliding and combining with her make the mundane world seem pale and tawdry." In some instances, people can be literally forced to act out scenes in ways that erode any mood of playfulness from their motions. Meanwhile, the weight of sexual and gender norms, memories and traumas may shape one's ways of being in the world to the degree of undermining the liveability of individual lives.

Simon and Gagnon (1986, 100), writing against Freudian theories of libido as an organic, unruly drive, argue that "Desire, in a critical sense, is not really desire for something or somebody ... but rather what we expect to experience from something or somebody." Berlant (2006, 21) further argues that investments in objects "and projections onto them are less about them than about a cluster of desires and affects we manage to keep magnetized to them". Therefore, "we are really talking about a cluster of promises we want someone or something to make to us and make possible for us" (Berlant 2006, 21). Understood in this vein, relationships with one's objects of desire – be these human, non-human or combinations thereof – are animated by a sense of potentiality in terms of the capacities to act that they afford, the possible registers of sensation that they evoke, and the modalities and directions that they may open up. The cluster of promises connected to sexual desire may involve momentary satiation or more long-term intimacies, the feeling of being accepted or the sense of exceeding one's boundaries. All this entails degrees of optimism concerning the possible shapes of things to come.

One point here would nevertheless be that the shape of the potential is not, in the realm of sexuality, necessarily all that clear in its outlines, or coherent in how it becomes envisioned. It is not possible to know precisely what one expects, wishes, enjoys or even craves before an encounter or experimentation has taken place. Rather, bodies and their appetites perpetually become through and in their affective relations to one another (Massumi 2002, xvi; Coleman 2009, 42–43). The sense of the potential, in its openness of possibilities and diverse clusters of more or less ephemeral promises, may well be the locus where desire becomes magnetised.

Understood as both bound to rules and resistant to them, as both routine-like and extraordinary, sex involves a degree of uncertainty, an openness of becoming. As exploration based on agreements between the partners involved, sexual play helps to set in motion the felt boundaries of imagination and bodily capacity. In experimentations of what and how bodies feel and do, play allows for them to become re-attuned in relation to one other and the events that bring them together, and to move beyond the limits within which their orientations, desires and palates may previously have been confined (cf. Massumi 2015, 59; Berlant and Edelman 2014, 117; Bauer 2018).

A range of non-genital sexual play has been conceptualised as an eroticisation and affective intensification of the whole body (e.g. Foucault

1997, 165), yet the bodily capacities of giving and receiving intensity can be applied to conceptualisations of sexual pleasure much more broadly. For Grosz (1995a, 289), the intensification of bodily zones often occurs through the unexpected, "through a kind of wild and experimental free play that re-marks, reinscribes orifices, glands, sinews, muscles differently". In the course of sexual play, heightened affective intensity may emerge unpredictably or result from bodily training and techniques acquired through a sustained repetition of movements (Weiss 2011, 6, 10–11; Spatz 2015). Writing on enchantment Bennett (2001, 4) suggests that enthralling, disturbing and pleasurable experiences of aliveness emerge from surprising encounters, when something hits us, but they can also be fostered through deliberate strategies, such as giving "greater expression to the sense of play". The moods of enchantment that Bennett describes would not be sexual but mundane encounters and sensations of fullness, liveliness and plenitude, yet I find them to be readily applicable to studies of sex and its compelling qualities. Sexual pleasures occur, and can be discovered, in moments of affective resonance that move bodies in possibly unexpected ways, and transform them in the process.

Sexual play can come about spontaneously, or in response to life events, scripts and examples, and grow into routines, habits and tastes that gradually define the sexual self. Play can be a means of exploring and reworking the boundaries of sexual norms and that which bodies can or want to do. Play can equally generate new forms and patterns of sensation through improvisation. As Berlant – one of the few queer feminist scholars who has explicitly, albeit briefly, deployed the notion of play in discussing sexuality – points out, play "can provide a space of interest within which other rhythms and therefore forms of encounter with and within sexuality can be forged" (in Berlant and Edelman 2014, 6). Understood in this vein, play and playfulness are connected to the very contingency of intimate proximities and distances, pleasures and discomforts, libidinal pushes and pulls, as well as to "incongruities and paradoxes in sexual behaviors, attractions, thoughts, feelings, fantasies, and sensations" (Iasenza 2010, 292). This is also where the potential value of theorisations of play in the realm of sexuality lies.

The oscillating affective registers of interest and joy, disgust and shame rooted in personal histories and social norms are entangled in sexual lives and acts of play in complex ways. These acts, or scenes, are propelled by the fickleness of desire, supported by fantasy and playful mood, and geared towards bodily discovery, novelty and variations of pleasure. The disruptive intensities of sexual pleasure cannot be fully translated into or articulated through language. It remains nevertheless crucial to conceptualise these pleasures, to somehow grope at their edges in order to retain at least a little of their juiciness, are studies of sexuality to account for what makes the topic at hand so deeply compelling on levels both personal and social. Spaces of openness and opportunity that unfold in relation to and through an array of norms, scripts and rules are pivotal to the titillating, even engulfing force that sex and sexuality hold in individual fantasies, cultural representations and social arrangements. Theorisations of this force need to remain open to its unsettling qualities and volatile trajectories that resist capture in social categories of identity (no matter how intersectional these may be). It is my proposal that conceptualisations of playfulness and play can help in achieving some of this within studies of sexuality and sex.

Impelled by the "unpredictable and restless movement" (Grosz 1995a, 288) of desire, sexual play takes erratic routes but also follows carefully scripted choreographies resembling the ritual. Conceptualised as improvisatory openness towards variation and possibility, playfulness is a contingent dynamic of sexual orientations and identifications. Combined, the notions of play and playfulness make it possible to think through the mutability of sexual lives and to trace the circuits of sexual pleasure and desire in their splendid and miserable intensities, as well as the unexpected attachments and persistent aches that they engender.

References

Abramson, Paul R. and Steven D. Pinkerton. 2002. *With Pleasure: Thoughts on the Nature of Human Sexuality*. Revised edition. Oxford: Oxford University Press.

Adelman, Mara B. 1992. Healthy Passions: Safer Sex as Play. In *AIDS: A Communication Perspective*. Edited by Timothy Edgar, Mary Anne Fitzpatrick, and Vicki S. Freimuth, 69–89. Hillsdale: Lawrence Erlbaum.

Adesman, Andrew and Alexis Tchaconas. 2015. Why "Fifty Shades" Could Give Dangerous Messages to Teens. *Live Science*, February 12, www.livescience.com/49789-fifty-shades-of-grey-gives-dangerous-message-to-teens.html.

Agamben, Giorgio. 2011. *Nudities*. Translated by David Kishik and Stefan Pedatella. Stanford: Stanford University Press.

Ahmed, Sara. 2000. *Strange Encounters: Embodied Others in Post-Coloniality*. London: Routledge.

Ahmed, Sara. 2006. *Queer Phenomenology: Orientations, Objects, Others*. Durham, NC: Duke University Press.

Albury, Kath. 2002. *Yes Means Yes: Getting Explicit about Heterosex*. Crows Nest, NSW: Allen & Unwin.

Albury, Kath. 2014. Porn and Sex Education, Porn as Sex Education. *Porn Studies* 1, nos. 1–2: 172–181.

Albury, Kath. 2018. Heterosexual Casual Sex: From Free Love to Tinder. In *The Routledge Companion to Media, Sex and Sexuality*, 81–90. Edited by Clarissa Smith and Feona Attwood with Brian McNair. London: Routledge.

Allen, Samantha. 2015. Feeling Fetishes: Toward an Affective Theory of Sexuality. Unpublished PhD thesis, Women, Gender, and Sexuality Studies, Emory University.

Altenburger, Lauren E., Christin L. Carotta, Amy E. Bonomi and Anastasia Snyder. 2017. Sexist Attitudes among Emerging Adult Women Readers of *Fifty Shades* Fiction. *Archives of Sexual Behavior* 42, no. 2: 455–464.

Apter, Michael J. 1991. A Structural-Phenomenology of Play. In *Adult Play: A Reversal Theory Approach*. Edited by John H. Kerr and Michael J. Apter, 13–30. Amsterdam: Swets & Zeitlinger.

Armitage, Hugh. 2017. 50 Laughably Bad *Fifty Shades Darker* Quotes: Prepare to Have Your Insides Melted and Unfurled. *Digital Spy*, May 17, www.digitalspy.com/movies/fifty-shades-of-grey/feature/a820703/worst-50-shades-darker-quotes/.

Arthurs, Jane. 2004. *Television and Sexuality: Regulation and the Politics of Taste*. London: Open University Press.

Attwood, Feona. 2005. Fashion and Passion: Marketing Sex to Women. *Sexualities* 8, no. 4: 392–406.

Attwood, Feona. 2006. Sexed Up: Theorizing the Sexualization of Culture. *Sexualities* 9, no. 1: 77–94.

Attwood, Feona. 2007. No Money Shot? Commerce, Pornography and New Sex Taste Cultures. *Sexualities* 10, no. 4: 441–456.

Attwood, Feona. 2009. Introduction: The Sexualization of Culture. In *Mainstreaming Sex: The Sexualization of Western Culture*. Edited by Feona Attwood, xiii–xxiv. London: I.B. Tauris.

Attwood, Feona. 2011. Sex and the Citizens: Erotic Play and the New Leisure Culture. In *The New Politics of Leisure and Pleasure*. Edited by Paul Bramham and Stephen Wagg, 82–96. Berlin: Springer.

Attwood, Feona and Clarissa Smith. 2013. More Sex! Better Sex! Sex is Fucking Brilliant! Sex, Sex, Sex, SEX. In *Routledge Handbook of Leisure Studies*. Edited by Tony Blackshaw, 325–342. London: Routledge.

Barker, Martin. 2014. The "Problem" of Sexual Fantasies. *Porn Studies* 1, no. 1–2: 143–160.

Barker, Meg. 2005. On Tops, Bottoms and Ethical Sluts: The Place of BDSM and Polyamory in Lesbian and Gay Psychology. *Lesbian and Gay Psychology Review* 6, no. 2: 124–129.

Barker, Meg. 2013. Consent is a Grey Area? A Comparison of Understandings of Consent in *Fifty Shades of Grey* and on the BDSM Blogosphere. *Sexualities* 16, no. 8: 896–914.

Barker, Meg and Langdridge, D. 2010. Silencing Accounts of Already Silenced Sexualities. In *Secrecy and Silence in the Research Process*. Edited by Róisin Ryan-Flood and Rosalind Gill, 67–79. London: Routledge.

Barker, Meg, Camelia Gupta and Alessandra Iantaffi. 2007. The Power of Play: The Potentials and Pitfalls in Healing Narratives of BDSM. In *Safe, Sane and Consensual: Contemporary Perspectives on Sadomasochism*. Edited by Darren Langdridge and Meg Barker, 197–216. Basingstoke: Palgrave Macmillan.

Bataille, Georges. 1986. *Erotism: Death and Sensuality*. Translated by Mary Dalwood. San Francisco: City Lights.

Bauer, Robin. 2018. Bois and Grrrls Meet their Daddies and Mommies on Gender Playgrounds: Gendered Age Play in the Les-Bi-Trans-Queer BDSM Communities. *Sexualities* 21, nos. 1–2: 139–155.

Beasley, Chris. 2011. Libidinous Politics: Heterosex, "Transgression" and Social Change. *Australian Feminist Studies* 26, no. 67: 25–40.

Beasley, Chris, Mary Holmes and Heather Brook. 2015. Heterodoxy: Challenging Orthodoxies about Heterosexuality. *Sexualities* 18, no. 5–6: 681–697.

Beckmann, Andrea. 2001. Deconstructing Myths: The Social Construction of "Sadomasochism" versus "Subjugated Knowledges" of Practitioners of Consensual SM. *Journal of Criminal Justice and Popular Culture* 8, no. 2: 66–95.

Bennett, Jane. 2001. *The Enchantment of Modern Life: Attachments, Crossings, and Ethics.* Princeton: Princeton University Press.

Bergson, Henri. 2007. *Matter and Memory.* Translated by Nancy Margaret Paul and W. Scott Palmer. New York: Cosimo.

Berlant, Lauren. 2000. Intimacy: A Special Issue. In *Intimacy.* Edited by Lauren Berlant, 1–8. Chicago: University of Chicago Press.

Berlant, Lauren. 2006. Cruel Optimism. *Differences: A Journal of Feminist Cultural Studies* 17, no. 3: 20–36.

Berlant, Lauren. 2008. Against Sexual Scandal. *The Atlantic*, March 12, www.thenation.com/article/against-sexual-scandal/.

Berlant, Lauren. 2012. *Desire/Love.* New York: Punctum Books.

Berlant, Lauren and Lee Edelman. 2014. *Sex, or the Unbearable.* Durham, NC: Duke University Press.

Berlant, Lauren and Michael Warner. 2000. Sex in Public. In *Intimacy.* Edited by Lauren Berlant, 311–330. Chicago: University of Chicago Press.

Bollen, Jonathan and David McInnes. 2006. What Do You Like to Do? Gay Sex and the Politics of Interaffectivity. *Gay & Lesbian Issues and Psychology Review* 2, no. 3: 107–113.

Bonomi, Amy E., Lauren E. Altenburger and Nicole L. Walton. 2013. "Double Crap!" Abuse and Harmed Identity in *Fifty Shades of Grey. Journal of Women's Health* 22, no. 9: 733–744.

Bonomi, Amy E., Julianna M. Nemeth, Lauren E. Altenburger, Melissa L. Anderson, Anastasia Snyder and Irma Dotto. 2014. Fiction or Not? *Fifty Shades* is Associated with Health Risks in Adolescent and Young Adult. *Journal of Women's Health* 23, no. 9: 720–728.

Boscagli, Maurizia. 2014. *Stuff Theory: Everyday Objects, Radical Materialism.* New York: Bloomsbury Academic.

Bragg, Sara and David Buckingham. 2009. Too Much Too Young? Young People, Sexual Media and Learning. In *Mainstreaming Sex: The Sexualization of Western Culture.* Edited by Feona Attwood, 129–146. London: I.B. Tauris.

Branfman, Jonathan, Susan Stiritz and Eric Anderson. 2018. Relaxing the Straight Male Anus: Decreasing Homohysteria around Anal Eroticism. *Sexualities* 21, nos. 1–2: 109–127.

Brown, Ashley. 2012. "No One-Handed Typing": An Exploration of Gameness, Rules and Spoilsports in an Erotic Role Play Community in World of Warcraft. *Journal of Gaming and Virtual Worlds* 4, no. 3: 259–273.

Brown, Ashley M.L. 2015. *Sexuality in Role-Playing Games.* London: Routledge.

Bryan, Scott. 2015. I Read the New "Fifty Shades" Book, and It Is Absolutely Batshit. *BuzzFeed*, June 18, www.buzzfeed.com/scottybryan/i-read-the-new-50-shades-book-and-it-is-absolutely-batshit?utm_term=.wnqXJYjJM#.jwwAdoGdO.

Buckingham, David and Despina Chronaki. 2014. Saving the Children: Childhood, Pornography and the Internet. In *Thatcher's Grandchildren*. Edited by Stephen Wagg and Jane Pilcher, 301–317. Basingstoke: Palgrave Macmillan.

Butler, Judith. 1988. Performative Acts and Gender Constitution: An Essay in Phenomenology and Feminist Theory. *Theatre Journal* 40, no. 4: 519–531.

Butler, Judith. 1990. *Gender Trouble: Feminism and the Subversion of Identity*. London: Routledge.

Butler, Judith. 1993. *Bodies that Matter: On the Discursive Limits of "Sex".* London: Routledge.

Caillois, Roger. 2001. *Man, Play and Games*. Urbana: University of Illinois Press (first published in French in 1958).

Califia, Pat. 1999. *Public Sex: The Culture of Radical Sex*. Second edition. San Francisco: Cleis Press.

Carrillo, Héctor and Amanda Hoffman. 2018. "Straight with a Pinch of Bi": The Construction of Heterosexuality as an Elastic Category among Adult US Men. *Sexualities* 21, nos. 1–2: 90–108.

Carse, James P. 2012. *Finite and Infinite Games: A Vision of Life as Play and Possibility*. New York: The Free Press.

Cervero, Fernando. 2012. *Understanding Pain: Exploring the Perception of Pain*. Cambridge, MA: MIT Press.

Clark-Flory, Tracy. 2013. 6 Tips for Trying Out Role Play. *Cosmopolitan*, December 5, www.cosmopolitan.com/sex-love/advice/a5143/tips-on-role-playing-first-time/.

Click, Melissa. 2015. Fifty Shades of Postfeminism: Contextualizing Readers' Reflection on the Erotic Romance Series. In *Cupcakes, Pinterest, and Ladyporn. Feminized Popular Culture in the Early Twenty-First Century*. Edited by Elana Levine, 15–31. Chicago: University of Illinois Press.

Coleman, Rebecca. 2009. *The Becoming of Bodies: Girls, Images, Experience*. Manchester: Manchester University Press.

Comella, Lynn. 2013. *Fifty Shades* of Erotic Stimulus. *Feminist Media Studies* 13, no. 3: 563–566.

Cooper, Charlotte. 2003. Swing It Baby! *Journal of Bisexuality* 3, no. 3–4: 87–92.

Cowie, Elizabeth. 1993. Pornography and Fantasy: Psychoanalytic Perspectives. In *Sex Exposed: Sexuality and the Pornography Debate*. Edited by Lynn Segal and Mary McIntosh, 132–152. New Brunswick: Rutgers University Press.

Cvetkovich, Ann. 2003. *An Archive of Feelings: Trauma, Sexuality, and Lesbian Public Cultures*. Durham, NC: Duke University Press.

Däumer, Elisabeth D. 1992. Queer Ethic; or, the Challenge of Bisexuality to Lesbian Ethics. *Hypatia* 7, no. 4: 91–105.

Davies, Sally Lloyd, Danya Glaser and Ruth Kosoff. 2000. Children's Sexual Play and Behavior in Pre-School Settings: Staff's Perceptions, Reports, and Responses. *Child Abuse & Neglect* 24 no. 10: 1329–1343.

DeLamater, John and William N. Friedrich. 2002. Human Sexual Development. *Journal of Sex Research* 39, no. 1: 10–14.

Deleuze, Gilles. 1991. *Bergsonism*. Translated by Hugh Tomlinson and Barbara Habberjam. New York: Zone Books.

Deller, Ruth A. and Clarissa Smith. 2013. Reading the BDSM Romance: Reader Responses to *Fifty Shades*. *Sexualities* 16, no. 8: 932–950.

Deller, Ruth A., Sarah Harman and Bethan Jones. 2013. Introduction to the Special Issue: Reading the *Fifty Shades* "Phenomenon". *Sexualities* 16, no. 8: 859–863.

Denfeld, Duane and Michael Gordon. 1970. The Sociology of Mate Swapping: Or the Family that Swings Together Clings Together. *Journal of Sex Research* 6, no. 2: 85–100.

Diamond, Lisa M. 2009. *Sexual Fluidity: Understanding Women's Love and Desire*. Cambridge, MA: Harvard University Press.

Dines, Gail. 2014. Rethinking *Fifty Shades of Grey* within a Feminist Media Context. *Journal of Women's Health* 23, no. 9: i–ii.

Duguay, Stephanie. 2016. Lesbian, Gay, Bisexual, Trans, and Queer Visibility through Selfies: Comparing Platform Mediators across Ruby Rose's Instagram and Vine Presence. *Social Media + Society* 2, no. 2: 1–12, http://journals.sagepub.com/doi/pdf/10.1177/2056305116641975.

Dymock, Alex. 2013. Flogging Sexual Transgression: Interrogating the Costs of the "Fifty Shades Effect". *Sexualities* 16, no. 8: 880–895.

Edelman, Lee. 2004. *No Future: Queer Theory and the Death Drive*. Durham, NC: Duke University Press.

Eng, David L., Judith Halberstam and José Esteban Muñoz. 2005. Introduction: What's Queer about Queer Studies Now? *Social Text* 23, no. 3–4: 1–17.

Enomoto, Tomoo. 1990. Social Play and Sexual Behavior of the Bonobo (*Pan paniscus*) with Special Reference to Flexibility. *Primates* 31, no. 4: 469–480.

Epstein, Steven. 1994. A Queer Encounter: Sociology and the Study of Sexuality. *Sociological Theory* 12, no. 2: 188–202.

Essa, Eva L. and Colleen I. Murray. 1999. Sexual Play: When Should You Be Concerned? *Childhood Education* 75, no. 4: 231–234.

Fernbach, Amanda. 2002. *Fantasies of Fetishism: From Decadence to the Post-Human*. New Brunswick: Rutgers University Press.

Flood, Alison. 2015. *Fifty Shades of Grey* Sequel Break Sales Records. *The Guardian,* June 23, www.theguardian.com/books/2015/jun/23/ fifty-shades-of-grey-sequel-breaks-sales-records.

Flore, Jacinthe. 2014. Mismeasures of Asexual Desires. In *Asexualities: Feminist and Queer Perspectives.* Edited by Karli June Cerankowski and Megan Milks, 17–34. New York: Routledge.

Foote, Nelson N. 1954. Sex as Play. *Social Problems* 1, no. 4: 159–163.

Foucault, Michel. 1990. *The History of Sexuality, vol. I: An Introduction.* Translated by Robert Hurley. London: Penguin.

Foucault, Michel. 1997. *Ethics: Subjectivity and Truth.* Edited by Paul Rabinow. New York: The New Press.

Fox, Nick J. and Pam Alldred. 2013. The Sexuality-Assemblage: Desire, Affect, Anti-Humanism. *The Sociological Review* 61, no. 4: 769–789.

Frank, Katherine. 2013. *Plays Well in Groups: A Journey through the World of Group Sex.* Lanham: Rowman & Littlefield.

Freud, Sigmund. 2011. *Group Psychology and the Analysis of the Ego.* Translated by James Strachey. Project Gutenberg, www.gutenberg.org/ebooks/35877.

Frey, Kurt S. 1991. Sexual Behaviour as Adult Play. In *Adult Play: A Reversal Theory Approach.* Edited by John E. Kerr and Michael J. Apter, 55–69. Amsterdam: Swets & Zeitlinger.

Furedi, Frank. 2003. *Therapy Culture: Cultivating Vulnerability in an Uncertain Age.* London: Routledge.

Gamson, Joshua. 1998a. *Freaks Talk Back: Tabloid Talk Shows and Sexual Nonconformity.* Chicago: University of Chicago Press.

Gamson, Joshua. 1998b. Publicity Traps: Television Talk Shows and Lesbian, Gay, Bisexual, and Transgender Visibility. *Sexualities* 1, no. 1: 11–41.

Gamson, Joshua. 1999. Taking the Talk Show Challenge: Television, Emotion, and Public Spheres. *Constellations* 6, no. 2: 190–205.

Gerbasi, Kathleen C., Penny L. Bernstein, Samuel Conway, Laura L. Scaletta, Adam Privitera, Nicholas Paolone and Justin Higner. 2008. Furries from A to Z (Anthropomorphism to Zoomorphism). *Society and Animals* 16, no. 3: 197–222.

Green, Emma. 2015. Consent Isn't Enough: The Troubling Sex of *Fifty Shades. The Atlantic* February 10, www.theatlantic.com/entertainment/archive/2015/02/consent-isnt-enough-in-fifty-shades-of-grey/385267/.

Grigordiadis, Vanessa. 2015. The Rocky Road to Making *The Fifty Shades of Grey* Movie. *Vanity Fair,* February, www.vanityfair.com/hollywood/2015/01/ fifty-shades-of-grey-sex-scenes.

Grossman-Scott, Amanda. n.d. The Fifty Shades Effect: Disempowering Young Girls and What We Can Do about It. *Educate Empower Kids*, https://educateempowerkids.org/fifty-shades-disempowers/.

Grosz, Elizabeth. 1994. *Volatile Bodies: Towards a Corporeal Feminism.* Bloomington: Indiana University Press.

Grosz, Elizabeth. 1995a. Animal Sex: Libido as Desire and Death. In *Sexy Bodies: The Strange Carnalities of Feminism.* Edited by Elizabeth Grosz and Elspeth Probyn, 278–299. London: Routledge.

Grosz, Elizabeth. 1995b. Bodies and Pleasures in Queer Theory. In *Who Can Speak? Authority and Critical Identity.* Edited by Judith Roof and Robyn Wiegman, 221–230. Urbana: University of Illinois Press.

Grosz, Elizabeth. 2005. Bergson, Deleuze and the Becoming of Unbecoming. *Parallax* 11, no. 2: 4–13.

Hakim, Jamie. 2016. Chemsex and the City: Queering Intimacy in Neoliberal London. Paper at the Crossroads in Cultural Studies Conference, University of Sydney, December 14.

Halberstam, Jack. 2015. Fifty Shades of Zzzzzzzzzz. *Bully Bloggers*, February 25, https://bullybloggers.wordpress.com/2015/02/25/fifty-shades-of-zzzzzzzzzz-by-jack-halberstam/.

Hale, C. Jacob. 1997. Leatherdyke Boys and their Daddies: How to Have Sex without Women or Men. *Social Text* 15 no. 3–4: 223–236.

Hall, Kimberley. 2016. Selfies and Self-Writing: Cue Card Confessions as Social Media Technologies of the Self. *Television & New Media* 17, no. 3: 228–242.

Hammers, Corie. 2014. Corporeality, Sadomasochism and Sexual Trauma. *Body & Society* 20, no. 2: 68–90.

Hammers, Corie. 2015. The Queer Logics of Sex/Desire and the "Missing" Discourse of Gender. *Sexualities* 18, no. 7: 838–858.

Harlow, Harry F. and Helen E. Lauersdorf. 1974. Sex Differences in Passion and Play. *Perspectives in Biology and Medicine* 17, no. 3: 348–360.

Harman, Sarah and Bethan Jones. 2013. Fifty Shades of Ghey: Snark Fandom and the Figure of the Anti-Fan. *Sexualities* 16, no. 8: 951–968.

Harrison, Katherine and Marie-Louise Holm. 2013. Exploring Grey Zones and Blind Spots in the Binaries and Boundaries of E.L. James' *Fifty Shades* Trilogy. *Feminist Media Studies* 13, no. 3: 558–662.

Harvey, Laura and Rosalind Gill. 2011. Spicing It Up: Sexual Entrepreneurs and *The Sex Inspectors*. In *New Femininities: Postfeminism, Neoliberalism and Subjectivity.* Edited by Rosalind Gill and Christina Scharff, 52–67. London: Palgrave.

Harviainen, J. Tuomas. 2011. Sadomasochist Role-Playing as Live-Action Role-Playing: A Trait-Descriptive Analysis. *International Journal of Role-Playing* 2: 59–70.

Harviainen, J. Tuomas and Katherine Frank. 2016. Group Sex as Play: Rules and Transgression in Shared Non-Monogamy. *Games and Culture*. Epub ahead of print August 16. DOI: 10.1177/1555412016659835

Harviainen, J. Tuomas, Ashley M. Brown and Jaakko Suominen. 2016. Three Waves of Awkwardness: A Meta-Analysis of Sex in Game Studies. *Games and Culture*. Epub ahead of print March 9. DOI: 1555412016636219.

Hawkinson, Kaitlyn and Brian D. Zamboni. 2014. Adult Baby/Diaper Lovers: An Exploratory Study of an Online Community Sample. *Archives in Sexual Behavior* 43, no. 5: 863–877.

Higonnet, Anne. 1998. *Pictures of Innocence: The History and Crisis of Ideal Childhood*. London: Thames & Hudson.

Hillis, Ken. 2009. *Online a Lot of the Time: Ritual, Fetish, Sign*. Durham, NC: Duke University Press.

Holmes, Mary, Chris Beasley and Heather Brook. 2011. Guest Editorial: Heterosexuality. *Australian Feminist Studies* 26, no. 67: 3–7.

Hongisto, Ilona. 2015. *Soul of the Documentary: Framing, Expression. Ethics*. Amsterdam: Amsterdam University Press.

Hoppe, Trevor. 2011. Circuits of Power, Circuits of Pleasure: Sexual Scripting in Gay Men's Bottom Narratives. *Sexualities* 14, no. 2: 193–217.

Huizinga, Johan. 1949. *Homo Ludens: A Study of the Play-Element in Culture*. London: Routledge & Kegan Paul.

Humphrey, W. Steven. 2015. Fifty Terrible Lines from *Fifty Shades of Grey*. The Stranger, February 4, www.thestranger.com/blogs/slog/2015/02/14/21710269/fifty-terrible-lines-from-fifty-shades-of-grey.

Iasenza, Suzanne. 2010. What is Queer about Sex? Expanding Sexual Frames in Theory and Practice. *Family Process* 49, no. 3: 291–308.

Illouz, Eva. 2007. *Cold Intimacies: The Making of Emotional Capitalism*. Oxford: Polity Press.

Illouz, Eva. 2014. *Hard-Core Romance: "Fifty Shades of Grey," Best-Sellers, and Society*. Chicago: University of Chicago Press.

Irvine, Janice. 2003. Introduction to "Sexual Scripts: Origins, Influences and Changes". *Qualitative Sociology* 26, no. 4: 489–490.

Jackson, Stevi and Sue Scott. 2007. Faking Like a Woman? Interpretive Theorization of Sexual Pleasure. *Body & Society* 13, no. 2: 95–116.

Jacobs, Tom. 2014. Why "Fifty Shades of Grey" Might Be Bad for Your Health. *The Huffington Post*, September 24, www.huffingtonpost.com/2014/09/24/fifty-shades-of-grey-health_n_5868340.html.

James, E. L. 2012a, *Fifty Shades of Grey*. New York: Vintage.

James, E. L. 2012b, *Fifty Shades Darker*. New York: Vintage.

James, E. L. 2012c, *Fifty Shades Freed*. New York: Vintage.

James, E. L. 2015. *Grey*. London: Arrow Books.

James, E. L. 2017. *Darker.* London: Arrow Books

James, R. and Lynn G. Smith. 1970. Co-Marital Sex and the Sexual Freedom Movement. *Journal of Sex Research* 6, no. 2: 131–142.

Jones, Steven. 2010. Horrorporn/Pornhorror: The Problematic Communities and Contexts of Online Shock Imagery. In *Porn.com: Making Sense of Online Pornography*. Edited by Feona Attwood, 123–137. New York: Peter Lang.

Kalish, Rachel and Michael Kimmel. 2011. Hooking Up: Hot Hetero Sex or the New Numb Normative? *Australian Feminist Studies* 26, no. 67: 137–151.

Kaplan, Louise C. 2006. *Cultures of Fetishism*. New York: Palgrave.

Karhulahti, Veli-Matti. 2013. A Kinesthetic Theory of Videogames: Time-Critical Challenge and Aporetic Rhematic. *Game Studies* 13, no. 1: http://gamestudies.org/1301/articles/karhulahti_kinesthetic_theory_of_the_videogame/.

Kincaid, James R. 1998. *Erotic Innocence: The Culture of Child Molesting*. Durham, NC: Duke University Press.

Kirby, Vicki. 2015. Transgression: Normativity's Self-Inversion. *Differences* 26, no. 1: 96–116.

Koivunen, Anu. 2010. The Affective Turn? Reimagining the Subject of Feminist Theory. In *Working with Affect in Feminist Readings: Disturbing Differences*. Edited by Marianne Liljeström and Susanna Paasonen, 8–29. London: Routledge.

Kontula, Osmo. 2009. *Between Sexual Desire and Reality: The Evolution of Sex in Finland*. Helsinki: The Family Federation of Finland.

Kulick, Don. 2000. Gay and Lesbian Language. *Annual Review of Anthropology* 29: 243–285.

Kulick, Don. 2005. Four Hundred Thousand Swedish Perverts. *GLQ: A Journal of Lesbian and Gay Studies* 11, no. 2: 205–235.

Kyrölä, Katariina. 2014. *The Weight of Images: Affect, Body Image and Fat in the Media*. Burlington: Ashgate.

Lamb, Sharon. 2001. *The Secret Lives of Girls: What Good Girls Really Do: Sex Play, Aggression, and their Guilt*. New York: The Free Press.

Lamb, Sharon and Mary Coakley. 1993. "Normal" Childhood Sexual Play and Games: Differentiating Play from Abuse. *Child Abuse & Neglect* 17, no. 4: 515–526.

Latta, Judie, Sigrid Hopf and Detlev Ploog. 1967. Observation on Mating Behavior and Sexual Play in the Squirrel Monkey (*Saimiri sciureus*). *Primates* 8, no. 3: 229–245.

Lauteria, Evan W. and Matthew Wysocki. 2015. Introduction. In *Rated M for Mature: Sex and Sexuality in Video Games*. Edited by Matthew Wysocki and Evan W. Lauretia, 1–9. London: Bloomsbury.

Laqueur, Thomas. 2003. *Solitary Sex: A Cultural History of Masturbation*. New York: Zone Books.

Larsson, IngBeth and Carl-Göran Svedin. 2002. Sexual Experiences in Childhood: Young Adults' Recollections. *Archives of Sexual Behavior* 31, no. 3: 263–273.

Levine, Caroline. 2017. *Forms: Whole, Rhythm, Hierarchy, Network*. Princeton: Princeton University Press.

Lewis, Angela. 2011. Ageplay: An Adults Only Game. *Counselling Australia* 11, no. 2: 1–9.

Lewis, Lionel S. and Dennis Brissett. 1967. Sex as Work: A Study of Avocational Counseling. *Social Problems* 15, no. 8: 8–18.

Liljeström, Marianne and Susanna Paasonen. 2010. Introduction: Feeling Differences: Affect and Feminist Reading. In *Working with Affect in Feminist Readings: Disturbing Differences*. Edited by Marianne Liljeström and Susanna Paasonen, 1–7. London: Routledge.

Love, Heather. 2011. Queers__this. In *After Sex? On Writing since Queer Theory*. Edited by Janet Halley and Andrew Parker, 180–191. Durham, NC: Duke University Press.

Lunt, Peter and Paul Stenner. 2005. *The Jerry Springer Show* as an Emotional Public Sphere. *Media, Culture & Society* 27, no. 1: 59–81.

McAlister, Jodi. 2017. True Tales of the First Time: Sexual Storytelling in the Virginity Loss Confessional Genre. *Sexualities* 20, no. 1–2: 105–120.

McCallum, E.L. 1999. *Object Lessons: How to Do Things with Fetishism*. Albany: SUNY Press.

McCormack, Mark. 2018. Mostly Straights and the Study of Sexuality: An Introduction to Special Issue. *Sexualities* 21, nos. 1–2: 3–15.

McKee, Alan, Katherine Albury and Catharine Lumby. 2008. *The Porn Report*. Melbourne: Melbourne University Press.

Marcus, Steven 1964. *The Other Victorians: A Study of Sexuality and Pornography in Mid-Nineteenth-Century England*. New York: Basic Books.

Marin, Vanessa. 2014. How to Role-Play in Bed without Feeling Like a Cheesy Porn Star (Unless You're into That). *Bustle* September 18, www.bustle.com/articles/40475-how-to-role-play-in-bed-without-feeling-like-a-cheesy-porn-star-unless-youre-into-that.

Marsh, Sarah. 2016. The Gender-Fluid Generation: Young People on Being Male, Female or Non-Binary. *The Guardian*, March 23, www.theguardian.com/commentisfree/2016/mar/23/gender-fluid-generation-young-people-male-female-trans.

Martin, Amber. 2013. *Fifty Shades* of Sex Shop: Sexual Fantasy for Sale. *Sexualities* 16, no. 8: 980–984.

Massumi, Brian. 2002. *Parables for the Virtual: Movement, Affect, Sensation*. Durham, NC: Duke University Press.

Massumi, Brian. 2015. *The Politics of Affect*. Cambridge: Polity Press.

Mercer, John. 2004. In the Slammer: The Myth of the Prison in American Gay Pornographic Video. *Journal of Homosexuality* 47, nos. 3–4: 151–166.

Morgan, Sophie. 2012. I Like Submissive Sex but Fifty Shades is Not about Fun: It's about Abuse. *The Guardian*, August 25, www.theguardian.com/society/2012/aug/25/fifty-shades-submissive-sophie-morgan.

Mortensen, Torill Elvira, Jonas Linderoth and Ashley M.L. Brown, eds. 2015. *The Dark Side of Game Play: Controversial Issues in Playful Environments*. London: Routledge.

Mulholland, Monique. 2013. *Young People and Pornography: Negotiating Pornification*. New York: Palgrave.

Nachamanovitch, Stephen. 2009. This is Play. *New Literary History* 40, no. 1: 1–24.

Nash, Jennifer C. 2014. *The Black Body in Ecstasy: Reading Race, Reading Pornography*. Durham, NC: Duke University Press.

Neville, Lucy. 2015. Male Gays in the Female Gaze: Women who Watch M/M Pornography. *Porn Studies* 2, nos. 2–3: 192–207.

Nielsen, Silja. 2014. "Ei kaikkea pidä sekoittaa ahdisteluun": Tyttöjen internetissä saamat ja lähettämät seksiin liittyvät viestit ("Not everything should be confused with harassment": Sexual messages that girls have received and sent on the Internet). MA thesis, Department of Media Studies, University of Turku, www.doria.fi/bitstream/handle/10024/101931/progradu_siljanielsen.pdf?sequence=2.

Nielsen, Silja, Susanna Paasonen and Sanna Spišák. 2015. "Pervy Role-Play and Such": Girls' Experiences of Sexual Messaging Online. *Sex Education: Sexuality, Education and Learning* 15, no. 5: 472–485.

Orgeur, P. and J.P. Signoret. 1984. Sexual Play and its Functional Significance in the Domestic Sheep (*Ovis aries L.*). *Physiology & Behavior* 33, no. 1: 111–118.

Osborne, Heather. 2012. Performing Self, Performing Character: Exploring Gender Performativity in Online Role-Playing Games. *Transformative Works and Cultures* 11. http://journal.transformativeworks.org/index.php/twc/article/view/411.

Pääkkölä, Anna-Elena. 2016. *Sound Kinks: Sadomasochistic Erotica in Audiovisual Music Performances*. Turku: Annales Universitatis Turkuensis, series B, vol. 422.

Paasonen, Susanna. 2010. Disturbing, Fleshy Images: Close Looking at Pornography. In *Working with Affect in Feminist Readings: Disturbing Differences*. Edited by Marianne Liljeström and Susanna Paasonen, 58–71. London: Routledge.

Paasonen, Susanna. 2011. *Carnal Resonance: Affect and Online Pornography*. Cambridge, MA: MIT Press.

Paasonen, Susanna. 2013. Grains of Resonance: Affect, Pornography and Visual Sensation. *Somatechnics* 3 no. 2: 351–368.

Paasonen, Susanna. 2018. Many Splendored Things: Sexuality, Playfulness and Play. *Sexualities* 21, no. 4: 537–551.

Paasonen, Susanna, Katariina Kyrölä, Kaarina Nikunen and Laura Saarenmaa. 2015. "We Hid Porn Magazines in the Woods": Memory-Work and Pornography Consumption in Finland. *Sexualities* 18 no. 4: 394–412.

Paasonen, Susanna, Kylie Jarrett and Ben Light. forthcoming. *Not Safe for Work: Sex, Humor and Risk in Social Media.* Cambridge, MA: MIT Press.

Paley, Vivian Gussin. 2004. *A Child's Work: The Importance of Fantasy Play.* Chicago: University of Chicago Press.

Parchev, Ofer and Darren Langdridge. 2017. BDSM under Security: Radical Resistance via Contingent Subjectivities. *Sexualities,* online before print, http://journals.sagepub.com/doi/abs/10.1177/1363460716688684?journalCode=sexa.lew

Picardo, Cheyenne and Phoebe Reilly. 2015. Whip Smart: Real-Life Dominatrix Takes on "Fifty Shades of Grey". *Rolling Stone,* February 13, www.rollingstone.com/movies/features/real-life-dominatrix-takes-on-fifty-shades-of-grey-20150213.

Plummer, Ken. 1995. *Telling Sexual Stories: Power, Change and Social Worlds.* London: Routledge.

Plummer, Ken. 2003a. *Intimate Citizenship: Private Decisions and Public Dialogues.* Seattle: University of Washington Press

Plummer, Ken. 2003b. Queers, Bodies and Postmodern Sexualities: A Note on Revisiting the "Sexual" in Symbolic Interactionism. *Qualitative Sociology* 26, no. 4: 515–530.

Probyn, Elspeth. 2000. *Carnal Appetites: FoodSexIdentities.* London: Routledge.

Proyer, René T. 2014. To Love and Play: Testing the Association of Adult Playfulness with the Relationship Personality and Relationship Satisfaction. *Current Psychology* 33: 501–514.

Race, Kane. 2015a. "Party and Play": Online Hook-up Devices and the Emergence of PNP Practices among Gay Men. *Sexualities* 18, no. 3: 253–275.

Race, Kane. 2015b. Speculative Pragmatism and Intimate Arrangements: Online Hook-up Devices in Gay Life. *Culture, Health & Sexuality* 17, no. 4: 496–511.

Radway, Janice. 1984. *Reading the Romance: Women, Patriarchy, and Popular Fiction.* Chapel Hill: University of North Carolina Press.

Raun, Tobias. 2016. *Out Online: Trans Self-Representation and Community Building on YouTube.* London: Routledge

Richards, Christina. 2015. Further Sexualities. In *The Palgrave Handbook of the Psychology of Sexuality and Gender,* edited by Christina Richards and Meg John Barker, 60–76. Basingstoke: Palgrave Macmillan.

Richardson, Diane. 2007. Patterned Fluidities: (Re)imagining the Relationship between Gender and Sexuality. *Sociology* 41, no. 3: 457–474.

Robards, Brady. 2018. "Totally Straight": Contested Sexual Identities on Social Media Site Reddit. *Sexualities* 21, nos. 1–2: 49–67.

Rossi, Leena-Maija. 2011. "Happy" and "Unhappy" Performatives: Images and Norms of Heterosexuality. *Australian Feminist Studies* 26, no. 67: 9–23.

Ruberg, Bonnie. 2010. Sex as Game: Playing with the Erotic Body in Virtual Worlds. *Rhizomes* 21. Available at: www.rhizomes.net/issue21/ruberg.html.

Rubin, Gayle. 1989. Thinking Sex. In *Pleasure and Danger: Exploring Female Sexuality*. Edited by Carole S. Vance, 267–319. London: Pandora.

Rulof, Paul. 2011. *Ageplay: From Diapers to Diplomas*. Las Vegas: The Naxca Plains Corporation.

Rust, Paula C. 1995. *Bisexuality and the Challenge to Lesbian Politics: Sex, Loyalty, and Revolution*. New York: New York University Press.

Ryan, Kathryn M. and Sharon Mohr. 2005. Gender Differences in Playful Aggression during Courtship in College Students. *Sex Roles* 53, no. 7–8: 591–601.

Ryberg, Ingrid. 2012. *Imagining Safe Space: The Politics of Queer, Feminist and Lesbian Pornography*. Acta Universitatis Stockholmiensis. Stockholm: University of Stockholm.

Sager, Jessica. 2015. 17 Dumbest, Most Disturbing Aspects of "50 Shades of Grey". *Your Tango*, www.yourtango.com/2015251910/17-dumbest-most-disturbing-moments-50-shades-grey.

Satinsky, Emily and Denise Nicole Green. 2016. Negotiating Identities in the Furry Fandom through Costuming. *Critical Studies in Men's Fashions* 3, no. 2: 107–123.

Savin-Williams, Ritch C. 2014. An Exploratory Study of the Categorical versus Spectrum Nature of Sexual Orientation. *Journal of Sex Research* 51, no 4: 446–453.

Savin-Williams, Ritch C. and Zhana Vrangalova. 2012. Mostly Heterosexual and Mostly Gay/Lesbian: Evidence for New Sexual Orientation Identities. *Archives of Sexual Behavior* 41, no 1: 85–101.

Scoats, Ryan, Lauren J. Joseph and Eric Anderson. 2018. "I Don't Mind Watching Him Cum": Heterosexual Men, Threesomes, and the Erosion of the One-Time Rule of Homosexuality. *Sexualities* 21, nos. 1–2: 30–48.

Sedgwick, Eve Kosofsky. 2003. *Touching Feeling: Affect, Pedagogy, Performativity*. Durham, NC: Duke University Press.

Sedgwick, Eve Kosofsky and Frank, Adam. 1995. Shame in the Cybernetic Fold: Reading Silvan Tomkins. In *Shame and its Sisters: A Silvan Tomkins Reader*. Edited by Eve Kosofsky Sedgwick and Adam Frank, 1–28. Durham, NC: Duke University Press.

Segal, Lynn. 1994. *Straight Sex: The Politics of Pleasure*. London: Virago.

Seigworth, Gregory J. and Melissa Gregg. 2010. An Inventory of Shimmers. In *The Affect Theory Reader*. Edited by Melissa Gregg and Gregory J. Seigworth, 1–28. Durham, NC: Duke University Press.

Shaw, Adrienne and Elizaveta Friesem. 2016. Where is the Queerness in Games? Types of Lesbian, Gay, Bisexual, Transgender, and Queer Content in Digital Games. *International Journal of Communication* 10: 3877–3889.

Sicart, Miquel. 2014. *Play Matters*. Cambridge, MA: MIT Press.

Silva, Tony J. 2018. "Helpin' a Buddy Out": Perceptions of Identity and Behaviour among Rural Straight Men that Have Sex with Each Other. *Sexualities* 21, nos. 1–2: 68–89.

Simmel, Georg. 1949. The Sociology of Sociability. Translated by Everett C. Hughes. *American Journal of Sociology* 55, no. 3: 254–261.

Simon, William and John H. Gagnon. 1986. Sexual Scripts: Permanence and Change. *Archives of Sexual Behavior* 15, no 2: 97–120.

Simon, William and John H. Gagnon. 2003. Sexual Scripts: Origins, Influences and Changes. *Qualitative Sociology* 26, no. 4: 491–497.

Smith, Anna. 2015. *Fifty Shades of Grey*: What BDSM Enthusiasts Think. *The Guardian,* February 15, www.theguardian.com/film/2015/feb/15/ fifty-shades-of-grey-bdsm-enthusiasts.

Smith, Clarissa. 2007. *One for the Girls! The Pleasures and Practices of Reading Women's Porn*. Bristol: Intellect.

Smith, Clarissa. 2009. Pleasing Intensities: Masochism and Affective Pleasures in Short Porn Fictions. In *Mainstreaming Sex: The Sexualization of Western Culture*. Edited by Feona Attwood, 19–35. London: I.B. Tauris.

Smith, Clarissa, Feona Attwood and Martin Barker. 2015. Figuring the Porn Audience. In *New Views on Pornography: Sexuality, Politics and the Law*. Edited by Lynn Comella and Shira Tarrant, 267–285. Santa Barbara: Praeger.

Snitow, Ann. 1983. Mass Market Romance: Pornography for Women is Different. In *Powers of Desire: The Politics of Sexuality*. Edited by Ann Snitow, Christine Stansell and Sharon Thompson, 245–263. New York: Monthly Review Press.

Snitow, Ann, Christine Stansell and Sharon Thompson. 1983. Introduction. In *Powers of Desire: The Politics of Sexuality*. Edited by Ann Snitow, Christine Stansell and Sharon Thompson, 9–47. New York: Monthly Review Press.

Soldat, Jan. 2014. *Kontrolliert einlassen – Begrenzungen und Grenzüberschreitungen meiner dokumentarischen Methode*. Schriftliche Diplomarbeit. Berlin: Hochschule für Film und Fernsehen "Konrad Wolf" Potsdam-Babelsberg.

Spatz, Ben. 2015. *What a Body Can Do: Technique as Knowledge, Practice as Research*. London: Routledge.

Spinoza, Baruch. 1992. *The Ethics, Treatise on the Emendation of the Intellect and Selected Letters*. Edited by Seymour Feldman. Translated by Samuel Shirley. Indianapolis: Hackett.

Spišák, Sanna. 2016a. "Everywhere They Say that It's Harmful but They Don't Say How, so I'm Asking Here": Young People, Pornography and Negotiations with Notions of Risk and Harm. *Sex Education. Sexuality, Society and Learning* 16, no. 2, 130–142.

Spišák, Sanna. 2016b. Negotiating Norms: Girls, Pornography and Sexual Scripts in Finnish Question and Answer Forum. *Young: Nordic Journal of Youth Research* 25, no. 4: 1–16.

Spišák, Sanna. forthcoming. The Intimacy Effect: Girls' Reflections about Pornography and Expectations of Intimacy. *Sexualities.*

Spišák, Sanna and Susanna Paasonen. 2017. Bad Education? Childhood Recollections of Pornography, Sexual Exploration, Learning and Agency in Finland. *Childhood* 24, no. 1: 99–112.

Steel, Lady Velvet. 2015. "Fifty Shades of Grey": A Dominatrix's View. *The Hollywood Reporter*, February 14, www.hollywoodreporter.com/news/ fifty-shades-grey-a-dominatrixs-773577.

Steele, Valerie. 1996. *Fetish: Fashion, Sex and Power.* New York: Oxford University Press.

Stenros, Jaakko. 2015. Playfulness, Play, and Games: A Constructionist Ludology Approach. PhD dissertation, Tampere University Press.

Storr, Merl. 2003. *Latex and Lingerie: Shopping for Pleasure at Ann Summers Parties.* Oxford: Berg.

Strauss, Neil. 2005. The Game: Penetrating the Secret Society of Pickup Artists. New York: HarperCollins.

Sundén, Jenny. 2009. Play as Transgression: An Ethnographic Approach to Queer Game Cultures. Paper presented at Breaking New Ground: Innovations in Games, Play, Practice, and Theory, Proceedings of DiGRA 2009, the annual conference of the Digital Games Research Association. West London,September 1–4, 2009. Available at www.digra.org/wp-content/uploads/digital-library/09287.40551.pdf.

Sundén, Jenny and Malin Sveningsson. 2012. *Gender and Sexuality in Online Game Cultures: Passionate Play.* London: Routledge.

Sutton-Smith, Brian. 1997. *The Ambiguity of Play.* Cambridge, MA: Harvard University Press.

Thomas, Marlo. 2012. Fifty Shades of Success: Behind the (Sex) Scenes with E.L. James. *The Huffington Post*, April 10, www.huffingtonpost.com/marlo-thomas/fifty-shades-of-success_ b_1923039.html.

Thorn, Katy. n.d. From the Experts: The Importance of Fantasy in Relationships. *Volonté*, www.lelo.com/blog/from-the-experts-the-importance-of-fantasy-in-relationships/.

Tomkins, Silvan S. 1995. *Exploring Affect: The Selected Writings of Silvan S. Tomkins.* Edited by Virginia Demos. Cambridge: Cambridge University Press.

Tomkins, Silvan S. 2008. *Affect Imaginary Consciousness: The Complete Edition.* New York: Springer.

Tosenberger, Catherine. 2008. Homosexuality at the Online Hogwarts: Harry Potter Slash Fanfiction. *Children's Literature* 36: 185–207.

Tripodi, Francesca. 2017. Fifty Shades of Consent? *Feminist Media Studies* 17, no. 1: 93–107.

Tsaliki, Liza. 2016. *Children and the Politics of Sexuality: The Sexualization of Children Debate*. London: Palgrave Macmillan.

Tsjeng, Zing. 2016. Teens These Days are Queer AF, New Study Says. *Broadly*, March 10, https://broadly.vice.com/en_us/article/teens-these-days-are-queer-af-new-study-says.

Vance, Carole S. 1989/1984. Pleasure and Danger: Towards a Politics of Sexuality. In *Pleasure and Danger: Exploring Female Sexuality*. Edited by Carole S. Vance, 1–27. London: Pandora.

Vörös, Florian. 2015. Les usages sociaux de la pornographie en ligne et les constructions de la masculinité: Une sociologie matérialiste de la réception des médias. PhD thesis, École des Hautes Études en Sciences Sociales, France.

Ward, Jane. 2015. *Not Gay: Sex between Straight White Men*. New York: New York University Press.

Warner, Michael. 2000. *The Trouble with Normal: Sex, Politics, and the Ethics of Queer Life*. Cambridge, MA: Harvard University Press.

Waskul, Dennis D. and Phillip Vannini. 2008. Ludic and Ludic(rous) Relationships: Sex, Play, and the Internet. In *Remote Relationships in a Small World*. Edited by Samantha Holland, 241–261. New York: Peter Lang.

Weeks, Jeffrey. 1998. The Sexual Citizen. *Theory, Culture & Society* 15, no. 3: 35–52.

Weiss, Margot D. 2006. Working at Play: BDSM Sexuality in the San Francisco Bay Area. *Anthropologica* 48, no. 2: 229–245.

Weiss, Margot D. 2009. Rumsfeld! Consensual BDSM and "Sadomasochistic" Torture at Abu Ghraib. In *Out in Public: Reinventing Lesbian/Gay Anthropology in a Globalizing World*. Edited by Ellen Lewin and William Leap, 180–121. Malden: Blackwell.

Weiss, Margot. 2011. *Techniques of Pleasure: BDSM and the Circuits of Sexuality*. Durham, NC: Duke University Press.

Wignall, Liam and Mark McCormack. 2017. An Exploratory Study of a New Kink Activity: "Pup Play". *Archives of Sexual Behavior* 46 no. 3: 801–811.

Williams, Linda. 2004. Porn Studies: Proliferating Pornographies On/Scene: An Introduction. In *Porn Studies*. Edited by Linda Williams, 1–23. Durham, NC: Duke University Press.

Williams, Raymond. 1977. *Marxism and Literature*. Oxford: Oxford University Press.

Wirman, Hanna. 2014. Games for/with Strangers: Captive Orangutan (*Pongo pygmaeus*) Touch Screen Play. *Antennae* 30: 105–115.

Wysocki, Matthew and Evan W. Lauretia, eds. 2015. *Rated M for Mature: Sex and Sexuality in Video Games*. London: Bloomsbury.

Index

Abramson, Paul, 29

Adesman, Andrew, 67

Adult Baby / Diaper Lovers (ABDL)
  Coming of Age, 95–98
  diaper play, 86–92
  Extreme Love, 92–94
  guidebooks on, 84
  Happy, Happy Baby, 98–100
  mainstream media coverage of, 86–92
  My Crazy Obsession, 92
  My Strange Attraction, 92–93
  overview of, 84

affect
  affective associations and sexual play, 21
  affective curve of excitement, 22, 32–33,
    95, 110
  affective intensities, 22, 150–151
  affective intensity and identity, 134
  affectus (Spinoza), 41–42
  bodily affectation, 31–32, 38, 42–43,
    150–151
  excitement and the self, 131
  and feminist enquiry, 7, 8
  non-instrumentality of affect, 6
  and normativity, 110
  and pain, 6, 10–11, 42
  positive affect and sexual play, 3, 11, 12
  registers of affect, 94–95, 109–110
  re-working of affect in BDSM play,
    104–105
  sexual desire and affective
    amplification, 40–43
  sexual experimentation and, 132
  slave play as bodily intensification, 105
  transgression and negative affect, 10–11

affect theory
  affective curve of enjoyment–joy, 40,
    95, 122

and queer theory, 109–110

and resonance, 59–60

age-play *see also* Adult Baby / Diaper
    Lovers (ABDL)
  as comfort following childhood abuse, 94
  diaper play, 95–100
  mainstream media coverage of, 86–92
  manifestations of, 84–86
  motivations, 86

Ahmed, Sara, 140

Albury, Kath, 18

Alldred, Pam, 42–43

Allen, Samantha, 40, 110

Altenburger, Lauren, 67–69, 86

amateurism, 144–145

Ann Summers, 54–55

asexuality, 32

Attwood, Feona, 17, 45–46, 138–139

autoerotic play, 20–21

Barker, Martin, 57–58, 79, 80–81

Barker, Meg, 61, 106

BDSM culture
  cannibalism, 124–125
  commercialisation of, 127
  control within, 94, 103, 106
  doing and being distinctions, 127–128
  in *Fifty Shades of Grey* (James), 54–55,
    66–67, 106
  kink paraphernalia, 22
  normative codes for, 121–122
  pathologisation of, 66, 106, 118
  power exchange in, 118–119
  role of play in, 127–129
  slaughter play, 122–124
  theatrical terms of, 120–121
  therapeutic possibilities of, 103–108
  transgression and, 104, 127

Beasley, Chris, 7, 140, 141
Beckmann, Andrea, 93
becoming process, 8, 104–105, 125, 133, 146–147
Bennett, Jane, 64
Bergson, Henri, 73–74
Berlant, Lauren, 8, 56, 60–61, 150
bestsellers, 55, 59
binary models, 30, 32, 135, 136, 137, 140, 141, 142–143
bisexuality, 135
bodies see also embodiment; intensification, bodily
    absence from in sex research, 38–39
    absence from sexual script theory, 37–39
    affective intensity, 31–32, 38, 42–43, 150–151
    capabilities of, 38
    corporeal resonance in Fifty Shades of Grey (James), 59–60
    memories of bodily encounters, 147–148
    perceptions of, 145–147
    resonance between, 59–60
    and sensation, 38, 147–148
    sex and affect, 40–43
    sexuality as detached from, 37–38
    slave play as bodily intensification, 105
Bonomi, Amy, 67–69
Boscagli, Maurizia, 22
Brissett, Dennis, 45–46
Brook, Heather, 7, 140, 141
Brown, Ashley, 25, 26
Bustle, 46
Butler, Judith, 5, 34–35

Caillois, Roger, 24–25, 28, 31, 64, 101, 139
Califia, Pat, 128–129, 131, 135, 136–137, 139, 149
Carse, James P., 32
Cartesianism, 26
childhood sexual play
    adolescent sex-play, research, 77
    as distinct from adult sexuality, 73–74

exposure to pornography, 82–83
goSupermodel research, 74–78, 81, 82–83
memories of, 81–82
research on, 79–80
and sexualisation, 80–81
trauma from early sexual experiences, 82–83
understandings of, 79–80
children, figures of, 85–86
cognition, 38, 40, 43
Coming of Age, 95–98
confession, 78, 87
consumer culture, 49, 55, 69–70, 127, 138–139
control
    within BDSM culture, 94, 103, 106
    and gender power dynamics, 50–51, 56–57, 61–62
Cosmopolitan, 46–47, 48
Cowie, Elizabeth, 61
CSI (television show), 86–87, 92

Deleuze, Gilles, 42, 142
Deller, Ruth, 60, 70
desire
    and affect, 40–43
    enchantment and insatiable desire, 64–65
    and identity categories, 131–132
    as key driving force (Freud), 39–40
    potentiality and, 149–150
    and primary trauma (Freud), 56
    in relation to love, 60–61
    in relation to pain, 41–42
Diamond, Lisa M., 132, 136
Diaper Pail Fraternity/Friends, 87
Dines, Gail, 68
dirty talk, 20
Doctor Phil, 87
drive theory, 39–41, 74, 149–150

Edelman, Lee, 85
embodiment
    bodily memories, 147–148
    and childhood sexual play, 79

embodied play, 32
and kink paraphernalia, 22
sexuality as embodied capacities, 74
emotions
and affectus, 41
emotional risks, 10
responses to playfulness, 30-32
and sexual instincts, 39-40
enchantment, 64, 151
enjoyment
affective curve of enjoyment–joy, 40,
95, 122
of age-play, 85, 99-100
blocks to, 10
and registers of affect, 94-95, 110-111,
119-120
through play, 2, 6, 9, 18
Epstein, Stephen, 29, 135-136
erotica, 60, 134
excitement, affective curve of, 22, 32, 95, 110
Extreme Love, 92

fan fiction, 49, 51
fandom
furry fandom, 133-134
snark fandom, 70
fantasy
in *Fifty Shades of Grey* (James), 55,
57-58, 60-61
mimicry, 24-25
and play, 148
and primary trauma (Freud), 57-58
in relation to reality (Freud), 56
and the exploration of other possibilities,
58-59, 79
feminist theory
and bisexuality, 135
research on sex and play, 2
on sexuality, 6-8, 29, 110
on trauma, 109
fetishism, 22-23
Fetlife, 85
Fifty Shades of Grey (James)

acceptable "kink" in, 50, 54-55
BDSM in, 54-55, 66-67, 106
commercial success of, 49
as commodified depiction of sexual play,
48-49, 66-67
consent and sexual violence, critiques of
portrayals, 66-70
control and gender power dynamics,
50-51, 56-57, 61-62
corporeal resonance of, 59-60
criticism of, 65-66, 70
depictions of sex, 62-64
enchantment and insatiable lust, 64-65
eroticisation of violence n, 67-68, 69
fantasy in, 55, 57-58, 60-61
generic gendered roles of, 50-51
mainstream circulation of sexual
fantasies, 50
narrative, 49, 52, 53-55, 56, 57, 59, 60, 65
overview of, 49-50, 54
reader reactions to, 58, 70
as romantic genre fiction, 52-54
as self-help guidebook for gender
relations, 55
sexual fantasy and, 55, 57-58, 60-61
transgression in, 54-55, 65
violence and consent in, 66-70
flexisexuality, 136-137
flirtation, 23, 81, 148
Foote, Nelson E., 17
foreplay, 46
Foucault, Michel, 34, 102, 128
Fox, Nick, 42-43
Frank, Adam, 109-110
Frank, Katherine, 19
Freud, Sigmund, 39, 40, 56, 74
Frey, Kurt, 30-31
Furedi, Frank, 108
furries, 133-134, 135

Gagnon, William, 20, 33-34, 36, 37, 39,
149-150
game studies, 25-26

gamification, 27
Gamson, Joshua, 87
gay male culture, 1, 17, 18
goSupermodel research
    cultural materials for sexual
        role-play, 77–78
    messaging, 74–75
    pervy role-play, 75–77, 78, 81
    trauma and sexual messaging, 82–83
Green, Emma, 67
Grosz, Elizabeth, 8–9, 142, 146–147, 151
Guattari, Félix, 42
guidebooks
    for Adult Baby/Diaper Lovers
        (ABDL), 84
    sex as domestic skill for healthy
        relationships, 45–46, 48
    sexual role-play scenarios, 46–48

Hakim, Jamie, 149
Halberstam, Jack, 66
Hammers, Corie, 104–105
Happy, Happy Baby, 98–100
Harman, Sarah, 70
Harviainen, J. Tuomas, 19, 25, 122
heteronormativity
    and non-binary categories, 136–138
    vs. non-normative playfulness, 139–140
heterosexuality
    circular figure of, 141
    flexisexuality, 136–137
    heterosexual sex as the norm, 24, 25
    non-normative heterosexual
        practices, 140
    research on human sexual play, 30–31
History of Sexuality (Foucault), 34, 102, 128
Holmes, Mary, 7, 140, 141
homosexuality, 135
hook-up apps, 18, 47
hook-up culture, 1, 17–18
Hotel Straussberg, 111, 115–116
Huizinga, Johan, 18–19, 23–24, 36, 139,
    148–149

identification, 25, 78, 137
identities
    and desire, 131–132
    excitement and the self, 131
    flexisexuality, 136–137
    non-binary categories in adolescents,
        137–138
    perceptions of the body, 145–147
    and pornography, 143–145
    power of the individual over, 138–139
    taxonomies of sexual identity, 135–136,
        142–143
    transformed through sexual play, 134
identity politics, 135–136
ideology, 43
ilinx play, 24–25
Illouz, Eva, 55, 56, 59
improvisation
    role in sexual play, 33
    within sexual script theory, 33–34
The Incomplete, 101–104, 105, 106–108, 111
intensification, bodily
    affective intensity, 22, 31–32, 38, 42–43,
        150–151
    affective intensity and identity, 134
    practices of, 28
    slave play as, 105
    through sex play, 3, 28, 151
intimacy
    in Fifty Shades of Grey (James), 50, 53,
        60, 106
    and sexual play, 1, 21, 26, 30, 151
    through affect, 94

Jackson, Stevi, 35
James, E.L., 49, 51, 53
James, E.L., 58
Jeremy Kyle Show, 87–92
Jerry Springer Show, 87
Jones, Bethan, 70

Kalish, Rachel, 18
Kimmel, Michael, 18

kink
    acceptable "kink" in *Fifty Shades of Grey*, 50, 54–55
    and the character of Christian (*Fifty Shades of Grey*), 49–50
    commercialisation of, 127
    depictions of in *Fifty Shades of Grey*, 66, 67
    mainstream media coverage of, 126–127
    paraphernalia, 22, 127
Kinsey Report, 29
Kinsey, Alfred, 143
Kirby, Vicky, 141–142
Kontula, Osmo, 35
Kulick, Don, 134

Lacan, Jacques, 109
Langdridge, Darren, 106, 122
Lauteria, Evan W., 26
Law and Order, 111
Lemon Party, 114
Lewis, Lionel S., 45–46
libido, 39
ludus, 24–25, 85, 101–103

magic circles, 17–23
Marcus, Steven, 65
marriage manuals, 45–46
masculinity, 52, 53, 124
masochism, 42, 56, 60, 61, 127, 134
masturbation, 4, 17, 20, 81, 84
media effects, 67, 69–70
memories
    of bodily encounters, 147–148
    of childhood exposure to pornography, 82
    of childhood sexual play, 81–82
messaging, 74–75, 78, 81
Messina, Sergio, 144–145
methodology, 143–144
mimicry play, 24–25
monogamy, 91
My Crazy Obsession, 92
My Strange Attraction, 92–93

narratives
    in *Fifty Shades of Grey* (James), 49, 52, 53–55, 56, 57, 59, 60, 65
    online sexual narratives, 78
    in Soldat's documentaries, 113–114, 123
    trauma narratives, 106
Nash, Jennifer C., 7–8
new materialism, 42, 146–147
Nielsen, Silja, 74–75
non-human, 42
normativity
    and affect theory, 110
    and "in-line" straightness, 140
    and queer theory, 141–142
    and transgression, 135, 139

objectification, 8
obscenity, 112–113
ontology, 73–74, 83, 143
oral sex, 48, 62–63, 77
orgasm, 27–28, 45–46

paedia play, 24–25
paedophilia, 86, 91
pain *see also* trauma
    as amplifier of desire, 41–42
    and negative affective registers, 10–11
    and positive affect, 6, 42
    and sexual pleasure, 7, 23, 122
    somatic pain, 104–105
paraphernalia, 22, 32, 54–55, 127, 133
Parchev, Ofer, 106, 122
pathologisation, 66, 106, 118
performativity, 34–35
Pinkerton, Steven, 29
play parties, 19
play *see also* childhood sexual play; sexual play
    in adulthood lives, 83
    as autotelic, 26–27
    Caillois' taxonomy of, 24–25
    definitions of, 8–10, 11–12, 21, 23
    finite/infinite division, 32–33

play (cont.)
  and the hierarchies of sex, 3–6
  improvisation and, 20–21
  as improvisation and learning, 95–98
  incorporated into everyday lives, 101–103
  magic circle notion and, 18–19
  notion of and sex, 1–2, 8, 23–27, 151–152
  as serious, 148–149
  as unproductive activity, 28
  as variations of pleasure, 2, 6
Playboy, 1, 2
playboy sensibilities, 17
playfulness
  and the moods of the participants, 30–32
  notion of, 2–3
  and sexual desire, 3
  and the sexual self, 3
Pleasure and Danger, 6
Plummer, Ken, 38–39
pornification, 77
pornography
  and identities, 143–145
  memories of childhood exposure to, 82
  online, 78
  parallels with romance genre, 65
  trauma and childhood exposure to, 82–83
Powers of Desire, 6
prison play, 115–121
Prison System 4614, 116, 119–120, 127
props, 21–22, 32
Protocols, 123–125
psychoanalysis, 109–110
psychology, 109–110
puberty, 25, 74
pup-play, 86
puritanism, 19–20, 25, 29, 42, 91–92
purity, 54, 85–86

Queer Phenomenology, 140
queer theory
  anti-normativity in, 141–142
  and the notion of normalcy, 139–140
  research on sex and play, 2

  on sexuality, 8, 29, 110
  on trauma, 109

race, 7, 131, 145–147
Race, Kane, 1, 21
Radway, Janice A., 52, 54, 55
rape, 104–105
religion, 146
reproduction, 24, 29–30, 43, 89, 122
resonance
  notion of, 59–60
  and structures of feeling, 59
role-play
  cultural materials for, 77–78
  and improvisation, 33
  pervy role-play (goSupermodel research), 75–77, 78, 81
  prison play, 115–121
  as psychotherapy for trauma, 103–104
  stock fantasy scenarios for, 46–48
romance genre
  Fifty Shades of Grey (James) as, 52–54
  the heroine's virginity, 54
  overwhelming sexuality in, 64–65
  parallels with pornography, 65
Rousseau, Jean-Jacques, 85
Ruberg, Bonnie, 23–24
Rubin, Gayle, 4–5, 73
Rulof, Paul, 84–86, 87

Scott, Sue, 35
Sedgwick, Eve Kosofsky, 109–110, 147
semen, 39, 62–63
sensation
  affective curve of enjoyment–joy, 40, 95, 122
  and the body, 38, 147–148
  and enchantment, 64
  for fursuits, 133
  intensification of through sex play, 3, 28, 151
  safety and comfort in age play, 92–94, 99
  and sex toys, 22

surprises, 131–132
variation in, 37
sensationalism, 86–87, 91–92
sex
Cartesian dualism and, 26
conceptions of, 17–18
as unproductive activity, 28
sex experts, 1
sex parties, 18
sex research, 29, 38–39
sex toys, 1, 4, 21, 22, 45, 46, 50, 148
sex work, 31
sexology, 30
sexting, 76, 81
sexual drive, 39–41, 74, 149–150
sexual hedonism, 17–18
sexual play
and affect, 3, 11, 12, 21
amongst mammals, 29–30
identities and, 134
intimacy and, 1, 21, 26, 30, 151
repeatability of, 36–37
research on human sexual play, 30–31
spaces for, 19–20
as "work", 45–46
sexual script theory
absence of sexual bodies from, 37–39
concept of sexuality in, 33–34, 37
as fluid, 35, 36–37
gendered normative scripts, 34–35
interpersonal scripts, 34
sex and individual intelligibility, 34
sexual shame, 10–11
sexuality
in childhood, 73–74
defined, 8–9, 74
as embodied capacities, 74
feminist and queer theories on, 8,
29, 110
in sexual script theory, 33–34, 37
trauma and, 109
Shame and Its Sisters, 109
Sicart, Miquel, 2, 9, 25, 26, 85

Simon, John H., 20, 33–34, 36, 37, 39,
149–150
The Sixth Season, 120
slave play, 101–104, 105, 106–108, 111, 124
Smith, Clarissa, 60, 70, 127, 134
Snitow, Ann, 6–7, 8, 54, 55, 64, 65
social media, 65, 67, 70, 93
Soldat, Jan
access to the work of, 114–115
Coming of Age, 95–98
documentary films, 103, 108, 110–111
film style, 111–112, 125–126
Happy, Happy Baby, 98–100
Hotel Straussberg, 111, 115–116
The Incomplete, 101–104, 105,
106–108, 111
Law and Order, 111
outness of sex play and daily life,
112–114
Prison System 4614, 116, 119–120, 127
Protocols, 123–125
The Sixth Season, 120
The Visit, 116–118
A Weekend in Germany, 111
Spinoza, Baruch, 38, 41
Spišák, Sanna, 137
Stansell, Christine, 6–7, 8
straightness, 140, 141
Suominen, Jaakko, 25
Sutton-Smith, Brian, 26, 30

taboos, 124–125, 148
talk shows
coverage of sexual nonconformity,
87, 91–92
Jeremy Kyle Show, 87–92
Jerry Springer Show, 87
taste cultures, 138
Tchaconas, Alexis, 67
therapy culture, 108
Thompson, Sharon, 6–7, 8
Tomkins, Silvan S., 6, 40–41, 42, 43, 64, 94,
99, 109–111, 131

transgression
  and age-play, 85–86
  and BDSM, 104, 127
  in *Fifty Shades of Grey* (James), 54–55, 65
  and negative affective registers, 10–11
  and normativity, 135, 139
  and queer theory, 141
  and taboos, 124
  within lifestyle events, 19
trauma
  and adolescent sexual messaging, 82–83
  age-play as response to childhood
    abuse, 92–94
  in analysis of sexuality, 109
  BDSM as trauma play, 103–108
  and childhood exposure to
    pornography, 82–83
  feminist theory and, 109
  notion of, 108–109
  primary trauma (Freud), 57–58
  role-play as psychotherapy for, 103–104
trauma narratives, 106
Twilight, 51, 52

Usenet, 75, 87, 144, 145

Vance, Carole S., 7, 10
vanilla, 5, 50, 106

violence
  childhood play as sign of sexual
    violence, 80
  and consent in *Fifty Shades of
    Grey*, 66–70
  eroticisation of in *Fifty Shades of Grey*,
    67–68, 69
  and the notion of play, 9
  rape, 104–105
virginity, 54
The Visit, 116–118
Vörös, Florian, 37–38

Walton, Nicole, 67–69
Ward, Jane, 136
A Weekend in Germany, 111
Weiss, Margot, 22, 104, 116–118, 120–121,
  127, 128, 129, 139
whiteness, 50, 52, 60, 136–138
Whitman, Walt, 65
Williams, Raymond, 59
With Pleasure, 29
Wolf, Klaus Johannes, 101–104, 105,
  106–108, 111
Wysocki, Matthew, 26

Zing Tsjeng, 137
zoophilia, 86